Contemporary HRM Issues in the 21st Century

Praise for *Contemporary HRM Issues in the 21st Century*

'This succinct, tightly written book moves beyond the 'usual' (and much covered) issues of standard HRM texts to address some of the livelier current debates on the subject. It includes talent management, career management, crisis management, mental health and well-being, drug testing, employee vetting and sustainable HRM. By updating knowledge on these contemporary issues, this book is a valuable addition to any scholar's bookshelf.'

Chris Brewster, Professor of International HRM,
Henley Business School, University of Reading, UK

'This excellent book makes a valuable contribution to the broadly based HRM discipline in Australia. The author is clearly at the cutting edge of the development of HRM in Australia in the context of a growing Asia-Pacific economic area. I highly recommend this book for students, academics and HR practitioners.'

Peter J. Dowling, Emeritus Professor of International Management & Strategy,
La Trobe University, Melbourne, Australia

Contemporary HRM Issues in the 21st Century

Edited By

Peter Holland

Swinburne Business School, Australia

United Kingdom – North America
Japan – India – Malaysia – China

Emerald Publishing Limited
Howard House, Wagon Lane, Bingley BD16 1WA, UK

First edition 2019

Reprints and permissions service
Contact: permissions@emeraldinsight.com

British Library Cataloguing in Publication Data
A catalogue record for this book is available from the British Library

ISBN: 978-1-78973-460-7 (Print)
ISBN: 978-1-78973-457-7 (Online)
ISBN: 978-1-78973-459-1 (Epub)

ISOQAR certified
Management System,
awarded to Emerald
for adherence to
Environmental
standard
ISO 14001:2004.

Certificate Number 1985
ISO 14001

INVESTOR IN PEOPLE

Contents

Lists of Figures and Tables

Figures

Tables

About the Contributors

Timothy Bartram
Timothy Bartram is a Professor of Management at RMIT University, Australia. His expertise covers human resource management (HRM) and high-performance work systems, employment relations, nursing management, workers with disability, Men's Sheds and Indigenous communities. Much of Tim's research is multidisciplinary and promotes the innovative use of HRM especially in the healthcare sector inclusive of hospitals and healthcare industry.

Jillian Cavanagh
Jillian Cavanagh is a Senior Lecturer at RMIT. Her commitment to research is predominantly in the area of human resource management, employer support and the employment of workers with disabilities, men's groups and sheds, community development and engagement, Aboriginal and Torres Strait Islander men's health, and participation in men's sheds.

Ross Donohue
Ross Donohue is an Associate Professor in the Department of Management at Monash University. He has published in leading international journals such as the *Journal of Vocational Behavior, Human Resource Development International* and the *Journal of Employment Counseling*. He has also authored book chapters on careers and employment.

Kirsteen Grant
Kirsteen Grant is an Associate Professor of HRM at Edinburgh Napier University, UK. She draws on complementary backgrounds in organisational practice and academia. Her research interests centre on professional, responsible and precarious work; (changing) nature and expectations of work; talent management; workplace skills utilisation; and high-performance working.

Peter Holland
Peter Holland is a Professor of Human Resource Management and Director of the Executive MBA at Swinburne University of Technology, Melbourne. His current research interests include employee voice and silence, workplace electronic monitoring and surveillance and simulation-based learning. He has authored/co-authored 12 books and over 120 journal articles, monographs and book chapters on a variety of human resource management and employee relations issues.

Debora Jeske

Debora Jeske is a Work and Organisational Psychologist in Berlin, Germany. Prior to that, she worked as a lecturer at University College Cork in the Republic of Ireland. In her research, she combines her interest and knowledge of technology to understand which solutions work for individuals, teams and organisations.

Xiaoyan (Christiana) Liang

Xiaoyan (Christiana) Liang is a Lecturer at Central Queensland University, Melbourne Campus. Her research interests include business ethics, leadership and voice. She has experience working in industry as a Consultant in Shanghai before moving to Australia.

Hannah Meacham

Hannah Meacham is a Lecturer in the Department of Management at Monash University. She holds a PhD in the creation of meaningful and inclusive work for people with intellectual disabilities. She previously worked within the HR industry both in Australia and the UK specialising in strategic HR management and workplace relations.

Renee Paulet

Renee Paulet has worked for Federation University since its inception in 2014. Prior to this, she had been a Lecturer with Monash University. She has a research and teaching focus on human resource management (HRM), exploring topics such as sustainable HRM, the impact of place on HRM, HRM in call centres, and managing HR in small businesses.

Cathy Sheehan

Cathy Sheehan has 25 years of research experience in strategic human resource practice. She has successfully led an Australian Research Council-funded project, completed research with the Australian Human Resource Institute, Australian Senior HR Roundtable and the Victorian Workcover Authority as well as extensively publishing in leading internationally refereed journals.

Katharina Spaeth

Katharina Spaeth is a PhD candidate at Monash University. Her research focuses on human resource management and employment relations studies particularly employee engagement, employee voice and well-being. She received the Joe & Golda Isaac Scholarship for her research. Before commencing her studies, she worked for five years as an HR manager focussing on talent management and recruitment in Germany.

Tse Leng Tham

Tse Leng Tham is a Lecturer of Human Resource Management at the School of Management, RMIT University, Australia. She has published in the *Journal of Manpower* and *International Journal of Nursing Practice*. Her research interests include workplace well-being, workplace climate and voice.

Preface

As we enter the third decade of the twenty-first century a reflection of the changes we have experienced in the context of work and employment this century can be encapsulated in the phrase 'accelerated disruption'. The concept of the global internet which was in its infancy at the start of the twenty-first century has facilitated the rise of social media and the gig economy. Both these phenomena have had a significant influence on new and traditional forms of work and employment. Combined with the increasing interconnectivity of the global economy and further economic deregulation in many advanced market economies (AMEs), these changes have been the catalyst for further transformation and disruption.

With this disruption which in and of itself is progress, the pace and change have created fundamental adjustments in work and employment and facilitated new and emerging issues to deal within the workplace. Indeed, at the cusp of the fourth industrial revolution the focus is increasing becoming how or will we retain employment as we know it, or will artificial intelligence do it for us? Whilst a subject for a future edition of this book, the point is that change is unstoppable and accelerating. It would be fair to say that such change has not been seen in living memory.

As we grapple with these changes and attempt to understand them and how in the context of work and employment we can manage them, this is where this book attempts to make a small contribution by providing an insight into these new and emerging issues and challenges. In the field of human resource management, the complexity of the issues has come thick and fast, to the extent that human resources managers, academics and students cannot rely on the case law which does not exist or is still emerging, as such there are limited benchmarks. Whilst this book is not an attempt to address the fundamental changes we have seen – its focus is on helping HRM professional and scholars navigate some of the rapidly changing aspect from a human resource management and employee relations perspective.

Section I provides an overview of the changes we have and are experiencing. Despite the accelerated deregulation of work, employment and economies, the issues of fair and equitable treatment remains a key aspect of the employment relationship. This is emphasised in the second chapter on managing talent. Talent in and of itself can be seen to reflect the nature of the contemporary work environment in that it is highly mobile and demanding. As such organisations need to spend increasing time and resources managing this critical resource.

Building on the issue of the changing nature of work and employment and talent management from Section I, Section II of this book looks at the heart of the employment relationship. In the chapter on psychological contracts, as well as looking at the formation and development of the contract, the chapter explores the types of contracts and how they can be managed. This leads into the chapter on career management and some of the fundamental changes we have and are seeing in the nature of contemporary careers, and aspect of managing these new relationships in the twenty-first century. The final chapter in this section reflects on the emergence of the service sector as part of the changing profile of the workforce of most AMEs. The chapter explores how this change has fundamentally reshaped the nature of work and the implication for human resource managers.

The next section focuses on issues which have emerged as key aspects of the contemporary workplace. Whilst risk and crisis management have been characteristics of most organisations policies and practices, the globalisation of many organisations workforces means they need to manage issues such as terrorism threats, kidnappings and pandemics as well as the threat of natural disasters. In an era of global news and the internet, organisations require quick and effective responses as they are often under immense public scrutiny. This chapter explores the various aspects of risk and crisis management and the role of HRM. The following chapter focuses on the increasingly important issue of mental health and well-being in the workplace. The chapter outlines the issues and approaches to deal with this important subject and provides a detail case study of the nursing profession and the multifaceted nature of these issues in action. The final chapter in this section explores what is termed the dark side of workplace behaviour or dysfunctional behaviour. The chapter examines issues of violence in the workplace and the emergence of what is known as the corporate psychopath. The chapter concludes with strategies for dealing with these issues.

Section IV of this book picks up on issues which could be seen as of this century. These chapters are designed to reflect the debates on these emerging or challenging issues. The first of these issues is the increasing availability of biological testing in particular drug testing and genetic testing. The implication of what this information can provide an employer raises many issues around the boundaries of employment, privacy and ethics. This is followed by the twenty-first century phenomena of cyber-vetting and the pro and cons of such strategies in a cyber-linked society. The chapter on sustainable HRM explores this emerging issue and HRMs role in an increasing focus on sustainability within organisations. The following chapter looks at the impact of technology on work design in the context of what we have learned from these relationships in the past and whether in fact we have forgotten these lessons. A case study on airline pilots explores how the technology is advancing at the potential detriment to the skills of the pilot. The final chapter explore the role of code of conduct. Whilst not considered a contemporary issue in itself, the nature of the twenty-first century internet connected workplace and society means that issue can become high profile and common knowledge very quickly. As such management under intense scrutiny need guiding principle often in the glare of the public and media. The chapter explores these issues through three high profile case studies.

In addressing these issues, exploring case studies which map out and examine these changes and approach, it is anticipated that the book will help the reader in addressing the challengers in their changing workplace underpinned by accelerating change and disruption.

Peter Holland

Section I

The Contemporary Workplace

Chapter 1

HRM in the Contemporary Workplace

Peter Holland

Introduction

> The world of work is not going to *be* disrupted it *is* disrupted.
>
> (Ross, Ressia, & Sander, 2017, p. xvii)

> We all sense it – something big is going on.
>
> (Freidman, 2016)

> There is a tremendous upside to technological change… (this) does not mean dismissing the real fears that people have about where, or *whether*, they fit in a workforce increasingly dominated by machines.
>
> (Chalmers & Quigley, 2017, p. 1)

As the preceeding quotes indicate, the workplace is becoming an ever more dynamic, complex and pressured environment as new technology and globalisation challenges the way we think and work. These changes in the first two decades of the twenty-first century have been described as a seismic shift in the employment landscape, not only in the amount and type of changes workers can expect but also in the type of work emerging (Emerson, 2013). The major changes we have experienced in the twenty-first century have a narrative of accelerating change and disruption underpinned by major technological innovation increasingly supported by artificial intelligence (AI) and globalisation (Friedman, 2016). As a recent Australian Federal Government (2018) inquiry reported:

> *[...] there is increasing evidence to suggest that our workplace laws, designed to provide a balanced framework for cooperation and productive workplace relations have failed to keep pace with emerging trends, such as the rise in non-standard work. Casual work, labour hire, sham contracting, the gig economy.... They are forms of work which in certain guise reduce workers rights and protections, and often deny workers access to basic rights and conditions... (APH, p. xi)*

3

Within this environment increasingly described as the fourth industrial revolution (Schwarb, 2016), the effective management of human resources (HRs) still remains a critical issue. Indeed, it could be argued this is even more so in the so-called 'war for talent' in these turbulent times. Whilst the emerging world of work has major implication for the employment relationship (ER), key aspects underpinning this relationship of fairness and well-being remains. This places HRs at the centre of the management of these resources or talent (which is also increasingly mobile), in a way that will enable the organisation to retain them and become considered an 'employer of choice' for these employees to remain with, recommend to others, or if they leave, return to in the future. Underpinning this is the notion that, in the midst of all this change, complexity and dynamism, the organisation's decision-making processes are founded on a 'bedrock' of clear and concise philosophical approaches to how HRs should be managed. Whilst this book address many contemporary challenges in human resource management (HRM), the key foundations upon which it is built include organisational justice, ethical behaviour and trust. Indeed, this goes to the heart of contemporary HRM, with its emphasis on building relationships between employee and management based upon mutual trust and respect (Boxall & Purcell, 2016; Lawler, 2003), in an era of accelerated deregulation of labour standards and labour markets.

As Burke (2008) notes, 'treating people right' is very difficult. As the chapters of this book will illustrate, the nature of the issues (current and emerging) faced by HR managers is complex and requires an in-depth understanding. For example, the psychological contract in Chapter 3 illustrates that issues of breach and violation of contract are viewed by different people in different ways, based upon individual perceptions and perceived relationships with the organisation – a core aspect of this is a sense of justice or injustice and trust. The issues explored with regard to monitoring and surveillance illustrate how these policies can impinge on employee privacy and create an oppressive environment underpinned by a lack of ethics and trust. Equally where employees feel betrayed, stressed and emotionally drained, what we describe as the *Dark Side* of the workplace emerges where workplace theft and violence emerge. In addition, this book provides a section on contemporary debates around the emergence of new technology such as cyber-vetting as well as traditional aspects of work such as Codes of Conduct in a twenty-first century context, as well sustainable HRM in an era of climate change.

Whilst the complex and dynamic nature of the workplace can potentially be seen to overwhelm the ability of management to 'treat people right', Burke (2008) argues that, by placing strong emphasis on and resources into developing fair and equitable systems to manage these issues, organisations can attract and retain quality employees whilst motivating them to perform at higher levels. Whilst the research on justice, ethics and trust largely emerged out of the field of social psychology (Blau, 1964; Cropanzano & Randall, 1993), these concepts have increasingly been applied to HRM issues and, from an applied perspective, offer new insights into the effective management of the organisation's key asset – people. One particular aspect is that of flexibility of work which has, through the application of technology, fundamentally changed the nature of 'being at work'. This can result in empowering workers to work away from the office and manage their own time and schedule, which requires a significant amount of trust on behalf of management. Or it can, as has been illustrated by research on call centres show high levels of monitoring and surveillance due to lack of trust. This is reflected in the discussion on monitoring and surveillance which points to the fact that despite the paradigm shift of the twenty-first century in the intensity of workplace surveillance – it is not a given that monitoring and surveillance should occur.

Why these aspects are increasingly important in the contemporary workplace may be better understood from the perspective of not addressing them. The consequences of not addressing issues of justice ethics and trust manifest in problems associated with a poor workplace climate, including health and well-being, morale, turnover, commitment and satisfaction. Indeed, Schabracq and Cooper (2000, 2003) argue that the way organisations approach these issues will become critical factors in competitiveness. So, what type of framework can an organisation develop to sustain itself as a place that is perceived to be 'treating people right'? The following sections explore the issues of organisational justice, ethics and trust, to illustrate the key features and interrelated aspects of these practices that provide the bedrock to effective HRM in arguably the most challenging time in the history of modern work patterns and practices.

Justice at Work – A Theoretical Perspective

A key aspect of employees' attraction, retention, well-being and organisational climate is how the employee views and evaluates organisational decisions in terms of their perceived fairness, equity, outcomes and treatment – or what has become increasingly understood as organisational justice (Boxall & Purcell, 2016). As Gibson and Campbell-Quick (2008) note, the concepts of organisational justice are defined as the degree of equity and fairness employees are shown by the organisation (management), and influence employee attitudes, emotions, trust, their sense of what is morally right and wrong, and increasingly whether this is an organisation that they want to work for or be associated with. So, if justice in the workplace is an increasingly critical issue, what is it, and how can it be managed?

The Concept of Organisational Justice

As a concept, the idea of justice can be taken back to Plato and Aristotle and, as noted, is bound with the concepts of fairness and equity. These ideas have been subsequently developed by Locke and Rousseau through to contemporary research by Rawls (1971) and Nozick (1974) – see Sen (2010) and Shaw and Barry (2004). With the increasing changes that are taking place in the workplace (see earlier quotes) in terms of relationships (types of employment contracts) and the way we work (increasingly in cyberspace), the notion of justice has become an important area of research that focuses on better understanding and dealing with issues in the workplace that have never been conceived preciously; for example, genetic testing and cyber-vetting, which are discussed in this book. In this context, research indicates that the notion of justice has been developed to the extent that it is now seen to be made up of several components which need to be managed both separately and in unison in order for a robust framework to develop within an organisation. Organisational justice focuses on the perception of employees of the fairness and equity of the organisation's policies, processes and practices. These are played out in terms of decision-making, the communication of information, allocation of resources, and the treatment of individual employees and other stakeholders in the organisation (Lewis, Thornhill, & Sanders, 2003). Within this context, organisational justice can be viewed from four interrelated perspectives:

distributive justice, procedural justice, interactional justice and informational justice. These perspectives are developed below.

Distributive Justice

Distributive justice focuses on the fairness of the outcomes of a process or decision. One of the most important theories underpinning distributive justice is J. Stacy Adams' 'equity theory' (1965). Equity theory focuses the individual making social comparisons with similar employees. The individual assesses their effort and outcomes against other individuals (fairness). Where there is a perceived disparity (either lower or higher), the employee will have a feeling of inequity (Folger, 2005; O'Donnell & Shields, 2006). It is argued that the greater the perceived inequity (particularly negative), the greater the perceived discontent, and the greater is the motivation to achieve equity (Grant, 1999). Thus, it is the perceived comparative reward rather than the absolute reward that determines satisfaction or dissatisfaction (Cropanzano & Randall, 1993). The consequences of perceived inequity are reduced effort and commitment, and increased absenteeism, turnover and 'dark' or counterproductive work behaviours (Boxall & Purcell, 2016).

Generally, Adams' equity theory is seen as a reasonable account of employees' responses to equity and inequity, with studies showing employees adjusting their behaviour and effort where the reward is perceived to be inequitable. For example, studies show that increase and decrease of perceived workplace status correlate with performance (Greenberg, 1988; Greenberg & Ornstein, 1983; Watson, 1986). However, research on employees who are over-rewarded indicates that whilst improved performance can occur in response to the over-reward, employees are just as likely to rationalise this over-reward by inflating the perception of their performance through a 'self-serving bias' and not increase their performance overall (Boxall & Purcell, 2016; Kruger, 1999). This appears, therefore, to support equity theory (Greenberg, 1990). This is important, as distributive justice is very much focussed on perceived fairness of outcomes, and potentially has major implications in an organisational context (Cohen-Charash & Spector, 2001).

Interpersonal Justice

Interpersonal justice refers to the social aspects of distributive justice and focuses on the consequences of the decision-making (Cropanzano & Randall, 1993). In practice, interpersonal justice reflects the way employees feel they have been treated in terms of respect and sensitivity to the issue or issues facing them; for example, biological monitoring and surveillance. This is often seen as a reflection of the value an organisation puts on the relationship with its employees (Greenberg & Baron, 2006). This is also known as the group value explanation of organisational justice, where value and perceived importance to the organisation are interpreted from the effort made by the organisation to communicate decisions to the employees (Greenberg & Baron, 2006).

Procedural Justice

A key aspect of justice in organisations is the underlying system for determining decisions and outcomes, how they are made, whether they are fair and equitable, and if they are consistently enforced without prejudice or personal bias (Boxall & Purcell, 2016; Gilliland, 1993). This is known as procedural justice. Procedural justice can mediate perceptions of distributive justice if the process has been seen to be fair and equitable (Cox, 2000). This is particularly important where employees receive unfavourable managerial decisions (Colquitt & Greenberg, 2003); for example increasing biological monitoring and surveillance. In an era in advanced market economies (AMEs) of declining trade union density and unitarist-based HRM systems, the extent to which there is genuine employee voice is also an important factor in procedural justice as it ensures that employees have an opportunity to participate in and influence the decision-making process (Boxall & Purcell, 2016; Donaghey & Cullinane, 2014; Holland, Cooper, & Sheehan, 2016; Pyman, Holland, Teicher, & Cooper, 2010). As Pearce, Bigley, and Branyiczki (1998) note, studies focussing on the effects of voice in the workplace where it is perceived to be valued are positive in terms of fairness and equity. Importantly also in a period of increasing war for talent, procedural justice can be a way an employee evaluates the (on-going) relationship or psychological contract with management and with the organisation (Fischer & Smith, 2004; Tyler & Lind, 1992). It is also important for organisation with websites like '*glassdoor*', where employees and ex-employees can post about their experience within an organisation for all to read (see Chapter 10 on cyber-vetting). Leventhal (1980) argues there are six rules which determine whether procedural justice has been followed. These are:

(1) *The consistency rule*: Procedures should be consistent across all employees over time.
(2) *The bias-suppression rule*: self-interest should be prevented from operating in decision-making processes.
(3) *The accuracy rule*: the best quality information should always be used in decision-making.
(4) *The correctable rule*: the system allows for the remedy of unfair decisions.
(5) *The representative rule*: all stakeholders affected by a decision are represented.
(6) *The ethicality rule*: allocation of resources is undertaken in an ethical and moral way.

Interactional Justice
To this point the concept of procedural justice has focussed on the structural aspects of fairness. A further dimension to procedural justice is the social dimension. As Bies and Moag (1986) identified, individuals assess justice in organisations based on the quality of treatment and communication they receive throughout the process. This enacted characteristic of procedural justice has been termed 'interactional justice' (Cropanzano & Randall, 1993). Specifically, interactional justice involves communicating information in a socially appropriate and respectful way (Colquitt, 2001; Tomlinson & Greenberg, 2005). Significant research into this aspect of justice across a range of organisational issues has identified several perspectives to interactional justice. These are truthfulness, respect, propriety and justification, and processes where an injustice may be rectified by an adequate justification (Boxall & Purcell, 2016; Cropanzano & Randall, 1993). Research (Bies, 1987; Shapiro, 1993) indicates that an effective way of achieving this is by communicating to employees an account of the process and procedures undertaken in making a decision (Fuchs & Edwards, 2012). This is what Cohen-Charash and Spector (2001) describe as the human side of organisational practices. Thus, a negative response to perceived interactional justice is more likely to focus on the individual supervisor rather than the organisation as would be the case

with procedural justice (Crapanzano & Prehar, 1999) and can impact on the employees' psychological contract discussed in Chapter 3.

The Context of Organisation Justice

Whilst the above framework clearly identifies the *content* of organisational justice, of equal important are the *contextual* elements, which include culture and organisational structures and how organisations manage status and power. As James (1993) notes, these issues have a very important and wide-ranging effect on justice behaviour and perceived injustice. Boxall and Purcell (2016) and Lewis, Thornhill, and Sanders (2003) have noted the implications for justice on many aspects of HRM. As noted, with the increasing complexity and speed of change in the workplace, it is important for organisations to have a solid foundation upon which policies, practices and processes are developed and reviewed in order to ensure that organisational justice is perceived by all stakeholders. Where decisions are made that will be unfavourable to stakeholders, that is, employees – research indicates that where there is a sense of perceived fairness in the decision-making process, employees, whilst not necessarily agreeing with the outcomes, will more readily accept the decisions that are made. The alternative is a workforce that feels betrayal, and the repercussions that come from this including lower moral and commitment, and higher turnover, absenteeism, theft and violence (see Chapter 8 for the Dark Side of Work). As Cropanzano and Randall (1993) and Boxall and Purcell (2016) indicate, this applied perspective provides a new approaches and recommendations for more effective HRM.

Research on the issues of organisational justice has also identified the effects on the related aspect of employee voice (Folger, 1977; Wilkinson, Dundon, Donaghey, & Freeman, 2014). Organisational justice and voice are linked by the scope of the subjects negotiated, the organisational decision-making approach to participation, and the perceived influence employees or their representatives have at arriving at a decision. Understanding this framework of justice can guide HR managers in dealing with HR issues as they develop in a way that, whilst possibly not perfect, will allow a sense that they are attempting to deal with the issues in a fair and equitable way with all stakeholder. It is clear that a culture of strong organisational justice can be critical to developing a workplace that is perceived by all stakeholders as a place where decision-making is undertaken in consideration of all and on a fair and equitable basis, in a turbulent environment.

Ethics and HRM

The second element in guiding HR managers and decision makers in these changing times is the ethical dimensions of decision-making. In combination with the processes of organisational justice, ethical perspectives can allow a more nuanced assessment of the impact of decision-making and reasoning on the individual, group, organisation and society level (e.g. sustainable HR initiatives – see Chapter 11). Exploring these issues through the classical ethical theories – egoism, utilitarianism and deontology – allows for a more expansive view of the issue and the potential impact on stakeholders (Greenwood & Freeman, 2011).

Egoism and utilitarianism are both consequential theories (developed from the work of Mills and Bentham), which judge the morality of an issue based on the consequences it generates, in the formal case, consequences or costs for the decision makers under question and in the latter, consequences and costs for all parties (stakeholders) whose interests might be affected. Egoism suggests that an action is morally right if all decision makers in a given situation freely decide to pursue either their short-term desires or long-term interests (Crane & Matten, 2016). In a workplace context therefore, the perceived positive gains for the employer needs to be juxtaposed with the impact on other key stakeholders such as the workforce, society and the long-term organisational performance and image of the organisation (Greenwood & Freeman, 2011).

Utilitarianism or the 'greatest good principle' states that an action is morally justified if it brings about the greatest good for the greatest number of people affected by the action (Crane & Matten, 2016). This approach differs from egoism, by looking at not only the outcomes for the decision makers, but also the collective welfare that is produced by the action, calculated by a cost-benefit analysis. An action is deemed morally correct if it generates the highest aggregate economic value (i.e. utility) for all parties involved, regardless of the negative impact it has caused.

The deontology approach takes a differing perspective to the consequential theories by focussing on the morality of an issue or action above the context. Morality is defined by a set of rationally deduced a priori moral rules, which must be applied consistently across situations without any exception. Kant the most influential writer in this field, termed this set of rules 'categorical imperative', which is comprised of three universal principles. The basis of these principles was to act in accordance with 'universal law' and human dignity and not as a means to an end (Kant, 1994). Taken together, they form the basis of moral judgement. Using these classical ethical theories within the context of the new contested terrain of the fourth industrial (digital) age can facilitate more reliable and respected decision-making.

Trust

A key aspect of justice and ethics discussed above is trust. As Boxall and Purcell (2016, p. 247) state: 'Low levels of organisational trust are linked to perceptions that organisational justice has broken down'. Greenwood (2014) highlights the role of justice ethics as underpinned by trust in fair and equitable treatment of all, under the 'veil of ignorance'. As contemporary research is increasingly showing, trust in management is a critical element for organisations to foster (Holland et al., 2016; Searle et al., 2011). Not least because trust has been found to be positively associated with a range of employee attitudes and valued work behaviours, including organisational citizenship (Dirks & Ferrin, 2002). As Boxall and Purcell (2016) argue, management at all levels can ill-afford to ignore the influence of trust on employees' attitudes and their subsequent contributions to the organisation, as trust enables greater cooperation and is a key element in judging how employees view their relationship with management. Consequently, trust can act as an antecedent of competitive advantage for organisations (Holland et al., 2016; Searle et al., 2011).

HR policies and practices constitute, inter alia, an institutionalised organisational process which can influence employees' perceptions of the trustworthiness of an organisation (as represented by management), or the organisational climate of trust (Holland et al., 2016; Searle et al., 2011). These HR policies, principles and subsequent practices are central in developing what Fox (1974) describes as either a high trust informal

ERs and low-trust formal relationships. As such, HR policies, principles and practices are central to the ER and the 'exchange' between employees and management or what Blau (1964), described as *Social Exchange Theory* (SET).

Social Exchange Theory

The contemporary concept of trust in the ER originates from SET (Blau, 1964; Whitener, Brodt, Korsguard, & Werner, 1998). Whilst SET has been criticised for its ambiguity, and in a workplace context does not adequately address power relationships or distributive justice, it is a useful frame of reference in understanding the ER. In essence, SET views the ER as a series of on-going exchange relationships and unspecified obligations (Blau, 1964), which over time, establish the nature and structure of interaction (Boxall & Purcell, 2016; Holland et al., 2016). From a HR perspective, this helps us to understand interdependence and reciprocity in the ER, and explains how and why employees reciprocate the treatment they receive from management as the relationship unfolds (Farndale, Van Ruiten, Kelliher, & Hope-Hailey, 2011). As Boxall and Purcell (2016) note, the on-going management of the ER means taking a long-term view about the underlying processes in which trust is a key dynamic.

HRM and Trust

Whilst trust has been researched extensively in the HRM literature, its definition remains contested (Nichols, Danford, & Tasiran, 2009). However, in the context of the ER, trust is the basis for quality relationships, cooperation and stability. In focussing on collective trust, Korczynski's (2000) definition, gives a focus to trust and economic activity. Trust is defined and contextualised as the confidence that one party to the exchange will not exploit the other's vulnerabilities. This definition builds on the systems or institutional approach of Luhmann (1979), and is more reflective of the on-going nature of the ER, and the reliance upon exchange. As Korczynski (2000, p. 6) notes, the nature of advanced societies makes trust at the system level increasingly important. Similarly, Dietz and Fortin (2007) and Holland et al. (2016), argue that in contemporary knowledge-based workplaces, the disclosure and sharing of sensitive information is increasingly important to enable organisations to function effectively, and trust is a central component in this relationship.

The Context of Trust

From a HRM perspective, we can say the concept of trust is about developing employee commitment, which is seen as an antecedent of increased organisational performance (Nicholls et al., 2009). Given the dynamic, reciprocal nature of the ER, the actions of management are continually evaluated and assessed by employees and their representatives (Costigan, Iiter, & Berman, 1998). As Lewis and Welgert (1985) argue, the actions of others imply reciprocal trust; conversely, actions that violate trust and fairness and equity (justice and ethics) can create an atmosphere in which employees may be less willing to develop a committed relationship with management and/or the organisation – invasive monitoring and surveillance being a case in point. Employees therefore are continually appraising multiple sources of information and evidence to inform their impression of the overall trustworthiness of management (Dietz & Fortin, 2007). As Tzafrir (2005) and Nichols et al. (2009) point out, trust is a key outcome in the relationship between HR practices and employees' attitudes to management.

Summary

As economic and structural changes in the labour market, including a decline in trade union density and collective bargaining and now technology pervade the workplace. The danger of increased managerial prerogative these structural changes bring can undermine the trust in the ER (and perceptions of ethical behaviour and organisational justice). Thus the increasing focus on justice trust and ethical behaviour, can lead to more effective involvement and communication with employees and improve organisational effectiveness across a variety of indicators (Boxall & Purcell, 2016; Holland et al., 2016; Pyman, Cooper, Teicher, & Holland, 2006). This is because management as the principal creators of communication, involvement and decision-making have a variety of options in how they respond to, and engage with, the workforce in this turbulent era underpinned by accelerated change and disruption. Management's choice will reflect their ideology and style, and in turn, influence the level of trust within the ER (e.g. Dietz, 2004; Lamsa & Pucetaite, 2006).

Returning to the theme of the quotes at the start of this chapter, despite or as a result of these fundamental changes in and at work, HR managers need to be increasingly sophisticated in their approach to the many (emerging) issues in the workplace, several of which are explored in the following chapters. The focus argued here is that starting with a framework of ethical decision-making, organisational justice and trust, the processes practices and implementation of policy are likely to be more effective.

References

Adams, J. S. (1965). Inequity in social exchange. In L. Berkowitz (Eds.), *Advances in experimental social psychology* (Vol. 2, pp. 267–299). New York, NY: Academic Press.

Australian Federal Government Senate Select Committee on: *The Future of Work and Workers*. (2018). Commonwealth of Australia, Australia: APH.

Bies, R. (1987). The predicament of injustice. In L. Cummings & B. Shaw (Eds.), *Research in organizational behaviour* (pp. 289–319). Greenwich, CT: JAI Press.

Bies, R., & Moag, J. (1986). Interactional justice: Communication criteria of fairness. In R. Lewecki, B. Sheppard, & M. Bazerman (Eds), *Research on negotiation in organizations* (Vol. 1, pp. 43–55). Greenwich, CT: JAI Press.

Blau, M. P. (1964). *Exchange and power in social life*. New York, NY: Wiley.

Boxall, P., & Purcell, J. (2016). *Strategy and human resource management* (4th ed.). Basingstoke: Palgrave Macmillan.

Burke, R. J. (2008). Building more effective organisation's. In R. J. Burke & C. L. Cooper (Eds.), *Building more effective organisations* (pp. 3–35). Cambridge: Cambridge University Press.

Chalmers, J., & Quigley, M. (2017). *Changing jobs: The fair go in the new machine age*. Melbourne, Australia: Redback.

Cohen-Charash, Y., & Spector, P. (2001). The role of justice in organizations: A meta-analysis. *Organisational Behaviour and Human Decision Process, 86*(2), 278–321.

Colquitt, J. (2001). On the dimensionality of organisational justice: A construct validation method. *Journal of Applied Psychology, 86*, 386–400.

Colquitt, J., & Greenberg, J. (2003). Organisational justice: A fair assessment of the state of the literature. In J. Greenberg (Ed.), *Organizational behaviour: The state of the science* (2nd ed.). Mahwah, NJ: Erlbaum Associates.

Costigan, R. D., Iiter, S. S., & Berman, J. J. (1998). A multi-dimensional study of trust in organizations. *Journal of Managerial Issues, 10*, 303–317.

Cox, A. (2000). The importance of employee participation in determining pay system effectiveness. *International Journal of Manpower Review*, *2*(4), 357–375.

Crane, A., & Matten, D. (2016). *Business ethics: Managing corporate citizenship and sustainability in the age of globalization*. Oxford: Oxford University Press.

Cropanzano, R., & Prehar, C. (1999). Using social exchange theory to distinguish procedural from interactional justice. Paper presented to the annual meeting of the society for industrial and organizational psychology, Atlanta, GA.

Cropanzano, R., & Randall, M. (1993). Injustice and work behaviour. In R. Cropanzano (Ed.), *Justice in the workplace: Approaching a fairness in human resource management* (pp. 3–20). Mahwah, NJ: Lawrence Erlbaum Associates.

Dietz, G. (2004). Partnership and the development of trust in British workplaces. *Human Resource Management*, *14*(1), 5–24.

Dietz, G., & Fortin, M. (2007). Trust and justice in the formation of joint consultation committees. *Journal of International Human Resource Management*, *18*(7), 1159–1181.

Dirks, K., & Ferrin, D. L. (2002). Trust in leadership: Meta-analytic findings and implications for research and practice. *Journal of Applied Psychology*, *87*(4), 611–628.

Donaghey, J., & Cullinane, N. (2014). Employee silence. In A. Wilkinson, J. Donaghey, T. Dundon, & R. Freeman (Eds.), *The handbook of research on employee voice* (pp. 398–409). London: Edward Elgar.

Emerson, M. (2013). Trends away from the mainstream. *The Age*, October 12, p. 2.

Farndale, E., Hope-Hailey, V., & Kelliher, C. (2011). High commitment performance management: The role of justice and trust. *Personnel Review*, *10*(1), 5–23.

Farndale, E., Van Ruiten, J., Kelliher, C., & Hope-Hailey, V. (2011). The influence of perceived voice on organizational commitment, an exchange perspective. *Human Resource Management*, *50*(1), 113–129.

Fischer, R., & Smith, P. (2004). Values and organizational justice: Performance and seniority-based allocation criteria in UK and Germany. *Journal of Cross-Cultural Psychology*, *6*, 669–688.

Folger, R. (1977). Distributive and procedural justice: Combined impact of voice and improvement on experienced inequity. *Journal of Personality and Social Psychology*, *35*, 108–119.

Folger, R. (2005). *Justice and employment*. In J. Coyle-Shapiro, L. Shore., M. Taylor, & L. Tetrick (Eds.), *The employment relationship* (pp. 29–47). Oxford: Oxford University Press.

Fox, A. (1974). *Beyond contact: Work, power and trust relations*. London: Faber & Faber.

Friedman, T. L. (2016). *Thanks for being late: An optimist's guide to thriving in the age of accelerations*. New York, NY: Allen Lane.

Fuchs, S., & Edwards, M. (2012). Predicting pro-change behaviour. The role of perceived organizational justice and organizational identification. *Human Resource Management Journal*, *22*(1), 39–59.

Gibson, A., & Campbell-Quick, J. (2008). Best practice for work stress and well-being: Solutions for human dilemmas in organisations. In R. Burke & C. Cooper (Eds.), *Building more effective organizations* (pp. 84–109). Cambridge: Cambridge University Press.

Gilliland, S. (1993). The perceived fairness of selection systems: An organisational justice perspective. *Academy of Management Review*, *18*, 694–734.

Grant, D. (1999). HRM, rhetoric and the psychological contract: A case of 'easier said than done'. *International Journal of Human Resource Management*, *10*, 327–350.

Greenberg, J. (1988). Equity and workplace status: A field experiment. *Journal of Applied Psychology*, *73*, 606–613.

Greenberg, J. (1990). Organizational justice. *Journal of Management*, *16*, 399–432.

Greenberg, J., & Baron, S. (2006). *Behaviour in organizations* (9th ed.). London: Prentice Hall.

Greenberg, J., & Ornstein, S. (1983). High status job titles as compensation for underpayment. A test of equity theory. *Journal of Applied Psychology, 68*, 285–296.

Greenwood, M. (2014). *HRM and Ethics.* Wiley Encyclopaedia of Management. Hoboken, NJ: John Wiley & Sons, Ltd

Greenwood, M., & Freeman, R. E. (2011). Ethics and HRM: The contribution of stakeholder theory. *Business & Professional Ethics Journal, 30*(3/4), 269–292.

Holland, P., Cooper, B., & Sheehan, C. (2016). Employee voice, supervisor support and engagement: The mediating role of trust. *Human Resource Management, 50*(6), 915–929.

James, K. (1993). The social context of organizational justice. In R. Cropanzano (Ed.), *Justice in the workplace: Approaching a fairness in human resource management* (pp. 21–50). Mahwah, NJ: Lawrence Erlbaum Associates.

Kant, E. (1994). *The philosophy of Kant.* New York, NY: Modern Library.

Korczynski, M. (2000). The political economy of trust. *Journal of Management Studies, 37*(1), 1–23.

Kruger, J. (1999). Lake Wobegon be gone! The 'below average effect' and the geocentric effect of comparative ability judgement. *Journal of Personality and Social Psychology, 27*(2), 221–232.

Lamsa, A., & Pucetaite, R. (2006). Development of organizational trust among employees from a contextual perspective. *Business Ethics: A European Review, 15*(2), 130–141.

Leventhal, G. (1980). What should be done with equity theory? In K. Geergen, M. Greenber, & R. Willis (Eds.), *Social exchange: Advances in theory and research* (pp. 27–55). New York, NY: Plenum Press.

Lawler, E. E. (2003). *Treating people right.* San Francisco, CA: Jossey-Bass.

Lewis, J., & Welgert, A. (1985). Trust as a social reality. *Social Forces, 63*, 65–79.

Lewis, P., Thornhill, A., & Sanders, M. (2003). *Employee relations: Understanding the employment relationship.* London: Prentice Hall.

Luhmann, N. (1979). *Trust and power.* Chichester: John Wiley.

Nichols, T., Danford, A., & Tasiran, A. (2009). Trust, employer exposure and the employment relation. *Economic and Industrial Democracy, 30*(2), 241–265.

Nozick, R. (1974). *Anarchy, state and Utopia.* New York, NY: Basic Books.

O'Donnell, M., & Shields, J. (2006). The new pay: Performance related pay in Australia. In J. Teicher, P. Holland, & R. Gough (Eds.), *Employment relations in Australia* (2nd ed.). Australia: Pearson Education.

Pearce, J., Bigley, G., & Branyiczki, I. (1998). Procedural justice as modernism: Placing industrial and organizational psychology in context. *Applied Psychology, 47*, 371–396.

Pyman, A., Cooper, B., Teicher, J., & Holland, P. (2006). A comparison of the effectiveness of employee voice arrangements in Australia. *Industrial Relations Journal, 37*, 543–559.

Pyman, A., Holland, P., Teicher, J., & Cooper, B. (2010). Industrial relations climate, employee voice and managerial attitudes to unions. An Australian study. *British Journal of Industrial Relations, 48*(2), 460–480

Rawls, J. (1971). *A theory of justice.* Boston, MA: Harvard University Press.

Ross, P., Ressia, S., & Sander, E. (2017). *Work in the 21ˢᵗ century: How do your log in?* London: Emerald Publishing.

Schabracq, M., & Cooper, C. (2000). The changing nature of work and stress. *Journal of Management Psychology, 15*, 227–241.

Schabracq, M., & Cooper, C. (2003). To be me or not to be me: About alienation. *Journal of Counselling Psychology, 16*, 53–79.

Schwarb, K. (2016). *The fourth industrial revolution*. Switzerland: World Economic Forum.

Searle, R., Den Hartog, D. N., Weibel, A., Gillespie, N., Six, F., Hatzakis, T., & Skinner, D. (2011). Trust in the employer: The role of high-involvement work practices and procedural justice in European organizations. *The International Journal of Human Resource Management, 22*(5), 1069–1092.

Sen, A. (2010). *The idea of justice*. London: Penguin Books.

Shapiro, D. (1993). Reconciling theoretical differences among procedural justice researchers. In R. Cropanzano (Eds.), *Justice in the workplace: Approaching a fairness in human resource management* (pp. 50–78). Mahwah, NJ: Lawrence Erlbaum Associates.

Shaw, W. H., & Barry, V. (2004). *Moral issues in business*. Belmont, CA: Thompson.

Tomlinson, R., & Greenberg, J. (2005). Discouraging theft by managing social norms and prioritizing organizational justice. In R. Kidwell & C. Martin (Eds.), *Managing organizational deviance* (pp. 200–221). London: Sage Publications.

Tyler, T., & Lind, E. (1992). A relational model of authority in groups. In M. Zama (Eds.), *Advances in experimental social psychology* (pp. 101–120). San Diego, CA: Academic Process.

Tzafrir, S. (2005). The relationship between trust, HRM practices and firm performance. *International Journal of Human Resource Management, 16*(9), 1600–1622.

Watson, T. J. (1986). *Management, organisation and employment strategy: New directions in theory and practice*. London: Routledge.

Whitener, E., Brodt, S., Korsguard, M., & Werner, J. (1998). Managers as initiator of trust: An exchange relationship framework for understanding managerial trustworthy behaviour. *Academy of Management Review, 23*(3), 513–530.

Wilkinson, A., Dundon, T., Donaghey, J., & Freeman, R. (2014). *The handbook of research on employee voice* (2nd ed.). Cheltenham: Edward Elgar.

Chapter 2

Managing Talent: A Contemporary Issue or a Case of Old Wine in New Bottles?

Peter Holland

Introduction

At the end of the second decade of the twenty-first century there is a growing recognition of the significant changes in the nature of how when and where we work. Concepts such as the 'gig' economy, which has undermined or blown to bits, traditional organisational models in well-established industries (i.e. accommodation and transport), supported by an increasingly globalised and deregulated economic, growth, are re-framing the nature of work and employment as we know it (Friedman, 2016). However, it is interesting to note the emergence of talent and management, and the 'war for talent' in the late twentieth century (Michaels et al., 2001), remains a constant in the academic and practical field of management. Indeed, as Gunnigle, Lavelle, and Monagham (2013) and Thunnissen and Gallardo-Gallardo (2017) note, post the global financial crisis (GFC), talent and its management appeared to have gained a greater strategic role. What is also interesting is the lack of consistency about what we mean by talent management (TM) or managing talent. This chapter looks at the issues of talent and the management of talent to better guide how we see it and how we use it, and the key role of human resources in this process and policy development.

What is Talent Management?

In exploring TM, it is probably best to look at the debates over the last two decades. Whilst, TM itself is not a contemporary management term, indeed, Gallardo-Gallardo, Dries, and Gorzalez (2013), trace its origin to the twelfth century, the contemporary interest in it as a 'stand-alone' concept can be traced back to the late 1990s and the release of the McKinsey report titled: *War for Talent* (Micheals et al., 1997) and the subsequent book of the same name (Michaels, Handfield-Jones, & Axelrod, 2001). Both came out at a time of increased competitiveness, globalising, deregulation of (labour) markets and the emergence of strategic human resource management, with an emphasis of human resource as the key to competitive advantage (Boxall & Purcell, 2016). Reflecting on this a decade after these influential works, Lewis and Hackman (2006, p. 139) note that considering the number of consulting firms engaging in TM and articles on the subject, it would be assumed that the field of TM was a well-defined and researched area of management underpinned by a core set of principles. However, they go on to note the lack of definition and scope has led to confusion as to the nature of TM, be it focussed on outcomes, process or simply issues. Like Ashton and Martin (2005), they lament the lack a of clear concise definition. A further decade later Collings, Scullion, and Vaiman (2015, p. 233), continue to highlight TM as one of the fastest growing areas of academic research in the field of management but still lacking in clarity and substance. As such, Dries (2013) argues that the inability to develop a core structure to underpin TM leaves it open to be potentially seen as a management fad.

Much of the debate in trying gain insight in the management of talent in the early part of the twenty-first century centred around what was talent, where was it located in the organisation, and was it an inclusive or exclusive process or strategy? (Gallardo-Gallardo, Dries, & Gorzalez, 2013). The influential work of Michaels et al, (2001), defined talent into categories – 'A', 'B' and 'C'. 'A' being the top performers – the stars of the organisation, who they argue should be heavily invested in. Category 'B' being competent or the bedrock of the organisations who facilitate or enable the Category A stars to perform and finally category 'C' the bottom performers who ideally need to be developed to become 'B' or 'A' performers, but more likely are managed out (Michaels et al., 2001). In other words, this approach identified TM as very much an exclusive approach to the management of human resources.

Zuboff (1998), on the one hand focussed on the value an employee provides the organisation, noting importantly that an employee may be of relatively low value from an external labour market perspective but high value within the context of their organisational role. In other works, talent was an inclusive process. What both these approaches to understanding TM provided was a differentiated internal labour market and a temporal perspective where there is potential for people to be re-evaluated and move within these internal labour markets.

These approaches by Micheals et al. (2001) and Zuboff (1988), focussed the recognition of TM as based upon the individual employee as the primary source of competitiveness (Barney, 1991; Boxall, 1996; Boxall & Purcell, 2016). As a result of this focus on the employee, the HR function has the potential to assume an increasingly critical, strategic and dynamic role in generating sustainable competitive advantage through people by focussing on the development of diverse policies, practices and systems to attract, retain and develop these key resources (Holland, Hecker, & Steen, 2002). This infers that the strategic management of talent has become a core imperative for organisations, particularly multinational corporations (Mellahi & Collings, 2010; Scullion & Collings, 2010), as such failures in TM are an ongoing source of concern for executives in modern organisations (Cappelli, 2008). As Lewis and Heckman (2006) note this is often because TM is not part of the strategic development of the organisation but secondary to it, a point supported by others (see Boudreau & Ramstead, 2005; Schmidt & Schmidt, 2010). This is a fundamental issue that goes to the heart of the emerging world of work in the twenty-first century. If organisations are to develop sustained competitiveness, the management of talented employees will be a central focus and fundamentally different to that of the twentieth century (Baron & Armstrong, 2007; Thorne & Pellant, 2007). So how can TM and strategy be reconciled?

As noted, the recognition of the role of TM has come at a time of major change in the nature of the labour markets in the late twentieth and early twenty-first centuries. Increasing shortages of skills in many advanced economies, combined with a generation of workers focussed on employability rather than employment, have been the catalyst for a shift away from the traditional employer–employee relationship – even *with* the advent of the GFC. However, this rise of TM has also coincided (as noted) with that of strategic human resource management (Boxall & Purcell, 2016). As Lewis and Hackman (2006) argue, TM should be part of the architecture of organisation; as such, strategic human resource management could be the ideal vehicle for its integration into the organisation's 'DNA' systems as by its nature it places the focus on human resources front and centre of an organisation's strategic development. As such we can look at the core theories of strategic HRM to better understand how a framework can be developed.

Attraction and Retention: A Theoretical Perspective

As noted, TM has become an increasingly significant aspect in building sustained competitive advantage. However, Lewis and Hackman (2006) argue that TM seems to be a new phase in repackaging a standard solution to HR challenges – or what is often called 'old wine in new bottles'. Whilst this often has negative connotations, the focus on strategic HRM provides potentially what TM is lacking: a solid theoretical perspective. A review of the HRM literature reveals two theoretical perspectives, and provides an understanding and framework for analysing the strategic approach associated with the long-term development of the organisation's human resources (and talent). The first is human capital theory, which links investment in the organisation's key asset, its employees, to increased productivity and sustained competitive advantage (Smith, 1998; Walton & Valentin, 2014). The strategic aspect is the long-term enhancement of the firm's human resource base by linking employees' skill development with retention through training and development, career management, and progression (Garavan, Morley, Gunnigle, & Collins, 2001); a seminal role for the HR function (Farndale, Scullion, & Sparrow, 2010). This also aligns with both Zuboff (1988) and Michaels et als' (2001) focus on the internal labour makes where skill enhancement can move people into more valued positions. This is also consistent with the second theoretical perspective, the resource-based view of the firm (RBV) (Penrose, 1959). The focus of the RBV is on an organisation retaining and developing these human resources through investments such as human resource development (HRD) strategies. This retention and development will ensure that these assets become valuable, rare and difficult to imitate, thus further enhancing the organisation's sustained competitive advantage (Barney, 1991; Garavan et al., 2001; Walton & Valentin, 2014), by undertaking this on an ongoing and long-term basis. Many scholars have adopted these theoretical approaches in interpreting the essential elements of building sustained competitive organisational advantage (Boxall & Purcell, 2016; Boxall & Steenveld, 1999; Delery & Shaw, 2001; Wright, Dunford, & Snell, 2001). Whilst not providing a 'road map' to achieving these outcomes, these approaches provide the conceptual arguments for framing HR as central to organisational sustained competitive advantage.

In other words, these theories link the strategic focus of the management and the development of human resources and the deliberate promotion of a sustained competitive advantage strategy as a key criterion in the attraction, development and retention of talent. A critical element for these strategic platforms is that they enable a diverse range of strategies for staff enhancement and development across all levels and ability in this process. Organisations taking this strategic course will seek a long-term and diverse approach to managing and investing in their human resources (talent pools) to ensure that appropriate training, development and career management are available to all employees.

As noted, whilst, the theories above are put forward as 'road maps', it does emphasis that organisations must commit resources to develop a diverse and adaptive approach to TM in order to ensure that each area within the organisation has access to appropriate levels of HRD to meet diverse organisational objectives. However, this must be done in a coherent manner with the alignment of all aspects of the human resource architecture.

Building the Internal Architecture

To achieve the principles of building and retaining talent outlined above in practice means that organisations need to ensure that there is a cohesive and reinforcing HR framework. Research by MacDuffie (1995) and Wright et al. (1999) was the first to highlight this approach and shift the focus from examining HR practices in isolation to a system of 'internal fit' or 'bundles' of human resource practices. As Boxall and Purcell (2016) argue, the coherence in HRM practices implies designing policies that pull in the same direction. Research by Delery and Doty (1996), Wright et al. (2005) and Delery and Gupts (2016) indicates that in combination these HRM policies and practices can enhance the organisation's human resources and thereby organisational effectiveness. Storey (2007) and Conway, Fu, Monks, Alfes, and Bailey (2016) support this argument stating that organisational effectiveness results from a synergy of 'bundles' of human resources policies and practices. These policies and practices focus therefore on enhancing each other, or pulling together in the one direction (Monks & Loughnane, 2006), to create an internal fit of the capabilities to ensure human resources are attracted, develop and retained and managed to enhance organisational sustained effectiveness (Foss Pedersen, Reinholt-Fosgaard, & Stea, 2015; Gooderham, Parry, & Ringdal, 2008; Paauwe, Boon, Boselie, & Den Hartog, 2013).

However, whilst this theoretical perspective provides a logical, rational and coherent 'map' of HRM policies and practices, as Boxall and Purcell (2016) and Thompson and Harley (2007) argue, taking a critical perspective this approach is an oversimplified way to understand HRM. This is because of the way policies and practices evolve in an organisation, through the combination of short and long organisational goals, control and collaborative strategies, and new and mature perspectives which overlap mean that the perception and focus of various stakeholders will likely differ in understanding, interpretation and implementation (Conway et al., 2016). It is critical to understand that HR principles may be logical, but the actual combination of particular human resource policies in practices may create tensions and contradictions which can negate the development of organisational effectiveness by undermining the specific policies of attraction, retention and development of talent and its management. This outcome is known as 'deadly combinations' (Becker, Huselid, Pickus, & Spratt, 1997). These deadly combinations have the potential to develop when differing focus and/or time horizons and interpretations emerge and result in policies actively working against each other (Becker et al., 1997; Boxall & Purcell, 2016). For example, it is of little competitive advantage if your organisation has the best recruitment and selection processes and therefore attracts the best candidates only to have poor career management and rewards system, meaning this talent is lost to the market.

As such, Monks and Loughnane (2006) and Conway et al. (2016) point out it is critical to identify the potential of deadly combinations and manage them out. It is also important for HR to be aware that deadly combinations can occur for a variety of reasons. As McDonnell, Collings, Mellahi, and Schuler (2017) argue, organisations have at any one time multiple strategies and agendas, for example, retrenching staff in one area whilst simultaneously recruiting in another. Or, as noted, new or piecemeal policies and practices overlaid onto existing practices and work patterns which can lead to contradiction, inefficiencies and ultimately deadly combinations. The result of such work patterns and practices are likely to be negative on both the individuals and the organisation (Guest et al., 2012), leading to an inability to create sustained competitive advantage through internal fit and therefore through TM. Therefore, understanding deadly combinations can provide insight into why new work policies and practices brought in to improve organisational effectiveness create tensions and negative outcomes (Monks & Loughnane, 2006). As several researchers have identified there needs to be more cognisance around how and why deadly combinations and misalignment in internal fit occur and impact TM (Conway et al., 2016; Foss et al., 2015; Jiang, Lepak, Hu, & Beer, 2012; Monks & Longhnane, 2006).

Talent Management and the Individual

In attempting to quantify talent, Michaels et al. (2001) argue, that in its broadest sense talent was the sum of a person's abilities which included their intrinsic knowledge, skills and experience supported by their experience, intelligence, judgement, attitude, character and drive. It also included the temporal of their ability to learn and grow. These last points alluded to what has become an increasingly important aspect of managing talent – the psychology contract. In this context, Collings et al. (2015) and Farndale, Pai, Sparrow, and Scullion (2014) identify in their research a need to have a more balanced perspective between the needs of the organisation and the individual. This focus on the needs of the individual as a factor in attraction and retention, takes us into the realms of the changing psychological contract within the employment relationship (see Chapter 3: Psychological Contracts). A key aspect emerging from the contemporary psychological contract is that (potential) employees will look for employability not employment, and will want to be challenged, and where this is not occurring will change employers. These trends indicate that organisations that are prepared to understand the individual more will be in a stronger position to retain key human resources as the so-called 'war for talent' intensifies. It also reaffirms the point made earlier that strategic TM needs to differentiate policies and practices to the level of the individual to maximise competitive advantage from these core assets in the twenty-first century. Only in taking such an approach can an organisation differentiate its talent and human resource strategies to maximise sustained competitive advantage (Colling & Mellahai, 2009), and have the right people in the right place at the right time. This also fits well with the ability, motivation and opportunity (AMO) framework where there is also a need to provide the opportunities for this talent to develop and thrive otherwise they will leave. This also reflects the need for internal fit between the focus of the organisation and talent, the culture and talent, and the individual psychological contract and the work. From distilling these key points of this section, Thunnissen and Gallardo-Gallardo (2017, p. 3), articulate a holistic definition of TM:

> *TM can be described as the activities and processes that involve the systematic attraction, identification, development, engagement, retention and deployment of these talents in order to create strategic sustainable success.*

Talent Management: An Attitude and a Mindset

As the research continues to illustrate, TM has become an imperative in the face of an increasingly complex and dynamic environment. In the same context of strategic HRM and its framework theories of human capital and the resource-based view of the firm, what is required to underpin its successful development is a culture of cooperation and communication of managers through all levels of the organisation. This will facilitate the processes of TM being more strategic, connected and broad-based to increase internal fit and decrease deadly combinations. TM processes at all levels need to include workforce planning, talent-gap analysis, recruitment, selection, education and development, retention, talent reviews, succession planning, and evaluation. Only through integration and alignment of these processes will the framework for sustainable success be developed. By assessing available talent and by placing the right people in the right place at the right time, organisations can survive and thrive (McCauley & Wakefield, 2006; Oakes, 2006; Silverman, 2006). This is where strategic HRM plays a significant role in bringing TM to the senior management level.

It is also clear that the way organisations seek to retain these highly skilled resources will have to change. The simple assumption that people are recruited and stay or are poached needs to be seen in the long-term context of resource development. Again this places human resources at the centre of policy and systems development to achieve outcomes that promote TM and the organisation as an employer of choice for increasingly discerning current and potential employees. The structural changes driving the 'war for talent' are widespread across many of the more industrialised market economies. This creates what Michaels et al. (2001) describe as a 'new' business reality, in which management skills and the ability to embrace a new mindset are critical. As Thunnussen, Boselie, and Fruytier (2013) argues this new reality implies a consideration of the value of TM for the individual.

In the context of this twenty-first century environment, organisations will have to adapt to this paradigm in a variety of ways. The evolving psychological contract under which workers operate will continue to redefine the employee relationship. In contrast to the traditional 'relational' contract associated with a conventional (long-term) employment relationship based upon standard terms and conditions of employment, work will be organised to be conducive to the demands of these workers. Management must therefore pay careful attention to both the structural and cultural conditions that exist within the firm (Sims, 1994; Thomas, Au, & Ravlin, 2003), including more diverse and proactive strategies as key retention tools that include talent in the processes (Dries, 2013; Newell, Robertson, Scarbrough, & Swan, 2002; Thunnissen, Boselie, & Fruytier, 2013). As Michaels et al. (2001) have noted, the way organisations have managed talent in the past will not be sufficient in the future. The new approach to focus on the management of human resources, and in particular, HRD strategies linked to employee development and employability.

It is becoming increasingly clear that talent and TM is seen as a critical driver in sustaining corporate performance, and an organisation's ability to attract, develop and retain talent will be a major factor determining competitive advantage in the future, thus requiring organisations to invest significantly more resources in the battle for talent (Festing & Schafer, 2014; Michaels et al., 2001). The seminal work on TM by Michaels et al. (2001) identifies five key areas for organisations to act upon if they are going to make talent a source of competitive advantage. These are:

(1) embracing a talent mindset;
(2) crafting a winning employee value proposition (EVP);
(3) rebuilding their recruitment strategy;
(4) weaving development into their organisation; and
(5) differentiating and affirming their people.

The following section discusses these key areas more fully to help provide a 'road map' to more fully outline the nature of building a TM strategic framework.

Embracing a Talent Mindset

A key element in the McKinsey report was the idea that TM is a critical role for the CEO; a role that could not be delegated. In this context, the report's authors proposed several key actions that leaders must take (Michaels et al., 2001):

* involvement in people decisions;
* developing probing talent reviews;
* instilling a talent-focussed mindset within the organisation;
* investing real money in talent; and
* being accountable for TM.

This approach also reinforces the role of strategic HRM as a driver for this at a senior level, and as noted earlier the need for a diverse approach to the market. Its importance is highlighted in Article 2.1 in Box 1 (below).

Box 1.

Article 2.1: This is why your top talent leaves – and how to stop them.
Adapted from Emily Douglas, October 1, 2018.

Why do good employees leave? It's a question that HR leaders have been asking themselves for decades.

A report from Mercer found that one third of all employees plan on quitting their current role in the next 12 months – citing a lack of career support and opportunities as the main reason why.

So, how can employers keep their top talent from seeking out pastures new, if money isn't the deciding factor?

Essentially, it comes down to employees finding a place where they can personally make a difference, while also being able to grow and develop their own career ...., what keeps an employee loyal to an organisation is having that deep sense of resonance with the corporate purpose and values says Norm Sabapathy, executive vice president of people at Cadillac Fairview.

This hyper-personalization of the development plans is a key differentiator for brands, as well as being a sticky tactic to keep executives in place. Earlier this year, we spoke to Laura Sherbin, co-president at the Center for Talent Innovation. We learned that one third of new employees actually make the decision to leave their new employer just six months into the job.

'Flight risk is inevitable if employees experience barriers to their career progression – and, unfortunately, diverse employees frequently report facing unfair barriers', added Laura.

HR leaders can play a significant role in reducing this trend by ensuring diverse employees have access to sponsors, senior colleagues advocating for their career advancement. A study from the Center for Talent Innovation (CTI) called *The Sponsor Effect 2.0: Road Maps for Sponsors and Protégés* found that professionals who had sponsors were far more likely than those who lacked them to be satisfied with their rates of advancement – what CTI referred to as the 'sponsor effect'.

Crafting a Winning EVP

An EVP is everything an employee experiences within an organisation, including intrinsic and extrinsic satisfaction, values, ethics and culture. It is also about how well the organisation fulfils the employee's needs, expectations and aspirations (Festing & Schafer, 2013; Michaels et al., 2001). In their study, the McKinsey Group set out to determine what employees look for when making an employment decision. The key issues included job satisfaction, challenging, exciting work and development. These factors are followed closely by a good culture, commitment, organisational support and career advancement (see Box 2).

Rebuilding Your Recruitment Strategy

When managers restructure a recruitment strategy, a critical issue is being able to understand the new workforce. This means that even during downturns in the market, there is a need to maintain a creative recruitment-and-selection strategy, as the TM is a long-term proposition. Only in this way will organisations continue to absorb new talent. In terms of attraction, along with the primary areas of recruitment and selection, values and ethics act as important sources of attraction as employees become increasingly discerning about their employers. Websites like *glassdoor*, for example, allow potential employees to find out about real organisational culture and values. An understanding of how potential employees view or obtain information about the organisation can enhance the match between the person and the organisation, increasing person-organisational fit and retention.

Box 2.

Article 2.2: This is the real reason your talent pools are dying.
Adapted from Emily Douglas, October 16, 2018.

HR Tech News

Where once employers held all the cards, power is now firmly in the hands of candidates.

In fact, 42% of leaders worry they simply won't be able to find the skills they need – with three quarters struggling to find any relevant candidates. A recent survey from CareerBuilder found that 44% of employers are looking to hire full-time employees right now – however, 45% are reporting a total dearth of top talent.

Why? Simple – you're not making use of the recruitment technology out there to bridge your diversity gap.

A non-inclusive talent pool is worthless – both in terms of skills needed and organisational branding. Candidates will intentionally seek out organizations that practice a commitment to diversity – which is often being cited as one of the main reasons for taking a role. In fact, organisations that rate highly for inclusivity are more likely to have above-average financial returns.

Diversity comes in many forms: diversity of thought, of belief, of how one approaches challenges.

Removing bias

Employers could use AI in the screening processes in order to scrap any bias. Also tools can be used to neutralize CVs, to get rid of any names or genders or pictures, so that the candidate is chosen for interview based solely on their skills.

Implement neutral language

Recruitment doesn't start with an interview – it begins as soon as you write that job advert. Past studies have shown that organisations are sometimes guilty of using weighted language, which serves to alienate certain sub-sections of candidates. For instance, ads for male-dominated sectors tended to use masculine wording. The Harvard Kennedy School found that this discouraged women from applying because (1) women think more men work there; (2) women then assumed they wouldn't fit into the culture; and (3) they found the overall job description less appealing.

Weaving Development Into Your Organisation

In the twenty-first century, employees are looking for work that provides opportunities and is challenging. However, this is often given lip service in many organisations, in particular those in the Anglo-American region. As Michaels et al. (2001) have noted, talent seldom arrives fully developed; what people possess is potential that, when nurtured and challenged, can be brought to its maximum. In other words, organisations must develop their talent at all levels and weave it into the culture. This requirement is closely linked to areas such as job design, job analysis and team building, which contribute to the day-to-day experience on the job, determining what people actually do at work and how effectively they do it. Otherwise talent will leave to pursue more interesting work elsewhere. In an environment characterised by talent shortages and an increasingly discerning workforce, it is imperative for employers to review how they construct and connect jobs (see Box 3).

Differentiating and Affirming Your People

We can link approaching the workforce as a diverse set of resources to what are called the 'hard' and 'soft' approaches to HRM. In terms of soft HRM, organisations:

- invest heavily in star performers (the A team);
- develop solid employees (the B team) to contribute their best to retain them; and
- help poor performers (the C team) to improve their performance.

If the technique of soft HRM fails to change the performance of the C team, the organisation will use an exit strategy – hard HRM.

Note that this approach can be seen as producing a potential star-focussed culture that undermines a team culture. Michaels et al., however, disagree, arguing that it simply involves recognition of an individual's achievement – as long as it is not overt it will not affect the performance of the organisation. Despite this, organisations should carefully consider the issue if they are considering embarking on such policies.

Box 3.

Article 2.3: These startups are winning the talent war.
Adapted from Rachel Ranosa, September 7, 2018.

HR Tech News

LinkedIn has unveiled its list of the most sought-after startups in the United States – companies seven years old or younger that are attracting top talent.

'A breakthrough startup can scramble industries, alter how we work and live, and shift talent flows around the world', says Daniel Roth, editor-in-chief at LinkedIn. 'It's no wonder that we tend to follow the fortunes of these founders and those who choose to work for them so carefully'.

A list of 50 companies in the US was created from data on the interactions of 575 million LinkedIn users. The networking site focussed on four criteria: employee growth, jobseeker interest, user engagement with the company and its employees, and how well the startups pulled talent from LinkedIn's Top Companies list.

In the United States, ride-hailing service Lyft tops the list with a global head-count of more than 3,000 employees. The San Francisco-based company is known to look after the well-being of its workers, having introduced mental health benefits and training managers on how to detect distress signals from employees, LinkedIn said. At number two is Los Angeles food and beverage company Halo Top. A team of 100 is powering the hypergrowth startup's rise … One secret to keeping Halo Top employees happy: the company lets everybody work remotely.

United States

   (1) Lyft
   (2) Halo Top Creamery
   (3) Coinbase
   (4) Noodle.ai
   (5) Bird
   (6) Robinhood
   (7) Ripple
   (8) Glossier
   (9) Aurora
 (10) Rubrik

Summary

There is a clear indication that the negotiating position of employees in the twenty-first century workplace is increasing for the first time in a generation. This is beginning to have an impact on the employment relationship and subsequently, employment policies and practices as the 'war for talent' becomes increasingly intense. It is clear that the new workforce is discerning and skilled. Potential employees are exploring whether the organisation pays enough attention to them in terms of both opportunities and resources. It appears that organisations are, in some cases, actively pursuing the management of talent as a source of sustained competitive advantage. In order to be effective and create long-term organisational success, TM strategies must align to business goals, integrate all related processes and systems, and create a talent mindset (Ashton & Morton, 2005). Over the next decade, it will be interesting to see how TM strategies change further. As labour markets continue to tighten and workers become even more discerning in a globalised, complex and dynamic business environment, global TM will continue to become increasingly important for multinational enterprises (Makela, Bjorkman, & Ehrnrooth, 2010; McDonnell, Lamare, Gunnigle, & Lavelle, 2010; Scullion & Collings, 2011; Tarique & Schuler, 2010).

References

Ashton, C., & Morton, L. (2005). Managing talent for competitive advantage: Taking a systemic approach to talent management. *Strategic HR Review*, 4(5), 28–31.

Barney, J. (1991). Firm resources and sustained competitive advantage. *Journal of Management*, 17, 99–120.

Baron, A., & Armstrong, M. (2007). *Human capital management: Achieving added value through people*. London: Kogan Page.

Becker, B., Huselid, M., Pickus, P., & Spratt, M. (1997). HR as a source of shareholder value: Research and recommendations. *Human Resource Management*, 36(1), 39–47.

Boudreau, J. W., & Ramstad, P. M. (2005) Talentship, talent segmentation, and sustainability: A new HR decision science paradigm for a new strategy definition. *Human Resource Management*, 44(2), 129–136.

Boxall, P. (1996). The strategic HRM debate and the resource-based view of the firm. *Human Resource Management Journal*, 6(3), 59–75.

Boxall, P., & Steenveld, M. (1999). Human resource strategy and competitive advantage: A longitudinal study of engineering consultancies. *Journal of Management Studies*, 36(4), 443–463.

Boxall, P., & Purcell, J. (2016). *Strategy and human resource management* (4th ed.). Basingstoke: Palgrave Macmillan.

Collings, D., & Mellahi, K. (2009). Strategic talent management: A review of the literature. *Human Resource Management Review*, 19(4), 303–314.

Collings, D., Scullion, H., & Vaiman, H. (2015). Talent management: Progress and prospects. *Human Resource Management Review*, 25(1), 1–3.

Cappelli, P. (2008). Talent management for the twenty-first century. *Harvard Business Review*, 86(3), 74–81.

Conway, E., Fu, N., Monks, K., Alfes, K., & Bailey, C. (2016). Demands or resources? HR practices, employee engagement, and emotional exhaustion within a hybrid model of employment relations. *Human Resource Management*, 55(5), 901–917.

Delery, J., & Doty, D. H. (1996). Modes of theorizing in strategic human resource management: Test of universalistic, contingency and configurational performance. *Academy of Management Journal*, 39(4), 802–835.

Delery, J., & Gupts, N. (2016). Human resource management practices and organizational effectiveness: Internal fit matters. *Journal of Organizational Effectiveness*, 3(2), 139–163.

Delery, J., & Shaw, J. (2001). The strategic management of people in work organizations: Review, synthesis and extension. *Personnel and Human Resource Management*, 20, 165–197.

Dries, N. (2013). The psychology of talent management: A review and research agenda. *Human Resource Management Review*, 23(94), 272–285.

Farndale, E., Pai, A., Sparrow, P., & Scullion, H. (2014). Balancing individual and organizational goals in global talent management. *Journal of World Business*, 49(2), 204–214.

Farndale, E., Scullion, H., & Sparrow, P. (2010). The role of the corporate HR function in global talent management. *Journal of World Business*, 45, 161–168.

Festing, M., & Schafer, L. (2014). Generational challenges to talent management: A framework for talent retention based on the psychological contract perspective. *Journal of World Business*, 49(2), 262–271.

Foss, N., Pedersen, T., Reinholt-Fosgaard, M., & Stea, D. (2015). Why complementary HRM practice impact performance: The case of rewards, job design, and work climate in a knowledge-sharing context. *Human Resource Management*, 54(6), 955–976.

Friedman, T. L. (2016). *Thanks for being late: An optimist's guide to thriving in the age of accelerations.* New York, NY: Allen Lane.

Gallardo-Gallardo, E., Dries, N., & Gorzalez, T. (2013). What is the meaning of 'talent' in the world of work? *Human Resource Management Review, 25*(3), 264–279.

Garavan, T., Morley, M., Gunnigle, P., & Collins, E. (2001). Human capital accumulation: The role of human resource development. *Journal of European Industrial Training, 25*, 48–68.

Gooderham, P., Parry, E., & Rigdal, K. (2008). The impact of strategic human resource management practices on the performance of european firms. *International Journal of Human Resource Management, 19*(11), 2041–2056.

Guest, J., Paauwe, J. & Wright, P. (2012). HRM and performance: Achievements and challenges. Hoboken, NJ: John Wiley & Sons.

Gunnigle, P., Lavelle, J., & Monagham, S. (2013). Weathering the storm? Multinational companies and human resource management through the global financial crisis. *International Journal of Manpower, 34*(30), 214–231.

Holland, P., Hecker, R., & Steen, J. (2002). Human resource strategies and organisational structures for managing gold-collar workers. *Journal of European Industrial Training, 26*, 72–80.

Jiang, K., Lepak, D., Hu, J., & Beer, J. (2012). Does human resource management influence organizational outcomes? *Academy of Management Journal, 55*(6), 1264–1294.

Lewis, R. E., & Heckman, R. J. (2006). Talent management: A critical review. *Human Resource Management Review, 16*(2), 139–154.

MacDuffie, J. (1995). Human resource bundles and manufacturing performance: Organizational logic and flexible production systems in the world auto industry. *Industrial and Labour Relations Review, 48*(2), 197–221.

Makela, K., Bjorkman, I., & Ehrnrooth, M. (2010). How do MNCs establish their talent pools? Influences on individuals' likelihood of being labelled as talent. *Journal of World Business, 45*, 134–142.

McCauley, C., & Wakenfield, M. (2006). Talent management in the 21st century: Help your company find, develop and keep its strongest workers. *The Journal for Quality and Participation, 29*(4), 4.

McDonald, A., Lamare, R., Gunnigle, P., & Lavell, J. (2010). Developing tomorrow's leaders: Evidence of global talent management in multinational enterprises. *Journal of World Business, 45*(20), 150–160.

McDonnell, A., Collings, D., Mellahi, K., & Schuler, R. (2017). Talent management: A systematic review and future prospects. *Journal European Journal of International Management, 11*(1), 86–128.

Mellahi, K., & Collings, D. G. (2010). The barriers to effective global talent management: The example of corporate elites in MNEs. *Journal of World Business, 45*, 143–149.

Michaels, E., Handfield-Jones, H., & Axelrod, E. (2001). *The war for talent.* Boston, MA: Harvard Business School Press.

Monks, K., & Loughnane, M. (2006). Unwrapping the HRM bundle: HR systems design in Irish power utility. *International Journal of Human Resource Management, 17*(11), 1926–1941.

Newell, S., Robertson, M., Scarbrough, H., & Swan, J. (2002). *Managing knowledge work.* Basingstoke: Palgrave Macmillan.

Oakes, K. (2006). The emergence of talent management. *Training & Development, 60*(4), 21–24.

Paauwe, J., Boon, C., Boselie, C., & Den Hartog, D. (2013). Reconceputualizing fit in strategic human resource management: Lost in translation? In J. Paauwe & P. Wright

(Eds.), *HRM and performance: Achievements and challenges* (pp. 61–78). Chichester: Wiley.

Penrose, E. (1959). *The theory of growth of the firm*. Oxford: Blackwell.

Schmidt, M., & Schmidt, C. (2010, May). How to keep your top talent. *Harvard Business Review*, *88*(5), 54–61.

Scullion, H., & Collings, D. (2010). Global talent management. *Journal of World Business*, *45*, 105–108.

Scullion, H., & Collings, D. (Eds.) (2011). *Global talent management*. London: Routledge.

Silverman, L. L. (2006). How do you keep the right people on the bus? Try stories. *Journal for Quality and Participation*, *29*(4), 11–15.

Sims, R. R. (1994). Human resource management's role in clarifying the 'new psychology contact'. *Human Resource Management*, 33(3), 373–382.

Smith, A. (1998). *Training and development in Australia* (2nd ed.). Chatswood, NSW: Butterworth.

Storey, J. (2007). *Human resource management: A critical test* (thirrd ed.). London: Thomson International.

Tarique, I., & Schuler, R. S. (2010). Global talent management: Literature review, integrative framework and suggestions for further research. *Journal of World Business*, *45*, 122–133.

Thomas, D. C., Au, K., & Ravlin, E. C. (2003). Cultural variation and psychological contract. *Journal of Organizational Behaviour*, *24*(4), 451–471.

Thompson, P., & Harley, B. (2007). hrm and the worker: Labor process perspectives. In P. Boxall, J. Purcell, & P. Wright (Eds.), *The Oxford handbook of human resource management* (pp. 147–166). London: Oxford University Press.

Thorne, K., & Pellant, A. (2007). *The essential guide to managing talent: How top companies recruit, train and retain the best employees*. London: Kogan Page.

Thunnissen, M., Boselie, P., & Fruytier, B. (2013). Talent management and the relevance of context: Towards a pluralist approach. *Human Resource Management Review*, *23*(4), 326–336.

Thunnissen, M., & Gallardo-Gallardo, E. (2017). *Talent management in practice: An integrated and dynamic approach*. Bingley: Emerald Publishing.

Walton, J., & Valetin, A. (2014). *Strategic human resource development: Practices and orthodoxies*. Basingstoke: Palgrave Macmillan.

Wright, P., Dunford, B., & Snell, S. (2001). Human resources and the resource based view of the firm. *Journal of Management*, *27*, 701–721.

Wright, P. M., Gardner, T. M., Moynihan, L. M., & Allen, M. R. (2005). The relationship between HR practices and firm performance: Examining causal order. *Personnel Psychology*, 58, 409–446.

Wright, P. M., McCormick, B., Sherman, W., & McMahan, G. (1999). Human Resource Management and Sustained Competitive Advantage, *Personnel Psychology*, 58, 409–446.

Zuboff, S. (1988). *In the age of the smart machine: The future of work and power*. New York, NY: Basic Books.

Section I

Case Study

Talent Management

Case Study – AgencyCo

AgencyCo is the leading supplier of labour hire work also known as 'on-hire', 'temp' or 'agency' work. Their labour-hire staff can be employees who are then on-hired to a client firm (but are not employees of that firm) or self-employed contractors. Initially providing supplementary trades, AgencyCo developed a white-collar sector providing customer contact services, healthcare and general office placement staff in a diverse range of industries.

AgencyCo argues that to attract and keep talented workers the work needs to be not only about opportunity and variety but also about quality training, development and career progression, through developing each employee's skills base. The variety of jobs with different client firms is also an important learning feature of working for AgencyCo. Management at AgencyCo identifies working with different clients as a training and development opportunity and is interpreted this way by labour hire workers who value the new experiences.

AgencyCo aims to become an employer of choice by giving employees and potential employees 'a sense of belonging but not a sense of being owned' by providing a range of benefits and doing all the things a normal employer would do. AgencyCo treats both their temporary and permanent staff as if they are committed to the organisation, which allows them to demonstrate that although an assignment is limited or short-term it will not lead to disinterest or second-rate treatment on the part of the agency. This people management approach has led to turnover in employees being significantly lower than the industry average.

Becoming an employer of choice in labour-hire industry does raise the issue of talented staff being poached by client organisations. AgencyCo claims to be able to compete with any permanent employer. This is supported by the fact that they do not see themselves as a provider of peripheral workers but rather as working within a partnership to manage these key employees. AgencyCo sees their competitive advantage as working in areas where they have acknowledged expertise which also corresponds with areas of labour shortage. Since labour hire workers may be subject to conflicting policies and procedures on clients' sites, in many cases there will be an AgencyCo supervisor linked to the site who looks after the AgencyCo employee under every circumstance even if there is a client supervisor present.

Written by Rob Hecker and Peter Holland

Questions
  (1) What characteristics does AgencyCo exhibit with regard to being successful at talent management?
  (2) Why do you think this approach will/won't work in the long term?

Section II

Managing the Individual at Work

Chapter 3

Psychological Contracts

Ross Donohue and Tse Leng Tham

Introduction

As organisations attempt to utilise their human resources more effectively in order to improve their performance and achieve sustained competitive advantage, the relationship between organisations and employees has emerged as an issue of interest to human resource management researchers and practitioners. One construct that is central to understanding organisational–employee relationships is the psychological contract. At a general level, there is broad agreement that the psychological contract refers to the beliefs surrounding the terms of exchange between employees and employers. However, as researchers have attempted to refine and specify this construct, different constitutive definitions and operationalisations have emerged. For example, conceptualisations of the psychological contract differ according to the type of beliefs (e.g. obligations, expectations, promises) as well as the level at which the construct occurs (e.g. individual, dyadic, group, organisational, societal). Rousseau (1989), arguably the researcher who has contributed most to advancing our understanding of this construct, has focussed on the obligatory and promissory aspects of the beliefs that constitute the psychological contract. A variety of mechanisms may lead to a promise inference, including verbal discussion, representation by an organisational agent, or organisational policy and practice (Hornung & Glaser, 2010). Rousseau has consistently advocated that the appropriate unit of analysis is the individual level (Roehling & Boswell, 2004). Thus, according to Rousseau, the psychological contract refers to the informal, tacit and often unspoken and unwritten set of reciprocal obligations and promises held by the employee of the employer (Rousseau, 1990, 1995). These promises and obligations may involve promotion, responsibility, job security, training or career development.

In contrast to a formal employment contract, the psychological contract is essentially perceptual and, as a consequence, one party's perception of the obligations and entitlements within the contract may not align with the interpretation of the other party (Lester, Claire, & Kickul, 2001). According to Robinson and Rousseau (1994), the psychological contract is also conceptually distinct from expectations as expectations merely refer to what an employee expects to obtain from the employer. The psychological contract, however, also involves the *perceived* mutual obligations that characterise the relationship that an employee has with his or her employer. Therefore, the formative psychological contract may reflect not only formally stated, explicit obligations, but also perceived obligations spawned via implicit means (Rosen, Chang, Johnson, & Levy, 2009; Zhao, Wayne, Glibkowski, & Bravo, 2007), both of which extend beyond the boundaries of the legal employment agreement. Consequently, if a perceived obligation is not complemented by the belief that a promise has been conveyed (e.g. if the perceived obligation is based exclusively on previous experience in other employment relationships), then it falls outside the psychological contract. The psychological contract may involve any item that may be exchanged between the organisation and the employee. However, given that the psychological contract is dynamic, unwritten, informal, and internally constructed, it is difficult to articulate its specific constituents at the time the contract is formed (Hiltrop, 1996).

Psychological contracts exist for a number of reasons. First, they reduce the level of uncertainty that employees may experience by establishing agreed-upon conditions of employment. Second, psychological contracts direct employees' behaviour without direct management supervision and surveillance, with the assumption being that employees will self-monitor based on the expectation of rewards. Given its potential in helping define and comprehend contemporary employment relationships (Turnley & Feldman, 2000; Tyagi & Agrawal, 2010), psychological contracts have gained traction as a foundational aspect of the employee–employer relationship (Robinson & Morrison, 2000). They provide a means of comprehending the 'obscured' and 'soft' aspects of the relationship (i.e. attention to important shifts in the employment relationship) (Shore, Coyle-Shapiro, & Tetrick, 2012).

Formation, Maintenance and Evaluation of the Psychological Contract

The beliefs that constitute the psychological contract are formed as a result of the employee's interactions with agents or representatives of the organisation – particularly his or her direct superior – as well as the employee's perceptions of the organisational culture. Initially, these beliefs are developed during the recruiting process and through early experiences in the organisation (Turnley & Feldman, 1999). However, expectations may arise prior to meeting representatives of the organisation through information gleaned from the media, the Internet, and sites such as *glassdoor*, promotional material, or friends and family who have had dealings with the organisation (McFarlane Shore & Tetrick, 1994). Additionally, expectations may be formed by interpretations of past exchanges that the employee has had with earlier employers, or they may be influenced vicariously by observing others' experiences (Saunders & Thornhill, 2006). Rousseau (2001) described the successive phases of psychological contract development and maintenance against the employment phase. The first two phases (pre-employment and recruitment described above) are defined as contract *formation*, before the transition to the third phase of contract *maintenance*.

Once a psychological contract has been formed, it tends not to change radically over time. However, it should be noted that the formation of the psychological contract is not a 'one-shot' affair; instead, it is dynamic in that it is consolidated, adjusted, revised and reformulated throughout the course of the employee's tenure with his or her organisation (Robinson & Rousseau, 1994). Evidence of the fact that the psychological contract changes over time and indeed is asymmetrical was identified by Robinson, Kraatz, and Rousseau (1994) in a longitudinal study involving a sample of MBA alumni. Specifically, they found that employees' perceived obligations to their employers diminished over time, while the obligations that employees attributed to their employers increased temporally. It is also important to note that individuals, not organisations, have psychological contracts, as organisations are inanimate entities incapable of 'perceiving'. According to Rousseau (1989), organisations provide the context for the formation of the psychological contract; however, individual managers, that is, agents or representatives of the organisation – can personally perceive a psychological contract with their employees.

The maintenance phase of the psychological contract is distinguishable by the simultaneous reduction of information-seeking behaviour by the employee and socialisation efforts by the organisation. Largely, the transition to the maintenance phase is contingent on the outcomes of the formation process and the degree to which the new employee is capable of reconciling the information received and promises perceived, with his/her actual experiences in the organisation (Christeen, 2009). Once an employee transitions to this relatively stable maintenance stage, the challenge for employers is to ensure that future organisational or personal events do not engender adverse evaluations of contract status.

The shift from the maintenance phase to the *evaluation* phase can occur due to a number of events, but this results in the employee integrating beneficial or non-threatening change into their existing contract. Alternatively, the employee may view the assessment of change as incongruent, potentially leading to perceptions of contract breach. Even organisations with the best of intent cannot guarantee that all outcomes will be beneficial for all employees at all times. Moreover, employees typically engage in a sense-making process in an attempt to rationalise events. This sense-making process may give rise to the perception of contract status as variously fulfilled, breached, or violated by the individual contract holder (discussed below).

Types of Psychological Contracts

While psychological contracts have many commonalities, they may vary according to the type of work undertaken, the motives of employees and the human resource management strategy applied by organisations (Rousseau, 2004). A number of typologies have been developed to explain variations in psychological contract types; however, the majority of extant studies have applied the dichotomous relational versus transactional typology proffered by Rousseau (1989). In response to the shifts in work-related values particularly among the younger Gen Y and Millennial employees, researchers have begun acknowledging the birth of a new form of psychological contract known as the balanced psychological contracts (Hess & Jepsen, 2009; O'Neill & Adya, 2007).

The Traditional (Relational) Psychological Contracts

A relational psychological contract is established on the basis of an exchange of effort and loyalty on the part of the employee in return for job security and career development on the part of the employer. The conceptual development of the relational psychological contract is primarily based on Blau's (1964) social exchange theory. Essentially, social exchange theory holds that when an individual provides resources or benefits to another, there is an expectation that the other party will give something in return. Thus, if an employee obtains support – such as opportunities for training and career development – from the employer, the employee will feel compelled to recipro-cate, perhaps by providing high levels of performance or commitment.

Under the terms of the relational psychological contract, the employer adopts a pater-nalistic role, showing consideration for the well-being of employees and taking much of the responsibility for the management of their careers. Additionally, the employ-ment relationship is seen as broad, long-term and open-ended. Employees who per-form their tasks well are essentially guaranteed tenure with the organisation until their retirement. Thus, the motivators of the relational psychological contract for employees are: job security; working in a friendly interpersonal environment; personal support; flexible working conditions; and opportunities for personal, professional and career development. The employee's obligations under this relationship include: working on tasks that are not delineated in his or her job description; providing mentoring to less experienced colleagues; developing skills that are specific to the organisation; and accepting a transfer to another division or relocating to another region (Tsui, Pearce, Porter, & Tripoli, 1997). A central feature of relational psychological contracts is loy-alty, as both the employee and the employer commit to fulfilling the needs of the other. Employees who are valued by their organisations are more likely to receive relational psychological contracts than employees whose value is judged as marginal.

The Transactional Psychological Contracts
External factors – such as globalisation, deregulation and increased competition – have precipitated a number of organisational changes – such as restructuring, downsizing and the movement towards more flexible employment options. As a corollary, employ-ees have become increasingly mistrustful of their employers, more cynical about the motives underlying the actions of management, and more likely to feel betrayed by the organisation. There is also evidence to suggest that the level of loyalty and organ-isational commitment on the part of employees that once existed has decreased. For example, Stroh and Reilly (1997) examined managers' attachment to their organisa-tions retrospectively and found that respondents' sense of loyalty to their organisation had declined over a five-year period. One result of these changes is the demise of the traditional relational psychological contract and the advent of the newer transactional psychological contract. In fact, in tandem with such changes in the employment rela-tionship, some researchers have gone so far as to claim, 'the near death of the relational psychological contract' (Callanan, Perri, & Tomkowicz, 2017, p. 355).

Transactional psychological contracts are based on clearly defined, monetisable exchanges that occur between the employee and the employer over a predefined and typically short period of time (Robinson et al., 1994). While the relational psycho-logical contract is based on social exchange, the transactional psychological contract is grounded in an economic exchange. The transactional psychological contract dis-misses the obligations assumed in the traditional relational contract. Permanency and the notion of 'a job for life' in exchange for organisational commitment and organ-isational citizenship are no longer relevant in transactional relationships (Millward & Hopkins, 1998). Unlike its relational counterpart, the transactional psychological con-tract is characterised by limited personal involvement in the job and reduced organ-isational citizenship behaviour on the part of the employee. While intrinsic factors are the drivers of individuals with relational psychological contracts, employees with transactional psychological contracts are motivated by extrinsic factors such as career fast tracking and financial incentives. Additionally, while paternalism on the part of the employer is a hallmark of the relational psychological contract, the new transactional psychological contract is based on the principle of partnership where the new responsibility for employers is to create opportunities for employees to manage their own careers.

It would appear that a number of factors – such as industry type, status and the nature of the work undertaken – influence the likelihood of a transactional versus a relational psychological contract emerging. For example, employees working in highly volatile industries such as information technology or hospitality, employees whose roles are not seen as being part of the core business of the organisation or employees whose function is viewed as not being essential to attaining competitive advantage often have transactional psychological contracts (Rousseau, 2004).

Dispositional factors may also predispose individuals towards either a transactional or a relational psychological contract. Raja, Johns, and Ntalianis (2004) examined personality differences in terms of psychological contract type and found that employees who were 'equity sensitives' (i.e. those who closely compare their level of input against the outcomes they receive from the organisation) and neurotics (i.e. those who are anxious, emotionally unstable and mistrustful) were significantly more likely to hold transactional psychological contracts. Additionally, conscientiousness and self-esteem were also positively associated with the relational psychological contract type. A study by Tallman and Bruning (2008) broadly supports the findings of Raja et al. (2004); however, they also found that gender moderates the relationship between personality and psychological contract obligations. Specifically, they found that personality had a relatively small effect on the obligation attitudes of women; however, it had a significant effect on the obligation attitudes of men.

Beyond Transactional Psychological Contracts Today

Whilst research has generally advocated for the dichotomous relational versus transactional psychological contract typology, psychological contract scholars have also begun recognising that the changing and distinct work-related values, expectations, attitudes and behaviours the younger generation of employees (Gen Y, Millennials) hold have implications for the nature of psychological contracts formed (Kultalahti & Viitala, 2015; Lub, Bal, Blomme, & Schalk, 2016). More recent literature has proposed a new type of psychological contract known as the *balanced psychological contract* which features a combination of both relational (e.g. mutual concern and flexibility) and transactional (e.g. well-defined performance-reward criteria) characteristics (Hess & Jepsen, 2009; O'Neill & Adya, 2007). These constituents of the balanced psychological contracts are in line with the prevailing and preferred forms of career adopted by the younger generation such as the protean career (see Chapter 4 for more on protean careers). Along the lines of the mindset of a protean careerist, individuals accept certain well-specified obligations and balance them against benefits to secure continual employment (Hall & Moss, 1998).

In this newer form of psychological contract, researchers have also delved into understanding the changing emphasis on the content of the balanced psychological contracts. For instance, unlike their Gen X and Baby Boomer counterparts, younger employees such as those in the Millennial cohort do not place high importance on monetary expectations but instead, hold time as a crucial medium of exchange (Kultalahti & Viitala, 2015). Specifically, reciprocal flexibility particularly with time-tabling and working hours (Behrstock-Sherratt & Coggshall, 2010; Kultalahti & Viitala, 2015) and work-life balance (Cennamo & Gardner, 2008) are regarded to be of high significance. Younger Gen Y employees also hold high expectations with regards to the availability of a coaching supervisor, where individuals are provided with constant learning and developmental opportunities that will assist with not just career advancement (De Hauw & De Vos, 2010), but the development of competencies which would enhance the individual's value in the labour market (Kultalahti & Viitala, 2015). Job content is also hailed as an integral aspect of the newer psychological contract (De Hauw & De Vos, 2010). Specifically, individuals expect the actualisation of intrinsic benefits particularly from dynamic tasks wherein work is interesting, varied and challenging. Researchers have also emphasised the expectations of meaningful work, especially emphasising the need for congruence between the values held by the individual employee and the organisation (Dries, Pepermans, & De Kerpel, 2008). Lastly, the newer form of psychological contracts also features the cultivation and maintenance of a workplace environment where social relations are encouraged and perceived to be nurturing, supportive and cooperative (Cennamo & Gardner, 2008).

Psychological Contract Breach

A breach of the psychological contract occurs when the employee perceives that the organisation has not adequately fulfilled promised obligations. Breach of the psychological contract can adversely affect workplace attitudes and behaviours (Agarwal & Bhargava, 2013). Consequently, mitigating against psychological contract breach should be a primary concern of all organisations. Psychological contract breach is a subjective experience as it is based on an individual's perception, and not necessarily on the reality, that obligations have not been met. Furthermore, the modern organisational context is marked by intensification of the pace and nature of changes owing to growing business complexity, globalisation and shifts in the economic and social environment. Concomitant with such a turbulent and unpredictable landscape, is the redefinition of employee–organisation relationships, necessitating changes in its nature and expectations (O'Donohue, Donohue, & Grimmer, 2007). Consequently, researchers have even suggested that instances of psychological contract breach are becoming commonplace in today's workplaces, emphasising the importance of studying breach because preventing it is extremely difficult (Sims, 1994; Tyagi & Agrawal, 2010).

Morrison and Robinson (1997) have theorised that there are two factors that may give rise to psychological contract breach. The first, reneging, occurs when the organisation – or more correctly, an agent or agents of the organisation – is conscious that an obligation exists but intentionally fails to meet that obligation. Reneging may occur as a result of the organisation being unable to fulfil an obligation due to factors such as resource constraints. Thus, while the obligation may initially have been made in good faith, changing circumstances may subsequently make the fulfilment of that obligation untenable. Indeed, psychological contract breach may be more likely to occur under conditions in which an organisation's performance has declined (Robinson & Morrison, 2000). The second source of breach, incongruence, arises when an agent(s) of the organisation and the employee differ in their views about whether an obligation exists, or are at variance in terms of the nature of that obligation. According to Robinson and Morrison, the strength of the influence of both reneging and incongruence on psychological contract breach is moderated by vigilance. Vigilance refers to the extent to which an employee monitors the organisation in terms of its fulfilment of the psychological contract. Parzefall and Coyle-Shapiro (2011) examined the events that trigger psychological contract breach and found that they could be grouped into four types: *specific obligation* (i.e. breaches arising from an unmet obligation at a single point in time); *connected events* (i.e. breaches triggered by an unfulfilled obligation embedded in a chain of unfulfilled obligations over a long period); *secondary breaches/knock-on effects* (i.e. breaches that lead to negative outcomes for the employee); and *everyday breaches* (i.e. the accumulation of low-level unmet expectations over time).

Employees who hold the perception that the psychological contract has been breached believe that the organisation is no longer supportive of their contribution (Zagenczyk, Gibney, Kiewitz, & Restubog, 2009). Consequently, they are likely to question their employer's commitment to the underlying exchange relationship (Lester, Kickul, & Bergmann, 2007). When breach occurs, contract terms may be subject to change. For example, the relational dimensions of the psychological contract may become more transactionally oriented (Chen & Chiu, 2009). Breach in turn can give rise to a number of negative outcomes for both the individual and the organisation, including reduced work performance, anti-citizenship behaviours (Kickul, Newman, Parker, & Finkl, 2001), withdrawal behaviours (Zhao et al., 2007) and counterproductive workplace behaviours (CWB) (Bordia, Restubog, & Tang, 2008; Restubog, Zagenczyk, Bordia, & Tang, 2013). For example, in a study of customer service employees working for an Australian telecommunications company, it was found that psychological contract breach was associated with reduced levels of organisational trust which, in turn, was related to perceptions of less cooperative employment relations as well as increased levels of absenteeism (Deery, Iverson, & Walsh, 2006). Similarly, Robinson (1996), in a longitudinal study involving newly hired managers, found that psychological contract breach was negatively related to: performance, civic virtue behaviour (i.e. involvement in and concern for the life of the company) and intentions to remain with the organisation. It would appear that trust plays an important role in reducing the likelihood of breach occurring, as Robinson found that trust in the employer at the time new managers were hired was negatively related to subsequent psychological contract breach and that initial trust in one's employer mediated the relationship between breach and employees' later contributions to the organisation. The negative consequences of psychological contract breach have been substantiated by a meta-analysis (Zhao et al., 2007) which identified more than 100 studies linking breach to outcomes such as lower job satisfaction, reduced organisational commitment, lower in-role performance and reduced likelihood of engaging in organisational citizenship behaviours.

Psychological Contract Violation

Psychological contract violation is distinct from psychological contract breach. While breach of the psychological contract is a cognitive response to unmet obligations, violation is 'an affective and emotional experience of disappointment, frustration, anger and resentment that may emanate from an employee's interpretation of a contract breach and its accompanying circumstances' (Morrison & Robinson, 1997, p. 242).

Thus, breach always occurs temporally prior to violation; however, perceived psychological contract breach does not always result in feelings of violation. It is also theorised to energise the individual physiologically and induce appropriate action. Several factors may mitigate the likelihood of violation occurring. For example, the magnitude of the breach may be perceived by the employee to be small and/or the psychological contract is sufficiently robust that feelings of violation do not arise. Scholars (Dulac, Coyle-Shapiro, Henderson, & Wayne, 2008; Restubog et al., 2013) have also identified the quality, nature, and perception of working relationships as critical contextual factors to be considered as to *when* perceptions of breach may escalate and translate into feelings of violation. Some researchers have found high-quality relationships such as perceived organisational support to desensitise or buffer the escalation of breach to violation (e.g. Dulac et al., 2008; Restubog et al., 2013). However, it must be noted that in some cases, researchers have found the opposite. For instance, Restubog and Bordia (2006) found that higher perceptions of workplace familism (i.e. where the organisation is seen as a 'surrogate parent') intensified negative reactions to breach as instances of undelivered promises on the parental organisation's part is seen as a form of betrayal.

In instances when violation of the psychological contract does occur, the empirical research indicates that there are several negative outcomes that can ensue. For example, Turnley and Feldman (1999), with a sample of over 800 managers, found that violation of the psychological contract leads to higher levels of turnover intention, increased voicing of complaints, greater neglect of in-role duties, and a decreased willingness to defend the organisation against external threats. Similarly, a study of Australian public sector managers found strong negative relationships between psychological contract violation and both job satisfaction and organisational commitment (Knights & Kennedy, 2005). Also, Robinson and Morrison (2000) found that employees experience more acute feelings of violation following a perceived breach of the psychological contract in circumstances when the breach is attributed to deliberate reneging on the part of the organisation rather than to incongruence. Finally, research also indicates that psychological contract violation mediates the relationship between psychological contract breach and workplace attitudes and behaviours such as organisational commitment (Cassar & Briner, 2011), turnover (Dulac et al., 2008) and revenge cognitions (Bordia et al., 2008).

Psychological Contract Fulfilment

Psychological contract fulfilment occurs when an employee believes that the employer has kept promises and met expectations. When employers fulfil the psychological contract, they indicate to employees that they are committed to them, that they value their contribution to the organisation, and that they intend to maintain the relationship. According to Coyle-Shapiro and Conway (2005), psychological contract fulfilment consists of two components: perceived employer obligations and inducements. Based on empirical research, Coyle-Shapiro and Conway argue that perceived inducements lead to perceived organisational support, which in turn reduce employees' perceptions of the organisation's obligations towards them.

Lester et al. (2001) examined aspects of the psychological contract that employees valued most and how well organisations were able to meet those expectations using a sample of MBA students. They found that those components of the psychological contract that employees placed most value on were, in fact, the obligations that organisations found most problematic to fulfil. Specifically, the provision of open and honest communication from the organisation, being assigned interesting and challenging work, and having competent management were aspects of the psychological contract rated by employees as most important. However, these dimensions were also found to have the greatest discrepancy in terms of fulfilment.

Robinson and Morrison (1995) found that, if employers failed to fulfil their obligations of the psychological contract, employees were significantly less likely to engage in organisational citizenship behaviours (i.e. discretionary, out-of-role behaviours). Similarly, Harwell (2003, cited in Barnett, Gordon, Gareis, & Morgan, 2004), in a study involving physicians, found that fulfilment of the psychological contract was negatively associated with intention to leave the organisation, intention to change career, burnout and career dissatisfaction. Lester et al. (2001) found that fulfilment of the psychological contract was negatively associated with intentions to leave the organisation and positively related to job satisfaction. Similarly, a study by Zhang and Agarwal (2009) found that psychological contract fulfilment led to perceptions of organisational justice, which in turn, was positively predictive of both organisational citizenship behaviours and intention to remain with the organisation.

With the growth in international business, organisations are increasingly required to manage expatriate employees working in host countries. It has been suggested that psychological contracts may be even more influential in expatriate situations than domestic employment relationships as the employer has a greater influence on an employee's life (Guzzo, Noonan, & Elron, 1994). If expatriates perceive that their psychological contracts have been fulfilled, they are less likely to identify incongruities between their expectation and their actual experience. Research supports this view as Chen and Chiu (2009) found that the psychological contract fulfilment of expatriates had a positive influence on both their psychological adjustment (involving subjective well-being and mood states) and their socio-cultural adjustment (encompassing general, interaction and work adjustment) to foreign environments.

Traditionally, it has been assumed that in situations in which an organisation provides inducements that exceed fulfilment of the psychological contract, the employee's level of satisfaction would increase commensurately. Consistent with this view, Lambert, Edwards, and Cable (2003) found that satisfaction did increase as delivered pay, recognition and relationships exceeded promised levels. Interestingly, however, they also found that there was limited marginal utility for inducements such as variety, skill development and career training and in fact the provision of these inducements beyond fulfilment actually engendered decreased satisfaction.

Rousseau (1989) has argued that, although breach and fulfilment fall along a continuum, once breach has occurred it is difficult to rectify. This suggests that the effects of breach and fulfilment are asymmetrical, with the former having a greater impact on outcomes than the latter. This contention is supported by research (Conway, Guest, & Trenberth, 2011) which indicated that breach and fulfilment impact differentially on individual level outcomes. Specifically, this study found that increasing levels of psychological contract breach was negatively related to job satisfaction, organisational commitment, contentment and enthusiasm. However, increasing levels of psychological contract fulfilment was only significantly associated (in a positive direction) with one of these outcomes (organisational commitment), and that this relationship was substantially weaker than the relationship between breach and organisational commitment.

Work Status and the Psychological Contract

In recent years, many organisations have witnessed an increased number of temporary, contingent and casual employees. Partially, this could be attributable to the evolution of human resource management strategies aimed at providing greater flexibility, but such trends may also be owed to the rise of 'new careers' (see Chapter 6 on boundaryless and protean careers) and the recent mushrooming popularity of the 'gig economy', where individuals are likely employed as independent contractors and the nature of work deviates significantly from the traditional linear career path with a single employing organisation Indeed, with such changes to the employer–employee relationship, some researchers have raised concerns regarding the effect of flexible employment contracts on employees' attitudes and behaviours. Saunders and Thornhill (2006) examined the impact of a change in work status on the psychological contracts of a group of permanent employees who were forced to take up temporary employment within an organisation. In this case study, the psychological contracts of employees within the firm whose work status remained unchanged, that is, remained on permanent employment contracts, were also assessed. Saunders and Thornhill found that permanent employees tended to continue to hold *relational* psychological contracts with the organisation while those forced to take temporary positions were more likely to hold *transactional* psychological contracts. However, it appears that the nature of the psychological contract is quite complex, as there was considerable variation within each group. For example, some employees who remained on permanent contracts but were unhappy with the change were concerned that their contracts were becoming more transactional in focus. Moreover, those permanent employees with a low preference for temporary work expressed concern that they, too, might be forced onto temporary contracts in the future. Within the forced temporary group there was even greater variation. For example, some of these employees quickly arrived at the realisation that their psychological contract was now transactional, while others became more calculative following an initial period of denial. Additionally, a number in this group still perceived their psychological contract as relational, despite the fact that the organisation's director defined the contract with temporary employees as transactional.

Van Dyne and Ang (1998) examined the psychological contracts of contingent and permanent professional service employees in Singapore and found that contingent employees had a more circumscribed psychological contract in terms of their perception of what the organisation was obliged to provide for them when compared to their permanent counterparts. Isaksson, De Cuyper, Oettel, and De Witte (2010) also found that permanent employees reported a wider range of entitlements in comparison to temporary employees. Interestingly, these authors disaggregated entitlements according to whether they were relational or transactional, and found that permanent employees reported a similar number of transactional entitlements but a higher number of relational entitlements.

Chambel and Castanheira (2006) compared temporary firm workers (i.e. temporary workers with employment contracts of a maximum duration of three years) with core workers, and compared direct-hire temporary employees (i.e. temporary workers with employment contracts of an indefinite duration) with core workers in two separate samples. They found that temporary workers perceived that the organisation offered them fewer inducements (e.g. promotional opportunities, training and career development) and that their psychological contracts were more transactional (i.e. placed less importance on socio-emotional factors and more importance on economic factors) than core workers. Interestingly, Chambel and Castanheira also found that temporary workers who had enduring relationships with the organisation and the possibility of converting to permanent employment contracts, that is, direct-hire temporary workers, tended to develop more relational psychological contracts that were similar to those of core workers.

Today, we increasingly see individuals being engaged in non-standard work arrangements, often termed gig employment, precarious work, independent contract work, freelancers and on-demand workers (Kalleberg, 2009). Indeed, in the United States, the number of employees engaged in alternative work arrangements has grown from 10% of the total workforce to almost 16% in just the last decade (Katz & Krueger, 2016). Such shifts in patterns are similarly witnessed in the European Union (Vacas-Soriano, 2015). A key feature of such alternative employment arrangements is the notion of diminishing permanence in the employer–employee relationships, which by extension, influences the nature of psychological contracts held by such employees.

Whilst research in this space is still relatively scant, some (e.g. Lemmon, Wilson, Posig, & Glibkowski, 2016) have begun investigating how managing the psychological contracts of individuals in non-standard employment (e.g. independent contractors may differ from what we know of psychological contracts in more traditional modes of employment). Studying a sample of independent contractors, Lemmon and colleagues found that much like in typical employment relationships, the conveyance of HR procedures is still very much fundamental to schema underpinning an individual contractor's psychological contract perceptions. For instance, if the organisation engages in forcing negotiation behaviours (e.g. forcing independent contractor to accept certain terms of engagement), this is more likely to encourage the formation of transactional psychological contracts. This, in turn, is likely to negatively impact perceptions of the organisation's distributive justice which has been shown to have negative implications on individual's workplace attitudes and behaviours such as job performance (Lemmon et al., 2016).

Implications for Human Resource Management

Human resource management policies and practices significantly influence the psychological contract by signalling to employees the expectations of the organisation as well as what employees can expect in return (Rousseau, 1995). HRM practices such as recruiting, training, performance and reward management need to be aligned as they are seen as a communicative choice by the organisation which sends employees messages on how it will treat people (Rousseau & Greller, 1994). It is therefore, not surprising that the function HRM practices play in influences psychological contract and related outcomes have been noted in the literature (Agarwal & Bhargava, 2008; De Vos & Meganck, 2009). Consequently, an important challenge for human resource managers is to ensure that the rhetoric of HRM matches the reality as perceived by employees. According to Grant (1999), when the espoused benefits of HRM appeal to employees and align with their perceptions of the policies and practices in operation, congruent psychological contracts are likely to emerge. Under this condition, high-trust relationships between management and employees are likely to develop, leading to stronger commitment and motivation from employees and to improved firm performance. However, if the rhetoric of HRM fails to appeal to employees and is incongruent with their perceptions of reality, mismatched psychological contracts are likely to arise – engendering cynicism, poor performance and reduced motivation. Additionally, while it has been established that the alignment of human resource functions is required for strategic success (Miles & Snow, 1984), most HRM activities undertaken in organisations may be subject to different time horizons – pay and performance, for example, which can lead to misalignments and impact the psychological contract. Thus, human resource managers need to carefully review their practices in terms of alignment to ensure that the signals they provide to employees regarding the nature of the psychological contract are consistent.

In light of the above, human resource managers and line managers should make a concerted effort to view the psychological contract from the employees' perspective by attempting to determine what employees perceive as the obligations that the organisation should fulfil. By being cognisant of these perceived organisational obligations, human resource managers are afforded the opportunity to ensure that they are met, or to identify if there has been miscommunication or misperception (Robinson & Morrison, 1995). Employers and employees need to continually manage, modify and renegotiate the terms of the psychological contract in order to accommodate changing circumstances.

Given that psychological contracts are often initially formed during recruitment and selection – coupled with the fact that the turnover of newly hired employees frequently occurs because the job fails to meet their expectations (Vandenberg & Scarpello, 1990) – human resource managers should ensure that they provide applicants with realistic job previews. Rather than 'marketing' the position and focussing inordinately on favourable aspects, human resource managers should provide an honest and down-to-earth preview of the job. This can be achieved by presenting accurate information in the job advertisement, or through work sample tests that allow candidates to experience the actual conditions and tasks, or by allowing them to discuss the job with incumbents in similar positions (Sims, 1994). According to Zhang and Agarwal (2009), realistic job previews that provide an accurate depiction of the inducements that the organisation can provide are likely to minimise employees' misperceptions of the psychological contract and therefore reduce the likelihood of subsequent breach.

Another factor that can reduce the likelihood of perceived breach or violation of the psychological contract is the early socialisation of new recruits. Formal socialisation processes such as induction and orientation programmes provide a process through which new employees can be indoctrinated with the beliefs, expectations, assumptions and obligations that are appropriate for the organisation. If the induction and orientation is sufficiently structured and comprehensive, new recruits are likely to develop beliefs and assumptions that are analogous to those held by the senior management (Robinson & Morrison, 2000). Additionally, socialisation processes such as induction and orientation allow new employees to develop and modify their cognitions in accordance with the available information, and it provides them with the opportunity to seek clarification in a proactive manner (Thomas & Anderson, 1998). Empirical support for the benefits of induction and orientation can be found in a study by Robinson and Morrison which indicates that perceived contract breach is significantly less likely to occur if employees experience a formal socialisation process.

Another mechanism through which human resource managers can positively influence the psychological contract is the design and implementation of an effective performance management process. Supervisory staff within organisations should receive training on how to provide their subordinates with feedback on their performance. In performance management meetings, supervisors can assess employee expectations and assumptions that converge with the organisation's objectives, clarify performance standards, highlight future rewards that are contingent on performance, and identify employee developmental needs (Lester et al., 2001). In order to be effective in terms of improving the psychological contract, performance appraisals should be conducted regularly (to accommodate the dynamic nature of the psychological contract) and accurate (due to social desirability, there is a positive bias in raters' assessments) (Rousseau & Greller, 1994). Indeed, Tran Huy and Takahashi (2018) found that participative performance appraisals not only serve to foster communication between supervisors and employees, but also play a crucial role in reducing employees' perceptions in psychological contract fulfilment.

Human resource managers should also pay particular attention to the psychological contracts of line managers and supervisors, as research indicates that perceptions of breach by senior employees can have a 'trickle-down' effect on lower-level employees and ultimately on customer relationships. For example, Bordia, Restubog, Bordia, and Tang (2010) found that supervisors who perceived that their organisation had breached their psychological contract were less likely to engage in organisational citizenship behaviours directed towards their subordinates. This resulted in subordinate perceptions that the supervisor had breached their psychological contract which, in turn, caused subordinates to reduce the quality of service they offered to customers.

The manner in which organisations terminate employment contracts also influences psychological contracts. Indeed, the perceived fairness of involuntary terminations not only affects the psychological contract of the victims, but also the performance and psychological contracts of employees who are retained (Brockner, 1988). Specifically, Rousseau and Aquino (1993) found that the obligation to retain an employee when making involuntary termination decisions can be ameliorated through procedural justice mechanisms such as giving advance warning of the termination and providing reasonable severance packages. Interestingly, two management practices – participation and justification – which are often espoused to promote procedural justice had no influence.

Given that psychological contracts are becoming increasingly transactional in nature, coupled with the prevalence of organisational change and delayering, it may be impractical for organisational leaders to expect the traditional conceptions of loyalty and commitment from their employees. Instead, some authors (Cavanaugh & Noe, 1999; Hakim, 1996) have advocated that employers and human resource managers need to focus on ways of building 'conscious loyalty'. The notion of conscious loyalty is consistent with the newer forms of psychological contract such as the transactional and balanced psychological contracts; however, it provides insights into how to foster high levels of commitment – which is typically associated with relational psychological contracts. Employees who are consciously loyal understand the necessity of developing their own independence, while simultaneously appreciating that they need to work interdependently with their organisation. Specifically, human resource managers need to provide employees with growth opportunities through personal development initiatives and the provision of challenging assignments, as well as clearly demonstrating via education, information and performance management how their career success contributes to organisational performance and vice versa.

Conclusions

Few concepts in recent years have generated the level of interest – in both human resource management researchers and practitioners – as the psychological contract. It refers to an informal set of reciprocal obligations and promises held by the employee of the employer, and it is initially formed based on factors such as early socialisation, the interpretation of past experiences, the media and vicarious observation. The traditional (relational) psychological contract – established on the basis of an exchange of effort and loyalty from the employee in return for job security and career development from the employer – is being replaced by the newer transactional and increasingly, the balanced psychological contract – where a key feature is clearly defined, monetisable exchanges that occur between the employee and the employer over a short, predefined period.

There are a number of negative consequences that can arise from breach and violation of the psychological contract, such as reduced performance, loyalty, trust, organisational citizenship behaviour, organisational commitment and job satisfaction as well as increased discretionary absenteeism, CWBs and turnover intentions – which all negatively impact upon the organisation's competitiveness. Conversely, fulfilment of the psychological contract appears to promote positive outcomes such as reductions in intention to leave the organisation, intention to change career, burnout and career dissatisfaction.

Human resource management practices, reward mechanisms and other organisational channels communicate promises and organisational intent. In terms of practical implications, human resource managers need to ensure: that their rhetoric matches the perceived reality; that their policies are consistent; and that obligations are made explicit. Additionally, human resource managers should make certain that they present realistic job previews to new hires, conduct formal induction and orientation programmes, provide support to employees, develop effective performance management processes, monitor supervisor psychological contracts, institute reward systems that facilitate fulfilment, and apply termination procedures that promote fairness. Effective management of psychological contracts is influential in terms of attracting, retaining, developing and motivating employees, and therefore it is an important weapon in the human resource manager's armamentarium in the war for talent.

References

Agarwal, U., & Bhargava, S. (2008). Reviewing the relationship between human resource practices and psychological contract and their impact on employee attitude and behaviours: A conceptual model. *Journal of European Industrial Training, 33*, 4–31.

Agarwal, U., & Bhargava, S. (2013). Effects of psychological contract breach on organisational outcomes: Moderating role of tenure and educational levels. *Vikalpa, 38*, 13–25.

Barnett, R. C., Gordon, J. R., Gareis, K. C., & Morgan, C. (2004). Unintended consequences of job redesign: Psychological contract violations and turnover intentions among full-time and reduced-hours MDs and LPNs. *Community, Work & Family, 7*(2), 227–246.

Behrstock-Sherratt, E., & Coggshall, J. G. (2010). Realizing the promise of Generation Y. *Educational Leadership, 67*, 28–34.

Blau, P. M. (1964). *Exchange and power in social life.* New York, NY: Wiley.

Bordia, P., Restubog, S. L. D., Bordia, S., & Tang, R. L. (2010). Breach begets breach: Trickle-down effects of psychological contract breach on customer service. *Journal of Management, 36*, 1578–1607.

Bordia, P., Restubog, S. L. D., & Tang, R. L. (2008). When employees strike back: Investigating mediating mechanisms between psychological contract breach and workplace deviance. *Journal of Applied Psychology, 93*, 1104–1117.

Brockner, J. (1988). The effects of work layoffs on survivors: Research, theory and practice. In B. M. Staw & L. L. Cummings (Eds.), *Research in organizational behavior* (Vol. *10*, pp. 213–255). Greenwich, CT: JAI Press.

Callanan, G. A., Perri, D. F., & Tomkowicz, S. M. (2017). Career management in uncertain times: challenges and opportunities. *The Career Development Quarterly, 65*, 353–365.

Cassar, V., & Briner, R. B. (2011). The relationship between psychological contract breach and organizational commitment: Exchange imbalance as a moderator of the mediating role of violation. *Journal of Vocational Behavior, 78*, 283–289.

Cavanaugh, M. A., & Noe, R. A. (1999). Antecedents and consequences of relational components of the new psychological contract. *Journal of Organizational Behavior, 20*, 323–340.

Cennamo, L., & Gardner, D. (2008). Generational differences in work values, outcomes and person-organisation values fit. *Journal of Managerial Psychology, 23*, 891–906.

Chambel, M. J., & Castanheira, F. (2006). Different temporary work status, different behaviors in organizations. *Journal of Business and Psychology, 20*, 351–357.

Chen, H., & Chiu, Y. (2009). The influence of psychological contracts on the adjustment and organisational commitment among expatriates: An empirical study in Taiwan. *International Journal of Manpower, 30*, 797–814.

Christeen, G. (2009). *The psychological contract: Managing and developing professional groups.* New York, NY: Open University Press.

Conway, N., Guest, D., & Trenberth, L. (2011) Testing the differential effects of changes in psychological contract breach and fulfilment. *Journal of Vocational Behavior, 79*(1), 267–276.

Coyle-Shapiro, J. A-M., & Conway, N. (2005). Exchange relationships: Examining psychological contracts and perceived organizational support. *Journal of Applied Psychology, 90*, 774–781.

De Hauw, S., & De Vos, A. (2010). 'Millennials' career perspective and psychological contract expectations: Does the recession lead to lowered expectations? *Journal of Business and Psychology, 25*, 293–302.

De Vos, A., & Meganck, A. (2009). What HR managers do versus what employees value: Exploring both parties' views on retention management from a psychological contract perspective. *Personnel Review, 38*, 45–60.

Deery, S. J., Iverson, R. D., & Walsh, J. T. (2006). Towards a better understanding of psychological contract breach: A study of customer service employees. *Journal of Applied Psychology, 91*, 166–175.

Dries, N., Pepermans, R., & De Kerpel, E. (2008). Exploring four generations' beliefs about career: Is "satisfied" the new "successful"? *Journal of Managerial Psychology, 23*, 907–928.

Dulac, T., Coyle-Shapiro, J. A.-M., Henderson, D. J., & Wayne, S. (2008). Not all responses to breach are the same: The interconnection of social exchange and psychological contract processes in organizations. *Academy of Management Journal, 51*, 1079–1098.

Grant, D. (1999). HRM, rhetoric and the psychological contract: A case of easier said than done. *International Journal of Human Resource Management, 10*, 327–350.

Guzzo, R. A., Noonan, K. A., & Elron, E. (1994). Expatriate managers and the psychological contract. *Journal of Applied Psychology, 79*, 617–626.

Hakim, C. (1996). Building conscious loyalty. In B. Hackett (Ed.), *The new deal in employment relationships* (pp. 19–21). Report Number 1162-96-CR. New York, NY: The Conference Board, Inc.

Hall, D. T., & Moss, J. E. (1998) The new protean career contract: Helping organizations and employees adapt. *Organizational Dynamics, 26*, 22–37.

Harwell, J. K. (2003). Making reduced-hours work: The role of psychological contract fulfilment on reduced-hour physicians' intent to leave their positions. Unpublished dissertation, Boston College, Boston, MA.

Hess, K., & Jepsen, D. M. (2009). Career stage and generational differences in psychological contracts. *Career Development Journal, 43*, 261–283.

Hiltrop, J. M. (1996). Managing the changing psychological contract. *Employee Relations, 18*, 36–49.

Hornung, S., & Glaser, J. (2010). Employee responses to relational fulfillment and work-life benefits: A social exchange study in the German public administration. *International Journal of Manpower, 31*, 73–92.

Isaksson, K., De Cuyper, N., Oettel, C. B., & De Witte, H. D. (2010). The role of the formal employment contract in the range and fulfilment of the psychological contract: Testing a layered model. *European Journal of Work and Organizational Psychology, 19*, 696–716.

Kalleberg, A. L. (2009). Precarious work, insecure workers: Employment relations in transition. *American Sociological Review, 74*, 1–22.

Katz, L. F., & Krueger, A. B. (2016). *The rise and nature of alternative work arrangements in the United States', 1995–2015*. Paper No. w22667. National Bureau of Economic Research, Cambridge, MA.

Kickul, J. R., Neuman, G., Parker, C., & Finkl, J. (2001). Settling the score: The role of organizational justice in the relationship between psychological contract breach and anticitizenship behavior. *Employee Responsibilities and Rights Journal, 13*, 77–93.

Knights, J. A., & Kennedy, B. J. (2005). Psychological contract violation: Impacts on job satisfaction and organizational commitment among Australian senior public servants. *Applied H.R.M. Research, 10*, 57–72.

Kultalahti, S., & Viitala, R. (2015). Generation Y–challenging clients for HRM? *Journal of Managerial Psychology, 30*, 101–114.

Lambert, L. S., Edwards, J. R., & Cable, D. M. (2003). Breach and fulfilment of the psychological contract: A comparison of traditional and expanded views. *Personnel Psychology, 56*, 895–934.

Lemmon, G., Wilson, M. S., Posig, M., & Glibkowski, B. C. (2016). Psychological contract development, distributive justice, and performance of independent contractors: The role of negotiation behaviors and the fulfillment of resources. *Journal of Leadership & Organizational Studies, 23*, 424–439.

Lester, S., Kickul, J., & Bergmann, T. (2007). Managing employee perceptions of the psychological contract over time: The role of employer social accounts and contract fulfilment. *Journal of Organisational Behaviour, 28*, 191–208.

Lester, S. W., Claire, E., & Kickul, J. (2001). Psychological contracts in the 21st century: What employees value most and how well organizations are responding to these expectations. *Human Resource Planning, 24*, 10–21.

Lub, X. D., Bal, P. M., Blomme, R. J., & Schalk, R. (2016). One job, one deal ... or not: Do generations respond differently to psychological contract fulfillment? *The International Journal of Human Resource Management, 27*, 653–680.

McFarlane Shore, L., & Tetrick, L. E. (1994). The psychological contract as an explanatory framework in the employment relationship. In C. L. Cooper & D. M. Rousseau (Eds.), *Trends in organizational behavior* (pp. 91–109). London: John Wiley & Sons.

Miles, R. E., & Snow, C. C. (1984). Designing strategic human resource systems. *Organizational Dynamics, 13*, 36–52.

Millward, L. J., & Hopkins, L. J. (1998). Psychological contracts, organizational and job commitment. *Journal of Applied Social Psychology, 28*, 1530–1556.

Morrison, E. W., & Robinson, S. L. (1997). When employees feel betrayed: A model of how psychological contract violation develops. *Academy of Management Review, 22*, 226–256.

O'Donohue, W., Donohue, R., & Grimmer, M. (2007). Research into the psychological contract: Two Australian perspectives. *Human Resource Development International, 10*, 301–318.

O'Neill, B. S., & Adya, M. (2007). Knowledge sharing and the psychological contract: Managing knowledge workers across different stages of employment. *Journal of Managerial Psychology, 22*, 411–436.

Parzefall, M. R., & Coyle-Shaprio, J. A.-M. (2011). Making sense of psychological contract breach. *Journal of Management Psychology, 26*, 12–27.

Raja, U., Johns, G., & Ntalianis, F. (2004). The impact of personality on psychological contracts. *Academy of Management Journal, 47*, 350–367.

Restubog, S. L. D., & Bordia, P. (2006). Workplace familism and psychological contract breach in the Philippines. *Applied Psychology: An International Review, 55*, 563–585.

Restubog, S. L. D., Zagenczyk, T. J., Bordia, P., & Tang, R. L. (2013). When employees behave badly: The roles of contract importance and workplace familism in predicting negative reactions to psychological contract breach. *Journal of Applied Social Psychology, 43*, 673–686.

Robinson, S. L. (1996). Trust and breach of the psychological contract. *Administrative Science Quarterly, 41*, 574–599.

Robinson, S. L., Kraatz, M. S., & Rousseau, D. M. (1994). Changing obligations and the psychological contract. *Academy of Management Journal, 37*, 137–152.

Robinson, S. L., & Morrison, E. W. (1995). Psychological contracts and organizational citizenship behaviour. *Journal of Organizational Behavior, 16*, 289–298.

Robinson, S. L., & Morrison, E. W. (2000). The development of psychological contract breach and violation: A longitudinal study. *Journal of Organizational Behavior, 21*, 525–546.

Robinson, S. L., & Rousseau, D. M. (1994). Violating the psychological contract: Not the exception but the norm. *Journal of Organizational Behavior, 15*, 245–259.

Roehling, M. R., & Boswell, W. R. (2004). Good cause beliefs in an at-will world? A focused investigation of psychological versus legal contracts. *Employee Responsibilities and Rights Journal, 16*, 211–231.

Rosen, C., Chang, C., Johnson, R., & Levy, P. (2009). Perceptions of the organisational context and psychological contract breach: Assessing competing perspectives. *Organisational Behaviour and Human Decision Processes, 108*, 202–217.

Rousseau, D. M. (1989). The "problem" of the psychological contract considered. *Journal of Organizational Behavior, 19*, 665–671.

Rousseau, D. M. (1990). New hire perceptions of their won and their employer's obligations: A study of psychological contracts. *Journal of Organizational Behavior, 11*, 389–400.

Rousseau, D. M. (1995). *Psychological contracts in organizations: Understanding written and unwritten agreements*. Thousand Oaks, CA: Sage.

Rousseau, D. M. (2001). Schema, promise and mutuality: The building blocks of the psychological contract. *Journal of Occupational and Organisational Psychology, 74*, 511–541.

Rousseau, D. M. (2004). Psychological contracts in the workplace: Understanding the ties that motivate. *Academy of Management Executive, 18*, 120–127.

Rousseau, D. M., & Aquino, K. (1993). Fairness and implied contract obligations in job terminations: The role of remedies, social accounts and procedural justice. *Human Performance, 6*, 135–149.

Rousseau, D. M., & Greller, M. M. (1994). Human resource practices: Administrative contract makers. *Human Resource Management, 33*, 385–401.

Saunders, M. N., & Thornhill, A. (2006). Forced employment contract change and the psychological contract. *Employee Relations, 28*, 449–467.

Shore, L. M., Coyle-Shapiro, J. A., & Tetrick, L. E. (Eds.). (2012). *The employee-organization relationship: Applications for the 21st century.* London: Routledge.

Sims, R. (1994). Human resource management's role in clarifying the new psychological contract. *Human Resource Management, 33*, 373–382.

Stroh, L. K., & Reilly, A. H. (1997). Rekindling organizational loyalty: The role of career mobility. *Journal of Career Development, 24*, 39–54.

Tallman, R., & Bruning, N. (2008). Relating employees' psychological contracts to their personality. *Journal of Managerial Psychology, 23*, 688–712.

Thomas, H. D. C., & Anderson, N. (1998). Changes in newcomers' psychological contracts during organizational socialization: A study of recruits entering the British army. *Journal of Organizational Behavior, 19*, 745–767.

Tran Huy, P., & Takahashi, K. (2018). Determinants of psychological contract breach: An empirical study of Vietnamese employees. *Management Research Review, 41*, 29–45.

Tsui, A. S., Pearce, J. L., Porter, L. W., & Tripoli, A. M. (1997). Alternative approaches to the employee-organization relationship: Does investment in employees pay off?. *Academy of Management Journal, 40*, 1089–1121.

Turnley, W. H., & Feldman, D. C. (1999). The impact of breaches of psychological contracts on exit, voice, loyality, and neglect. *Human Relations, 52*, 895–922.

Turnley, W. H., & Feldman, D. C. (2000). Research re-examining the effects of psychological contract violations: Unmet expectations and job dissatisfaction as mediators. *Journal of Organizational Behavior, 21*, 25–42.

Tyagi, A., & Agrawal, R. K. (2010). Emerging employment relationships: Issues & concerns in psychological contract. *Indian Journal of Industrial Relations, 45*, 381–395.

Vacas-Soriano, C. (2015). *Recent developments in temporary employment: Employment growth, wages and transitions* (98 pp.). Luxembourg: Publications Office of the European Union.

Van Dyne, L., & Ang, S. (1998). Organizational citizenship behavior of contingent workers in Singapore. *Academy of Management Journal, 41*, 692–703.

Vandenberg, R. J., & Scarpello, C. (1990). The matching model: An examination of the processes underlying realistic job previews. *Journal of Applied Psychology, 75*, 60–67.

Zagenczyk, T., Gibney, R., Kiewitz, C., & Restubog, S. (2009). Mentors, supervisors and role models: Do they reduce the effects of psychological contract breach? *Human Resource Management Journal, 19*, 237–259.

Zhang, H., & Agarwal, N. (2009). The mediating roles of organisational justice on the relationships between HR practices and workplace outcomes: An investigation in China. *The International Journal of Human Resource Management, 20*, 676–693.

Zhao, H., Wayne, S. J., Glibkowski, B. C., & Bravo, J. (2007). The impact of psychological contract breach on work-related outcomes: A meta-analysis. *Personnel Psychology, 60*, 647–680.

Chapter 4

Career Management in the 21st Century

Ross Donohue and Tse Leng Tham

Introduction

The way in which many individuals construct their careers has been transformed in recent years due to a number of significant environmental and attitudinal changes. Traditional career theories have generally been unable to explain or interpret these novel and burgeoning career paths, and therefore new approaches – such as the protean and boundaryless perspectives of careers and more recently, the kaleidoscope career model (KCM) – have emerged. This chapter describes the changes that have impacted on careers, and explains the modern protean, boundaryless and kaleidoscope career perspectives of career development. Some commentators (e.g. Baruch, 2003) have suggested that there has been inordinate emphasis in the careers literature on individual initiatives for managing non-traditional careers without sufficient consideration of organisational practices. To redress this oversight, this chapter examines the human resource management functions that can positively influence career management in the twenty-first century.

Traditional Perspectives of Career Development

Generally, a career can be defined as 'the evolving sequence of a person's work experiences over time' (Arthur, Hall, & Lawrence, 1989, p. 8). Established conceptions of career development – for example, Holland's (1973) theory of congruence and Super's (1953) life-span, life-space theory – tend to view career choice as a decision undertaken in early adulthood, and invariably careers are conceived as unfolding in a lockstep, stable-state, predictable and linear fashion. Thus, according to traditional perspectives the young adult, following some early exploration of potential career options, settles on an occupation and proceeds to advance in his or her career. These traditional theories of career were largely developed between the 1950s and 1970s, and they certainly reflected the career experiences of employees in industrialised societies up until that time. For most of the previous millennium, individuals were typically employed by the same organisation throughout the course of their careers. Workers who changed career were regarded as poor decision-makers, and those who had experienced multiple career transitions were considered unstable.

Most organisations were quite paternalistic and assumed much of the responsibility for managing the careers of their employees. Consequently, workers were largely dependent on opportunities provided by their organisation and had to trust that their employer would evaluate their career interests when making decisions. The training offered to employees was often quite focussed on developing firm-specific skills that were not readily transferable. The traditional career was based on the relational psychological contract between the employee and the employer (see Chapter 3: Psychological Contracts) where loyalty and continued organisational membership were offered in exchange for job security. Organisations were typically bureaucratic, and employees could expect to advance up the promotional hierarchy. Thus, career success was measured according to position within the hierarchy as well as the attendant benefits of higher salary, greater status and increased responsibility (Sullivan, 1999).

Environmental and Individual Changes

A number of major changes in recent years have significantly influenced the world of work and the construction of careers. In effort to survive competitive market turbulence at domestic and international levels, many organisations have had to undergo restructuring by removing multiple levels from their promotional hierarchies and downsized by cutting a large number of staff (Prahalad & Hamel, 1990). In addition, female participation in the workforce has also been on the steady rise (Blyton & Dastmalchian, 2006). In fact, reports also indicate that women are increasingly having greater career opportunities even in traditionally male-dominated industries (Valcour & Tolbert, 2003) and their growth in earnings outpaces male earnings by 45% since the early 1980s (Richardson, Healy, & Moskos, 2014). Coupled with changing societal expectations and cultural norms that are moving away from the traditional male breadwinner model, such changes have engendered an increase in the number of dual income families across generations, and are rapidly becoming the new norm (Sok, Blomme, & Tromp, 2014). Another major change in recent years is that organisations are increasingly outsourcing their human resource management – including recruitment, training and payroll – as well as finance, accounting, information technology and procurement functions in order to focus on their core business.

Additionally, in order to achieve greater flexibility and to improve responsiveness to changing market conditions, organisations are making much greater use of part-time and casual labour. Despite growth in sectors such as healthcare, hospitality and tourism, there is an increasing reliance on part-time and casual employment.

Today, the pace of change, amplified by technological advances and globalisation, has also led to the creation and growth of the 'gig economy'. Straying away from traditional employment relationships, work in the gig economy is instead typified by not only higher frequency of career transitions, but also alternative and often more precarious work arrangements including virtual and contingent work (Barley, Bechky, & Milliken, 2017; Katz & Krueger, 2017). Rather than relying on a predominant paternalistic organisation in cultivating one's career, those working in 'Uber-jobs' today are described as 'Self-Entrepreneurs', where individuals are essentially self-employed in the gig economy and are likely to be more self-directed in the craft and management of their own careers (Hall, Yip, & Doiron, 2018). Indeed, in Australia, the Australian Council of Trade Unions has commented that insecure work has burgeoned to 'crisis levels'. Statistics also demonstrate the steady rise in perceived precariousness of work for both men and women since 2012 (Cassells et al., 2018).

The expectations, goals and values of many individuals have also shifted during this period. Some employees have grown weary of the stress and demands associated with climbing organisational ladders, and instead have declined promotions in order to focus on personal development (Ibarra, 2003). Others have abandoned organisational careers and have attempted to gain greater work-life balance by establishing their own businesses that allow greater alignment of work and non-work activities (Callanan & Greenhaus, 2008; Moore, 2002). Particularly with employees of the younger generations, many have rejected the 'live to work' mentality their Baby Boomer parents have subscribed to in response to the context of rising job insecurity and perceived lack of reciprocated loyalty organisations show towards employees who are hard-working and loyal (McDonald & Hite, 2008). Such changes in the emphasis of work and life values are also reflected in the way in which younger employees plan, manage and enact their careers. The increasing emphasis on and determination in achieving greater work-life balance is also not limited to those with children, but research indicates that this is increasingly prevalent even amongst younger employees without children or elderly dependents (Twenge, Campbell, Hoffman, & Lance, 2010). Others have jettisoned the chase for the linear career progression and accompanying prestige and status within a hierarchical system in pursuit of work that is more closely aligned with their personal values and their meaning of work (Callanan & Greenhaus, 2008). Dispositional factors may also influence the decision to switch organisations or change careers. For example, Vinson, Connelly, and Ones (2007) found that individuals who were higher on extraversion, openness to experience and conscientiousness – three of the dimensions in Costa and McRae's (1992) five-factor theory of personality – were more likely to change employer than those who were lower on these constructs.

Contemporary Career Perspectives

In the context of the significant changes that have occurred, traditional theories of career appear anachronistic due to their inability to adequately represent contemporary career paths. Consequently, nascent perspectives such as boundaryless careers (Arthur & Rousseau, 1996), the protean careers (Hall & Mirvis, 1996) and now the KCM have emerged as the 'new career' which serve as an alternative, interorganisational lens to interpret the changing nature of careers.

Boundaryless Career Perspective

Arthur and Rousseau (1996) applied the term *boundaryless* to describe their theory in order to underscore the notion that workers no longer consider themselves bound to a single organisation and the traditional organisational career arrangement. This is predicated on the presumption that the organisation either lacks the ability or willingness to provide employees with job stability and lateral progressive careers in return for commitment and ongoing effort of the employee. As such, boundaryless workers are driven to operate independently and driven by subjectively determined career concepts.

They act as free-agents moving easily between organisations and careers. Thus, the boundaryless career does not describe a specific career form but rather represents a range of career manifestations that confound traditional career expectations and assumptions. In contrast to traditional perspectives, the boundaryless approach does not presume that an individual's career will consist of predictable and invariant advancement within a single organisation. Rather, according to Arthur and Rousseau, it is more likely that an individual's career will be comprised of lateral moves, occasional career plateauing and stagnation, periods outside of the labour market for familial reasons or to acquire human capital (i.e. education), and radical career change (Marler, Barringer, & Milkovich, 2002). Individuals following boundaryless career paths will need to apply a much broader set of criteria for gauging their career success by focussing on outcomes such as meaningful work, skill utilisation, work-life balance and fulfilling relationships (Hind, 2005).

In order to successfully navigate these unwieldy career paths, boundaryless workers will need to demonstrate agency, have strong internal and external marketability, be motivated by skill development rather than formal organisational rewards such as promotion or tenure, and be willing to take risks to capitalise on emergent career opportunities –all the whilst remaining confident in their 'marketability' in the labour market. It also implies that the individual should be both psychologically (e.g. changing their identity by using self-reflection allowing dramatic moves between occupational boundaries) and physically mobile (e.g. accepting career interruptions). A consistent theme in the literature regarding boundaryless careers is that they are liberating, as workers have greater autonomy, more flexibility to combine work and non-work activities, and expanded career options.

Rather than dichotomous either/or classification, researchers have clarified that the concept of a boundaryless career is rather one that is measured by degree of boundarylessness (Böhmer & Schinnenburg, 2016; Sullivan & Arthur, 2006). Indeed, whilst boundaries have generally become more permeable today than ever before, the permeability between job/organisational/career/industrial boundaries cannot be assumed to be identical across all individuals (Sullivan & Arthur, 2006). Research literature has also begun shedding light on some contextual factors which may act as 'boundaries' or obstacles to a higher degree of boundarylessness in an individual's career. For instance, gender discrimination in favour of men in certain industries or job roles may be more entrenched in some societies than others. This may allow men to have a higher degree of physical mobility in moving between jobs or industries in their careers (Malach-Pines & Schwartz, 2007). In Italy, Bagdadli, Solari, Usai, and Grandori's (2003) study highlight that top-level managers' boundaryless career can often be limited by obstacles that are competency-based (e.g. insufficient industry knowledge) and relationship-based (e.g. lack of professional networks to leverage to assist career movements). In more collectivistic cultures where tight familial connections are heavily emphasised (e.g. India and China), mobility and the degree of boundarylessness of an individual's career may be limited by parental authority and societal expectations around elder care (Hewlett & Rashid, 2010). For instance, the concept of the boundaryless career may clash with tenets of filial piety under Confucian culture where individuals are expected to care for older parents (Lau, Hsu, & Shaffer, 2013) particularly in instances where the country's social security system is perceived to be lacking.

Protean Career Perspective

The protean career approach has many characteristics in common with the boundaryless career perspective. The term *protean* is derived from the Greek god Proteus, who could transform himself into any form at will (Hall, 1996; Hall & Mirvis, 1996). This metaphor is used to evoke the image of an adaptable, flexible and independent worker, capable of reinvention in order to redirect and manage his or her career. Thus, protean careers are influenced more by the individual than the organisation, and they may be refocused periodically to accommodate individual needs and circumstances. Fundamentally, protean careerists are value-driven as they develop in accordance to their own values and goals (Böhmer & Schinnenburg, 2016). According to Hall (1996), protean workers are motivated by psychological success, continuous self-directed learning, autonomy, flexibility and intrinsic rewards from work including self-fulfilment. Research has indicated that the two most important personal values of individuals with a protean career orientation were making a contribution to society and maintaining work-life balance (Sargent & Domberger, 2007).

The protean career perspective also holds that careers should not be thought of as being nested in any one organisation or occupational field. Rather, this approach advocates a radical redefinition of the relationship between employee and employer where concepts such as job security, trust in the relational contract and loyalty are seen as irrelevant residuals from a bygone era (Hall, 1996).

Traditional perspectives have invariably coupled career with paid employment and work that is performed within the formal organisation, with little emphasis placed on non-work influences. However, Hall and Mirvis (1996) have argued that this is too circumscribed in a protean career context and instead have advocated the enlargement of career space. This involves the recognition that the demarcation between domains such as work and family are becoming diffuse and that work and non-work activities intersect and interact in a dynamic fashion to mutually shape the protean worker's career (Sullivan, 1999).

Traditional career theories typically view the organisation's needs as the primary consideration in career development decisions and view the employee's needs as secondary. From the protean perspective, however, the individual is seen as 'the figure' and the organisation is conceived as 'the ground' or context in which the protean worker can realise his or her aspirations. In this new relationship, the burden of responsibility for career development is shifted from the organisation to the individual and thus requires that protean workers self-manage their careers. Consequently, those individuals who are following the protean career path need to be flexible, self-directed, able to take risks in uncertain environments and focussed on acquiring and developing their human capital. Empirical evidence tends to support the benefits of adopting a protean orientation to career management in the contemporary employment context. For example, a recent longitudinal study of workers attempting to transition from unemployment to re-employment (Waters, Briscoe, Hall, & Wang, 2014) found that a protean career orientation was significantly associated with increased self-esteem, job search activity and reemployment.

Kaleidoscope Career Model (KCM) Perspective

Whilst the boundaryless and protean career perspectives have offered a means of more accurately and holistically understanding contemporary ways in which individuals plan, enact and manage their careers, researchers note that these 'new career' approaches still fall short in several crucial aspects (Mainiero & Gibson, 2018). More specifically, these perspectives do not take into consideration the critical influence of gender, identity, and culture and its combined impact on one's career development over the life-span (Savickas, 2003; Sullivan & Baruch, 2009).

In response to these identified shortfalls in 'new career' perspectives, Mainiero and Sullivan (2006) introduced the KCM. Underscoring the KCM is the presumption that an individual's career decisions over the life-span are shaped by the three parameters: authenticity, balance and challenge. Authenticity refers to the need to be able to make decisions that allows one to be true to oneself; the need for Balance considers the capacity to make choices that permits an individual to obtain equilibrium between the different spheres of life – work and non-work; the Challenge parameter refers to an individual's need to engage in work that is stimulating, where it provides opportunities of autonomy, responsibility, control, learning and growth (Clarke, 2015).

Analogous to how variant patterns are created when a kaleidoscope is rotated and the glass chips contained fall into new configurations, an individual alters the patterns of their careers by considering the relative and changing needs for authenticity, balance, and challenge given their current life context and associated obligations and opportunities. For instance, a new working mother in a more traditional family in China may follow what is known as a beta career pattern (Sullivan & Mainiero, 2007). She may emphasise *Challenge* in her early career but in consideration of societal and cultural norms around child-care responsibilities, the need for *Balance* may ascend to the foreground upon the arrival of her child, driving her to consider 'opting out' of the workforce (Cabrera, 2007; Clarke, 2015). Compared to a male counterpart, research indicates that an alpha career path may be pursued instead, where career interruptions are fewer and there are more opportunities to pursue a comparatively linear career, following a *Challenge-Authenticity-Balance* pattern (Cabrera, 2007). In this way, KCM provides a useful framework in considering, in the foreground, how gender influences the distinct ways in which men and women may fluidly prioritise and negotiate different parameters at various life stages. This, in turn, impacts an individual's motivations and driving decisions around their evolving careers across their life spans.

Beyond the consideration of gender, more recent research has also applied the KCM in understanding generational differences in career enactment and needs (e.g. Sullivan, Forret, Carraher, & Mainiero, 2009). For instance, Gen X employees are perceived to be less inclined to place work as the central part of their lives (Sullivan et al., 2009) whilst the more senior Baby Boomers are viewed as workaholics who flourish under conditions of increasing challenge in pursuit of extrinsic measures of career success (e.g. upward promotions, salary). Indeed, evidence suggests that Gen X employees exhibit significantly higher need for *Authenticity* than Baby Boomers, where their career decisions are guided by their ability to obtain a job in which the organisational values are congruent with their personal values and allows them to express their true selves fully (Callanan & Greenhaus, 2008; McDonald & Hite, 2008; Sullivan et al., 2009; Westerman & Yamamura, 2007). Gen X employees also tend to significantly place higher priority on *Balance* as compared to Baby Boomers as well (Sullivan et al., 2009). Such nuanced understanding of the cognitive reasoning behind different career needs and enactment of various groups of employees have significant implications for human resource planning, development and retention in workforces that are increasingly diverse. This will be discussed further in the proceeding sections of this chapter.

Cautionary Issues

Some researchers have raised concerns about the impact of increased job mobility on organisational commitment as individuals increasingly act of free-agents in the labour market and the employment relationship is increasingly loosening. Such concerns are particularly salient given the well-established relationships between organisational commitment and important variables such as turnover (Allen & Meyer, 1996), absenteeism (Hackett, Bycio, & Hausdorf, 1994), job performance (Meyer, Stanley, Herscovitch, & Topolnysky, 2002) and organisational citizenship behaviour (Meyer et al., 2002). Alonderienė and Šimkevičiūtė (2018) found that organisational mobility preference (i.e. the preference to move between organisations throughout a career) had a strong negative relationship with affective (i.e. emotional attachment and commitment) and continuance commitment (i.e. commitment to the organisation based on a perceived lack of alternatives and investments that would be lost by leaving). Indeed, this is supported by other research that has found that affective and continuance commitment were both significantly lower for external movers prior to exiting their organisation when compared with non-movers. Additionally, research evidence indicates that employees with self-directed career management (characteristic of protean careerists) who proactively manage their own careers are less likely to place a heavy emphasis on the perceived costs of leaving their organisations (Alonderienė & Šimkevičiūtė, 2018; Çakmak-Otluoğlu, 2012).

Whilst the number of workers following protean career paths is certainly increasing, it is important to note that the traditional career has not vanished from the organisational landscape. Reitman and Schneer (2003) longitudinally tracked a sample of MBA alumni over 13 years and found that 38% were pursuing a protean career; however, a not insubstantial 34% were following a traditional career path. (The residual 28% of the sample was excluded from analysis due to classification difficulties.) As Baruch (2006) has suggested, the descriptions in the literature of traditional and protean careers are best thought of as archetypical anchors at the extremes of the same continuum, with all careers falling somewhere along the continuum and most clustering towards the middle. Rodrigues and Guest (2010) have also questioned the inordinate emphasis that the boundaryless career perspective places on the individual as the primary agent for career management. These authors argued that this notion is implied rather than substantiated, and that the empirical research indicates that individuals are less agentic in managing their careers than espoused by the boundaryless career perspective. Similarly, Vinkenburg and Weber (2012), following a review of 33 empirical studies, concluded that upward mobility is still the norm and for many employees their organisations continue to play a pivotal role in managing their career development and advancement. Similar to our discussion earlier on the obstacles to the degree of boundarylessness in boundaryless careers, it is also important to bear in mind that protean career paths are uneven in their distribution of risks and opportunities; for well-educated and high-skilled workers these careers can provide challenges and avenues for self-development; however, for poorly educated and low-skilled workers such careers can provide precarious and discontinuous employment and may well engender stress and uncertainty, which is very much an issue in the emerging gig economy.

Human Resource Management and Career Management

Whilst the boundaryless, protean and KCM conceptions of career development place considerable emphasis on individual employees taking much of the responsibility for managing their career, there are a number of human resource management practices that can assist career development in the twenty-first century. Indeed, research indicates that human resource practices have a significant influence on the career management of employees (Portwood & Granrose, 1986), and satisfaction with organisational career management practices has been found to be negatively related to turnover intention (Herriot, Gibbons, Pemberton, & Jackson, 1994). As such, effectively managing the career development of employees can make a significant contribution to the organisation attaining a competitive advantage from within. Thus, the goal of human resource management practices that focus on career development is the alignment and mutual satisfaction of employee and organisational needs (Herriot & Pemberton, 1996).

Succession Planning

In light of the fact that organisational commitment and loyalty continue to decline, and employees are frequently changing employers, succession planning, that is, evaluating the promotion potential of each manager and deciding on a replacements for every management position, is a critical human resource management practice. However, there is evidence to suggest that many organisations are not placing sufficient emphasis on succession planning. For example, a study conducted in the United States found that 45% of leading corporations have no succession plan in place, and 50% rated their organisation as less than effective in terms of CEO succession (National Association of Corporate Directors, 2006). Hirsh (1990) identified the key concepts of succession planning undertaken by organisations and identified four distinct approaches: *as and when* – where a position is filled when it becomes vacant and there is no forward planning; *one step* – where successors are identified from the level below; *planned development* – where successors are identified from the level below but there is also fast tracking for high potential employees; and *developing potential* – where the employee rather than the position is the focus of the strategy, and consequently vacant positions are posted openly and there is a strong emphasis on training and development.

Paradoxically, the very factors cited above, that is, declining loyalty and commitment, and increasing turnover, as rationales for the importance of succession planning also limit its predictive ability (Baruch, 2004). As a consequence, succession planning needs to be flexible and broad in scope in order to adapt to the vagaries of the current context. Indeed, Leibman, Bruer, and Maki (1996) developed a dynamic approach that they refer to as succession management. With succession management: leadership templates rather than position descriptions are used as assessment criteria; replacement strategies are based on having cadres or pools of talent rather than on slating an individual to a specific position; and the assessment criteria are based on competence and networks rather than on skills and experience. Whilst succession management typically involves senior managers and line mangers, human resource managers also play a vital role. Specifically, human resource managers can contribute by developing and facilitating the process, managing important cross-boundary job transitions, ensuring that minority groups are not disadvantaged, and providing counselling and informational support to employees (Hirsh, 2000). Human resource managers also need to have extensive networks *within* the organisation in order to sense potential departures, but they also need excellent networks in the *external* labour market in order to identify potential replacements (Baruch, 2004).

Lateral Moves and Secondments
Lateral moves, secondments and high-quality job assignments provide employees with cross-functional experience in order to improve their skill development and extend their networks (Zaleska & de Menezes, 2007). Research (Hall, Gardner, & Baugh, 2008) indicates that employees are opting for lateral, or even downward, job shifts in order to realise their personal needs. The extent to which lateral moves and secondments can occur in organisations may be limited by prescriptive policies and procedures (Garavan & Coolahan, 1996). Consequently, human resource managers should attempt to 'free up' rigid and restrictive practices when developing their organisation's approach to lateral moves and secondments. There is evidence to indicate that cross-functional assignments have a positive influence on career development. For example, job assignments and projects that offer high levels of challenge and autonomy have been argued to rank higher in importance for performance as compared to training (Zaleska & de Menezes, 2007). This is particularly relevant to 'new careers' as such opportunities are likely to facilitate the building of a bank of experiences that will not only add to an individual's 'employability' but also positively impact future career moves and transitions. Whilst lateral moves may be beneficial in terms of advancement in the longer term, employees may interpret these transitions pejoratively. Thus, human resource managers are advised to explain to employees that advancement does not require vertical progression and that these horizontal shifts should be interpreted as successes rather than failures as they will improve their internal as well as their external marketability (Baruch, 2004).

Outplacement
In light of the significant job losses resulting from downsizing, human resource managers should consider offering outplacement services. Outplacement involves the organisation providing specialised career counselling to employees who have been terminated in order to assist them in finding employment elsewhere. The purpose of outplacement is to reduce disruptions for both the organisation and the individual by providing a smooth transition process. Outplacement also minimises the potential for litigation and grievance proceedings, improves the morale of remaining employees and protects the public image of the organisation. Traditionally, outplacement services have focussed on activities such as resume writing, interest assessment and interview training; however, in the context of boundaryless and protean careers they should also emphasise values exploration, the identification of transferable skills, developing and capitalising on networks and improving career resilience (Butterfield & Borgen, 2005).

Executive Coaching
It has been estimated that approximately 50% of individuals in managerial and executive positions are not performing to expectations, and as a consequence their career progression is limited (Burke & Cooper, 2006). Recently, executive coaching – which is a one-on-one relationship between a manager and an external coach in order to further the manager's professional development – has become an important career management practice (McCauley & Hezlett, 2001) and has been increasingly emphasised. There are three core elements to executive coaching: (1) one-to-one counselling

regarding work-related issues; (2) obtaining 360 degree feedback on the strengths and limitations of the executive; and (3) improving the executive's effectiveness in his/her current role (Feldman, 2001). According to Feldman and Lankau (2005), executive coaches are expected to be advisors (sharing their tacit knowledge about business success), career counsellors (helping executives identify their strengths and weaknesses), mentors (assisting executives perform more effectively) and therapists (helping executives change their behaviour). The outcomes of executive coaching will benefit those following boundaryless or protean careers as they are focussed on enhancing skill development, modifying interaction styles, improving performance, building career resilience, increasing adaptability to change, attaining work-life balance and facilitating career advancement (Witherspoon & White, 1996). As executive coaching is quite a nascent practice, there is little empirical evidence of its effectiveness; however, Smither, London, Flautt, Vargas, and Kucine (2003) found that executives who worked with coaches – compared to those who did not – set more specific goals, were open in sharing their feedback, received action ideas from their supervisors and improved their multi-source performance rating scores.

Dual Ladders
As organisational hierarchies are increasingly being de-layered and as the number of highly educated employees competing for fewer promotional opportunities expands, organisations are increasingly introducing dual promotional ladders. A dual ladder is a parallel promotional hierarchy that affords technical and professional employees advancement, remuneration and recognition without having to move to managerial positions. Moreover, it is often the case that very competent technical and professional staff do not necessarily make effective managers and perhaps have no aspiration to move into managerial roles. Thus, dual career ladders enable organisations to capitalise on the expertise of their technical and professional staff who are often in pivotal roles and whose knowledge is a source of competitive advantage. For individuals with considerable experience but little interest in taking on managerial position, dual career ladders provide an alternative career path. As a result, the opportunities for employees with considerable technical competence are expanded and negative outcomes such as poor person-environment fit, job dissatisfaction and turnover can be avoided (Levine, 2010). Many large organisations – particularly those in the health, education and science fields – utilise dual ladders. For example, Unilever introduced an alternative career pathway whereby highly skilled scientists could progress to become the equivalent of senior managers.

Mentoring
As much greater responsibility is being placed on individuals to manage their career development, the importance of having an effective mentor is particularly important. Mentoring occurs when a senior, more experienced employee (i.e. the mentor) provides career-related (e.g. sponsorship and coaching) and psychosocial (e.g. friendship and counselling) support to a junior, less experienced employee (i.e. the protégé) (Eby, Lookwood, & Butts, 2006). Many mentoring relationships are informal and occur naturally and spontaneously as a result of unstructured social interactions, mutual identification and interpersonal comfort. However, it is increasingly more common that organisations are introducing formal programmes where mentors are assigned or

paired with protégés. Unlike informal mentoring relationships, their formal counter-parts are structured by the organisation and often last for a predetermined duration.

In a meta-analytical review involving 14 studies, Underhill (2006) found that mentor-ing was associated with increased job satisfaction and with perceived promotion or career advancement opportunities. Additionally, Wanberg, Kammeyer-Mueller, and Marchese (2006) assessed formal mentoring relationships and found that the extent to which mentoring occurred was related to positive outcomes such as improved career clarity for both protégés and mentors. Additionally, this study indicated that men-tor proactivity, that is, taking responsibility for initiating meetings and maintaining contact, was positively related to both career mentoring and psychosocial mentoring. Research also indicates that organisational agents such as human resource managers play an important role in establishing, shaping and reinforcing the values that facili-tate effective mentoring relationships. In organisations where mentoring is supported, senior employees are more likely to devote the time and energy required to estab-lish relationships in order to develop junior employees. Allen, Poteet, and Burroughs (1997) found that the most important factor for facilitating mentoring relationships was perceived support by the organisation for employee learning and development. Similarly, Eby et al. (2006) found that as perceived management support for mentor-ing increased, there was a concomitant increase in the extent to which career-related mentoring occurred. A recent meta-analysis (Ghosh, 2014) examined the antecedents of mentoring support in organisational settings. This study found, at the individual level, that protégé's proactivity, protégé's learning goal orientation and mentor's trans-formational leadership were the important predictors of mentoring support. At the relational level, affect-based trust (i.e. trust based on a strong emotional bond between the mentor and the protégé) and perceived similarity between mentor and protégé were the key drivers of mentoring support. Finally, organisational support for mentoring and supervisory mentoring (i.e. an intense interpersonal exchange between mentor and protégé) were found to be the strongest predictors of mentoring support at the organisational level.

Despite the clear benefits of mentoring, there is some evidence to suggest that this career management practice may be under-utilised. For example, McAlearney (2005) found that only one third of healthcare organisations in her sample had formal men-toring programmes. Additionally, none of the executives and fewer than one quarter of chief executives who responded to the survey indicated that they had participated in formal mentoring programmes as a protégé. The reluctance to participate in men-toring programmes may be due to the difficulties that can potentially occur in these relationships. Eby and Lookwood (2004) examined the problems encountered in mentoring relationships and found that they related to factors such as mentor-protégé mismatches, problems with scheduling meetings, geographic distance, mentor neglect (by protégés), unmet expectations (by protégés), structural separation from mentors (by protégés) and perceptions of personal inadequacy (by mentors). Sullivan and Baruch (2009) argued that single mentoring relationships are no longer sufficient to satisfy the complex needs of protégés. They have recommended that employees estab-lish multiple within-firm mentoring relationships (and in some cases external mentor-ing relationships) in order to cope with growing performance pressures and increased protégé career mobility.

Performance Management and Career Management

A number of scholars (Baruch, 2004; Boswell & Boudreau, 1999; Hall, Posner, & Harder, 1989; Soens & De Vos, 2007) have highlighted the importance of establishing close links between the organisation's performance management system and career development. Additionally, Baruch (2004) has argued that as careers become more boundaryless or protean in nature, a robust performance management system is essential as it can identify employees who are eligible for promotion, those requiring skill development through training, and those who should be considered for redundancy during periods of downsizing. Moreover, the assessment should be oriented towards 'meta-criteria', such as the capacity to learn and adaptability in response to change as well as context performance (i.e. extra-role behaviours), the extent to which networks are maintained and extended, and the individual's contribution to team performance.

Facilitating Career Self-management

Career self-management, that is, the extent to which an employee gathers information and plans for career decisions), by definition is largely the responsibility of the employee, and indeed research conducted by Chiaburu, Baker, and Pitariu (2006) indicates that proactivity is positively related to career self-management. However, this study also found that the relationship is mediated by career resilience. Given the mediating role of this variable, human resource managers should consider introducing interventions to build career resilience, including: providing support for skill development, offering positive rewards for performance, using reinforcement contingencies and providing opportunities for success. Organisations should also consider introducing explicit career self-management training programmes where employees are encouraged to demonstrate agency in their own career building: by increasing their self-knowledge, through commitment to their career goals, and by the quality of their career plans. Indeed, Raabe, Frese, and Beehr (2007), using a quasi-experimental design, found that these three variables were related to career self-management behaviours which in turn were related to career satisfaction. Verbruggen and Sels (2008) examined whether career self-directedness could be enhanced though career counselling, focussing on self-awareness and flexibility, using a longitudinal design. They found that career self-directedness can be 'learned' via interventions aimed at improving self-awareness and flexibility. Moreover, career self-directedness was found to be predictive of involvement in career training and career mobility.

Human resource development activities should also focus on helping employees develop *know-why*, *know-how* and *know-whom* competencies in order to successfully manage boundaryless careers (Defillippi & Arthur, 1994). Know-why competencies require that employees acquire an understanding of their motivations, career goals and personal values. Know-why competencies also involve recognising the linkages between successive careers, thereby integrating these perhaps diverse work experiences into a coherent conception of one's career. Know-how competencies concern the extent to which employees are able to construct a portfolio of skills that are readily transferable between jobs and careers. Know-whom competencies relate to the establishment and maintenance of mentoring relationships, as well as networks that provide support, guidance, influence and tacit knowledge (i.e. knowledge that is not written down and only available from experienced individuals concerning issues such as what is rewarded by organisations, future directions or shifts within industries, etc.).

Whilst empirical research examining the importance of these competencies in relation to boundaryless careers is scant, initial evidence has been generally supportive. For example, Colakoglu (2011) found that career boundarylessness was positively related to both know-why and know-how competencies; however, it was unrelated to know-whom competencies. Additionally, this study found that all three competencies were positively related to career autonomy, which in turn was predictive of subjective career success. It should also be noted that the acquisition of such knowledge and competencies is increasingly shifting from more formalised training courses to sources that are less formalised such as via coaching (Zaleska & de Menezes, 2007). The role of HR here is then to be able to support such training and development that may take place in the more proximal social and organisational workplace context.

Other Structural and Cultural Changes

In consideration of more recent research emanating from the KCM perspective, organisations may need to pay closer attention to how they can provide support to the changing career needs of individuals who may be from different generations or life circumstances (e.g. starting a family, nearing retirement age, etc.). Such efforts could lead to higher rates of retention and more effective use of differences a diverse workforce for an organisation's strategic advantage (Gorman, Nelson, & Glassman, 2004). Particularly in satisfying the younger Gen X employees and women's need for balance, organisations should ensure flexible work policies are in place to enable employees to more effectively manage work–family interface (Bjornholt, 2010). These could include providing paid parental leave, flexible work arrangements, support for elder- and child-care, and other employee benefits such as sabbaticals (Sok et al., 2014). However, it is also crucial to ensure that the utilisation of these policies is not met with and inhibited by hostility, unsupportive leadership and negative management attitudes (Clarke, 2015). Instead, researchers have stressed on the need for organisations to take a proactive approach to driving a supportive culture.

Also taking into consideration the higher emphasis placed on *Authenticity* (the need to make decisions that suits the true self) in career decisions particularly amongst younger members of the workforce, researchers have emphasised the need to ensure good fit between employees and organisational values. Here, organisations may use of realistic job previews (Buckley et al., 2002) and chances for them to work on projects that may be meaningful to them (e.g. environmental conservation) to allow them to pursue a career that permits them expressing their full and true selves (Sullivan et al., 2009).

Integration

In order to be effective, the human resource management practices discussed above should not be introduced in isolation. Rather, these practices should be combined to form an integrative career system. Of course the sophistication of an integrated career system will vary according to organisational size, with larger firms requiring more complex systems. Additionally, larger organisations with internal labour markets are more likely to focus on career development with explicit policies and to offer greater training opportunities (Herriot et al., 1994). Baruch (2003) has argued that an organisation's career system requires integration at both the internal and external levels. Internal integration requires coordination of the various human resource practices; for example, in order for executive coaching to yield maximum results it should be guided by performance management data and supported by an internal mentor (Wasylyshyn, 2003). External integration, according to Baruch (2003), occurs when the career management system is aligned with both the organisational culture and strategy.

Conclusions

The traditional career theories – based on advancement, predictability, the relational psychological contract and organisational career management – have struggled to cope with the significant changes experienced by many individuals in the work environment. In response to these changes, new conceptions of career, that is, boundaryless and protean career and the KCM, have emerged which emphasise horizontal job moves, coping with uncertainty, transactional psychological contracts, networking and personal satisfaction. Whilst career self-management is a hallmark of these new and increasingly common career paths, human resource managers can assist employees in the development of modern careers through initiatives such as succession planning, lateral moves and secondments to increase cross-functional experience, outplacement, executive coaching, dual ladders, mentoring, performance management and explicit training in career self-management. It is important to note, however, that these practices should not be introduced in isolation, but rather as an integrated career management system and with the support of the right organisational culture.

References

Allen, N. J., & Meyer, J. P. (1996). Affective, continuance, and normative commitment to the organization: An examination of construct validity. *Journal of Vocational Behavior*, *49*, 252–276.

Allen, T. D., Poteet, M. L., & Burroughs, S. M. (1997). The mentor's perspective: A qualitative inquiry and future research agenda, *Journal of Vocational Behavior*, *51*, 70–89.

Alonderien , R., & Šimkevičiūtė, I. (2018). Linking protean and boundaryless career with organizational commitment: The case of young adults in finance sector. *Baltic Journal of Management*, *13*(4), 471–487.

Arthur, M. B., Hall, D. T., & Lawrence, B. S. (1989). *Handbook of career theory*. Cambridge: Cambridge University Press.

Arthur, M. B., & Rousseau, D. M. (1996). The boundaryless career as a new employment principle. In M. B. Arthur & D. M. Rousseau (Eds.), *The boundaryless career* (pp. 3–20). New York, NY: Oxford University Press.

Bagdadli, S., Solari, L., Usai, A., & Grandori, A. (2003). 'The emergence of career boundaries in unbounded industries: Career odysseys in the Italian New Economy. *International Journal of Human Resource Management*, *14*(5), 788–808.

Barley, S. R., Bechky, B. A., & Milliken, F. J. (2017). The changing nature of work: Careers, identities, and work lives in the 21st century. *Academy of Management Discoveries*, *3*(2), 111–115.

Baruch, Y. (2003). Career systems in transition: A normative model for organizational career practices. *Personnel Review*, *32*, 231–251.

Baruch, Y. (2004). *Managing careers: Theory and practice*. Harlow: Pearson Education.

Baruch, Y. (2006). Career development in organizations and beyond: Balancing traditional and contemporary viewpoints. *Human Resource Management Review*, *16*, 125–138.

Bjornholt, M. (2010). Part-time work and the career and life choices of the men from the worksharing couples study. *Equality, Diversity and Inclusion: An International Journal*, *29*(6), 573–592.

Blyton, P., & Dastmalchian, A. (2006). Work-life integration and the changing context of work. International perspectives on the balancing of multiple roles. In P. Blyton, B. Blunsdon, K. Reed, & A. Dastmalchian (Eds.), *Work-life integration* (pp. 17–27). Houndmills, Basingstoke, Hampshire: Palgrave Macmillan.

Böhmer, N., & Schinnenburg, H. (2016). How gender and career concepts impact global talent management. *Employee Relations, 38*(1), 73–93.

Boswell, W. R., & Boudreau, J. W. (1999). Separating the developmental and evaluative performance appraisal uses. Working Paper No. 99-09. Center for Advanced Human Resource Studies, Cornell University, Ithaca, NY.

Buckley, M., Mobbs, T., Mendoza, J., Novicevic, M., Carraher, S., & Beu, D. (2002). Implementing realistic job previews and expectation lowering procedures: A field experiment. *Journal of Vocational Behavior, 61*(2), 263–278.

Burke, R. J., & Cooper, C. L. (2006). The new world of work and organizations: Implications for human resource management. *Human Resource Management Review, 16*, 83–85.

Butterfield, L. D., & Borgen, W. A. (2005). Outplacement counseling from the client's perspective. *Career Development Quarterly, 53*, 306–316.

Cabrera, E. F. (2007). Opting out and opting in: Understanding the complexities of women's career transitions. *Career Development International, 12*(3), 218–237.

Çakmak-Otluoğlu, K. Ö. (2012). Protean and boundaryless career attitudes and organizational commitment: The effects of perceived supervisor support. *Journal of Vocational Behavior, 80*(3), 638–646.

Callanan, G. A., & Greenhaus, J. H. (2008). The baby boom generation and career management: A call to action. *Advances in Developing Human Resources, 10*(1), 70–85.

Cassells, R., Duncan, A., Mavisakalyan, A., Phillimore, J., Seymour, R., & Tarverdi, Y. (2018). *Future of work in Australia: Preparing for tomorrow's world.* Perth, Australia: Bankwest-Curtin Economics Centre.

Chiaburu, D. S., Baker, V. L., & Pitariu, A. H. (2006). Beyond being proactive: What (else) matters for career self-management behaviors?. *Career Development International, 11*, 619–632.

Clarke, M. (2015). Dual careers: The new norm for Gen Y professionals?. *Career Development International, 20*(6), 562–582.

Cleary, P. (1997). A revolution in the nation's workplace. *Sydney Morning Herald*, October 20, pp. 1–7.

Colakoglu, S. N. (2011). The impact of career boundarylessness on subjective career success: The role of career competencies, career autonomy, and career insecurity. *Journal of Vocational Behavior, 9*(1), 47–59.

Costa, P. T., Jr, & McCrae, R. R. (1992). A five-factor theory of personality. In L. A. Pervin & O. P. John (Eds.), *Handbook of personality: Theory and research* (pp. 139–153). New York, NY: The Gilford Press.

Defillippi, R. J., & Arthur, M. B. (1994). The boundaryless career: A competency-based perspective. *Journal of Organizational Behavior, 15*, 307–324.

Eby, L. T., & Lookwood, A. (2004). Protégés' and mentors' reactions to participating in formal mentoring programs: A qualitative investigation. *Journal of Vocational Behavior, 67*, 441–458.

Eby, L. T., Lookwood, A. L., & Butts, M. (2006). Perceived support for mentoring: A multiple perspectives approach. *Journal of Vocational Behavior, 68*, 267–291.

Feldman, D. C. (2001). Career coaching: What HR professionals and managers need to know. *Human Resource Planning, 24*, 26–35.

Feldman, D. C., & Lankau, M. J. (2005). Executive coaching: A review and agenda for future research. *Journal of Management, 31*, 829–848.

Garavan, T. N., & Coolahan, M. (1996). Career mobility in organizations: Implications for career development – Part 1. *Journal of European Industrial Training*, *20*, 30–40.

Ghosh, R. (2014). Antecedent of mentoring support: A meta-analysis of individual, relational, and structural or organizational factors. *Journal of Vocational Behavior*, *84*, 367–384.

Gorman, P., Nelson, T., & Glassman, A. (2004). The millennial generation: A strategic opportunity. *Organizational Analysis*, *12*(3), 255–270.

Hackett, R. D., Bycio, P., & Hausdorf, P. A. (1994). Further assessment of Mayer and Allen's (1991) three-component model of organizational commitment. *Journal of Applied Psychology*, *79*, 15–23.

Hall, D. T. (1996). Protean careers of the 21st century. *Academy of Management Executive*, *10*, 8–16.

Hall, D. T., Gardner, W., & Baugh, S. G. (2008). The questions we ask about authenticity and attainability: How do values and beliefs influence our career decisions? Careers division theme session panel discussion presented at the Academy of Management, Anaheim, CA.

Hall, D. T., & Mirvis, P. H. (1996). The new protean career: Psychological success and the path with a heart. In D. T. Hall (Ed.), *The career is dead: Long live the career* (pp. 15–45). San Francisco, CA: Jossey Bass.

Hall, D. T., Yip, J., & Doiron, K. (2018). Protean careers at work: Self-direction and values orientation in psychological success. *Annual Review of Organizational Psychology and Organizational Behavior*, *5*, 129–156.

Hall, J. L., Posner, B. Z., & Harder, J. W. (1989). Performance appraisal systems. *Group and Organizational Studies*, *14*, 51–59.

Herriot, P., Gibson, P., Pemberton, C., & Jackson, R. J. (1994). An empirical model of managerial careers in organizations. *British Journal of Management*, *15*, 113–131.

Herriot, P., & Pemberton, C. (1996). Contracting careers. *Human Relations*, *49*, 757–790.

Hewlett, S. A., & Rashid, R. (2010). The battle for female talent in emerging markets. *Harvard Business Review, May*, 101–106.

Hind, P. (2005). Making room for career change. *Career Development International*, *10*, 268–274.

Hirsh, W. (1990). *Succession planning: Current practices and future issues*. IMS Report No. 184, Brighton. Institute for employment studies.

Hirsh, W. (2000). *Succession planning demystified*. IMS Report No. 372, Brighton. Institute for employment studies.

Holland, J. L. (1973). *Making vocational choices: A theory of careers*. Englewood Cliffs, NJ: Prentice Hall.

Ibarra, H. (2003). *Working identity: Unconventional strategies for reinventing your career*. Boston, MA: Harvard Business School Press.

Katz, L. F., & Krueger, A. B. (2017). The role of unemployment in the rise in alternative work arrangements. *American Economic Review*, *107*(5), 388–392.

Lau, V. P., Hsu, Y. S., & Shaffer, M. A. (2013). Global careers in China. In C. Reis & Y. Baruch (Eds.), *Careers without borders* (pp. 247–266). London: Routledge.

Levine, D. (2010). Investigation of bullying, job analysis, dual career ladders. *HR Magazine*, November, pp. 20–21.

Leibman, M., Bruer, R. A., & Maki, B. R. (1996). Succession management: The next generation of succession planning. *Human Resource Planning*, *19*(3), 16–30.

Malach-Pines, A., & Schwartz, D. (2007). Now you see them, now you don't: Gender differences in entrepreneurship. *Journal of Management Psychology*, *23*, 811–832.

Mainiero, L. A., & Gibson, D. E. (2018). The Kaleidoscope career model revisited: How midcareer men and women diverge on authenticity, balance, and challenge. *Journal of Career Development*, *45*(4), 361–377.

Mainiero, L. A., & Sullivan, S. E. (2006). *The opt out revolt: Why people are leaving companies to create kaleidoscope careers*. Mountain View, CA: Davies-Black Publishing.

Marler, J. H., Barringer, M. W., & Milkovich, G. T. (2002). Boundaryless and traditional contingent employees: Worlds apart. *Journal of Organizational Behavior*, *23*, 425–453.

McAlearney, A. S. (2005). Exploring mentoring and leadership development in health care organizations. *Career Development International*, *10*, 493–511.

McCauley, C. D., & Hezlett, S. A. (2001). Individual development in the workplace. In N. Anderson, D. Ones, H. K. Sinangil, & C. Viswesvaran (Eds.), *Handbook of industrial, work, and organisational psychology* (pp. 313–335). London: Sage.

McDonald, K. S., & Hite, L. M. (2008). The next generation of career success: Implications for HRD. *Advances in Developing Human Resources*, *10*, 86–103.

Meyer, J. P., Stanley, D. J., Herscovitch, L., & Topolnysky, L. (2002). Affective, continuance, and normative commitment to the organization: A meta-analysis of antecedents, correlates, and consequences. *Journal of Vocational Behavior*. *61*, 20–52.

Moore, D. P. (2002). *Careerpreneurs: Lessons from leading women entrepreneurs on building a career without boundaries*. Palo Alto, CA: Davies-Black Publishing.

National Association of Corporate Directors. (2006, September 12). Corporate boards still challenged by CEO succession planning. Media Release, Washington, DC.

Portwood, J. D., & Granrose, C. S. (1986). Organizational career management programmes: What's available? What's effective?. *Human Resource Planning*, *19*, 107–119.

Prahalad, C. K., & Hamel, G. (1990). The core competence of the corporation. *Harvard Business Review*, *68*, 79–91.

Raabe, B., Frese, M., & Beehr, T. A. (2007). Action regulation theory and career self-management. *Journal of Vocational Behavior*, *70*, 297–311.

Reitman, F., & Schneer, J. A. (2003). The promised path: A longitudinal study of managerial careers. *Journal of Managerial Psychology*, *18*, 60–75.

Richardson, S., Healy, J., & Moskos, M. (2014). *From 'gentle invaders' to 'breadwinners': Australian women's increasing employment and earnings shares*. Adelaide, South Australia: National Institute of Labour Studies, Flinders University.

Rodrigues, R. A., & Guest, D. (2010). Have careers become boundaryless?. *Human Relations*, *63*, 1157–1175.

Sargent, L. D., & Domberger, S. R. (2007). Exploring the development of a protean career orientation: Values and image violations. *Career Development International*, *12*, 545–564.

Savickas, M. L. (2003). Advancing the career counseling profession: Objectives and strategies for the next decade. *The Career Development Quarterly*, *52*, 87–96.

Smither, J. W., London, M., Flautt, R., Vargas, Y., & Kucine, I. (2003). Can working with an executive coach improve multisource feedback ratings over time? A quasi-experimental field study. *Personnel Psychology*, *56*(1), 23–44.

Soens, N., & De Vos, A. (2007). Career counseling within organizations: Isolation or integration?. Working Paper No. 6482/10. Vlerick Leuven Gent Management School, Belgium.

Sok, J., Blomme, R., & Tromp, D. (2014). Positive and negative spillover from work to home: The role of organizational culture and supportive arrangements. *British Journal of Management*, *25*(3), 456–472.

Sullivan, S. E. (1999). The changing nature of careers: A review and research agenda. *Journal of Management*, *25*(3), 457–484.

Sullivan, S. E., & Arthur, M. B. (2006). The evolution of the boundaryless career concept: Examining physical and psychological mobility. *Journal of Vocational Behavior, 69*(1), 19–29.

Sullivan, S. E., & Baruch, Y. (2009). Advances in career theory and research: A critical review and agenda for future exploration. *Journal of Management, 35,* 1542–1571.

Sullivan, S. E., Forret, M. L., Carraher, S. M., & Mainiero, L. A. (2009). Using the kaleidoscope career model to examine generational differences in work attitudes. *Career Development International, 14*(3), 284–302.

Sullivan, S. E., & Mainiero, L. A. (2007). The changing nature of gender roles, alpha/ beta careers and work-life issues: Theory-driven implications for human resource management. *Career Development International, 12*(3), 238–263.

Super, D. E. (1953). A theory of vocational development. *American Psychologist, 8,* 185–190.

Twenge, J. M., Campbell, S. M., Hoffman, B. J., & Lance, C. E. (2010). Generational differences in work values: Leisure and extrinsic values increasing, social and intrinsic values decreasing. *Journal of Management, 36*(5), 1117–1142.

Underhill, C. M. (2006). The effectiveness of mentoring programs in corporate settings: A meta-analytical review of the literature. *Journal of Vocational Behavior, 68,* 292–307.

Valcour, P. M., & Tolbert, P. (2003). Gender, family and career in the era of boundarylessness: Determinants and effects of intra-and inter-organizational mobility. *International Journal of Human Resource Management, 14*(5), 768–787.

Verbruggen, M., & Sels, L. (2008). Can career self-directedness be improved through conseling?. *Journal of Vocational Behavior, 73,* 318–327.

Vinkenburg, C. J., & Weber, T. (2012). Managerial career patterns: A review of the empirical evidence. *Journal of Vocational Behavior, 80,* 592–607.

Vinson, G. A., Connelly, B. S., & Ones, D. S. (2007). Personality and organization switching: Implications for utility estimate. *International Journal of Selection and Assessment, 15,* 118–133.

Wanberg, C. R., Kammeyer-Mueller, J., & Marchese, M. (2006). Mentor and protégé predictors and outcomes of mentoring in a formal mentoring program. *Journal of Vocational Behavior, 69,* 410–423.

Wasylyshyn, K. M. (2003). Executive coaching: An outcome study. *Consulting Psychology Journal: Practice & Research, 55*(2), 94–106.

Waters, L., Briscoe, J. P., Hall, D. T., & Wang, L. (2014). Protean career attitudes during unemployment and employment: A longitudinal perspective. *Journal of Vocational Behavior, 84,* 405–419.

Westerman, J. W., & Yamamura, J. H. (2007). Generational preferences for work environment fit: Effects on employee outcomes. *Career Development International, 12*(2), 150–161.

Witherspoon, R., & White, R. P. (1996). Executive coaching: A continuum of roles. *Consulting Psychology Journal: Practice & Research, 48,* 124–133.

Zaleska, K. J., & de Menezes, L. M. (2007). Human resources development practices and their association with employee attitudes: Between traditional and new careers. *Human Relations, 60*(7), 987–1018.

Chapter 5

HRM and the Service Sector

Cathy Sheehan

Introduction

Technological advances and the speedy transfer of information have diminished the contribution that labour once made to manufacturing. Improvements in technology mean that products are now more readily produced and complex processes are more easily replicated. The rise of artificial intelligence (AI) has consolidated the reduction of the importance of a large, skilled production labour force (Wilson & Daugherty, 2018). It is expected that machines will continue to take over much of the tedious operational work. The work that will increasingly become more dominant and valuable will be interpersonal work: tasks that primarily require direct engagement with other people (AlphaBeta, 2017).

In response to the changing profile of the workforce, the focus of this chapter is on the rising importance of service workers not only in the delivery of products but also the cohort of service workers who are now responsible for providing emerging important personal service work. The 2017 AlphaBeta report *The Automation Advantage*, profiles the type of work that will arise as increasing levels of automation remove routine manual work. The expectation is that the future of work will focus on roles that computers and robots cannot provide such as personal care work and work that requires intuition and empathy.

The objectives of this chapter are to review the rise of service work, understand the challenges and opportunities that service work presents for employees and employers, and discuss the contribution that the human resources (HR) function can make in the management of some of the related issues.

The Decline of Manufacturing and Rise of Service Work

During the twentieth century, automotive developments reduced the intense labour requirements that had previously been associated with manufacturing assembly processes. More recently, technological advances in robotics and AI have continued to reduce labour opportunities associated with production. Declining employment in manufacturing in advanced market economies (AMEs) has been exacerbated by the off-shoring of manufacturing work to low-wage job markets overseas. As a result of these developments, the primary focus of employment in many developed countries has increasingly become service oriented. By the mid-1990s in the United States about 70% of work had shifted to service employment (Macdonald & Sirianni, 1996). In the UK in the years between 1971 and 2000, the number employed in manufacturing in Britain fell by almost four million – or almost 50%. In the same period, the number of employees in services rose by almost seven million – or an increase of over 60%. As a consequence, by 2000 more than four and half times as many people were employed in the service sector in Britain as in manufacturing (Noon & Blyton, 2002). The trend continues with employment sector developments reported by the International Labour Organisation (ILO) in the *World Employment Social Outlook – Trends 2018* showing that as of 2017, the service sector employed the largest share of the international workforce in all income groups (ILO, 2018).

The dominance of the service industry makes it an area of special interest in the study of human resource management (HRM). Success in the service industry relies heavily on the direct interaction between employees and customers. Adding value is therefore largely determined by the employees, an area that falls within the responsibility of the HR professional.

What is Service Work?

Before we consider the opportunities and challenges that service work presents for HR we need to understand what it is about jobs in the service industry that is different from jobs in manufacturing. There are several distinctions that are helpful in understanding the nature of service work. First, as suggested above, a job in the service industry primarily relies on human interactions rather than the production of physical goods that characterises manufacturing (Lovelock, Patterson, & Wirtz, 2015). The work is generated by people rather than machinery.

Second, with respect to the output of a service, it is intangible and therefore presented in a form that cannot be touched. The manufacturing process usually results in a three dimensional product that has mass and weight and can be handled. A service, however, does not possess these physical dimensions and its quality assessment therefore becomes more difficult as it is measured through the recipient's perceptions (Korczynski, 2002; Lovelock et al., 2015). This intangibility of a service means that it is also perishable – or temporary in nature. A service cannot be produced or stored in advance and taken out when needed; it has to be produced at the time it is required (Korczynski, 2002; Lovelock et al., 2015). Consistent with this perishability characteristic, the service is produced and consumed simultaneously (Korczynski, 2002: Lovelock et al., 2015).

Third, the service product highlights the active role of the customer with the service often relying on the information interaction between the provider and the customer (Korczynski, 2002: Lovelock et al., 2015). A service is therefore characterised by variability where the interaction between the provider and the customer contributes an added possible level of difference to each interaction. When a customer deals with a manufactured product, the product is usually relatively inert and predictable; with the creation of a service, however, the product relies on an interpersonal interaction and although the provider may be following a script and be trained to respond in a particular fashion, the interaction between each provider and customer has the potential to create quite a different outcome (Korczynski, 2002; Lovelock et al., 2015).

These characteristics of service work are useful in understanding how a service is quite different from a manufactured product. It is important to note, however, that not all service work is the same. In their discussion of how to classify service organisations, Mills and Margulies (1980) developed a useful typology that identified three basic types of service organisation: maintenance-interactive, task-interactive and personal-interactive. A maintenance-interactive service organisation primarily provides a service that dispenses a product and maintains an ongoing standard interaction that the customer trusts. Examples include banking and sales assistant work. The customer approaches the service with a clear idea about what they want and the interaction is routine and subject to few changes. In the task-interactive service organisation there is an added level of complexity as the service provider works with a customer to solve a problem and create a product that satisfies a particular set of customer needs: for example, an architectural company designing customised architectural plans or a catering company designing and delivering a menu for a specific event. Finally, Mills and Margulies (1980) identify a personal-interactive service organisation as one in which the service provided does not involve a separate product, but the service *is* the entire product, for example, psychological therapy, teaching or the assessment provided by a medical physician. In this interaction it is the knowledge of the provider, used to solve a problem and provide awareness for the customer, that is the key to the service. This feature of a personal-interactive service is in contrast to a maintenance-interactive service in which the customer arrives with a clear idea about what they want from the service.

Macdonald and Sirianni (1996) highlight a further distinction between types of service work by distinguishing between white collar service providers and the 'emotional proletariat'. The emotional proletariat are generally front-line service workers and para-professionals, whereas white collar service providers generally reside in managerial and professional roles. This differentiation on the basis of professional status is often accompanied by different guidelines about how the service is to be provided. For members of management and professional groups, for example, guidelines for appropriate emotional labour approaches will be generated collegially, and these individuals are to a great extent self-supervised. Front-line service jobs, however, are more likely to be given very explicit instructions concerning what to say and how to act, as is the case in call centres.

The discussion above highlights the wide variety of interactions that the service work label covers. Service work categories can be distinguished by the extent to which the customer determines the knowledge parameters of the service (Mills & Margulies, 1980), and also the level of professionalism of the service (Macdonald & Sirianni, 1996). The following sections highlight particular HR challenges faced by service providers in a range of situations as well as possible approaches to dealing with these challenges.

HR Challenges and Opportunities in the Services Sector

Recently there has been a general focus in the HRM literature on employee well-being (Guest, 2017). In 2018, for example, the *Academy of Management* set the theme of its annual conference as 'Improving Lives: Improving Health and Well-being in Society: How Can Organizations Help?'. An important aspect of this interest in employee well-being is the identification of workers who are involved in vulnerable employment or 'precarious work that places people at risk of continuing poverty and injustice resulting from an imbalance of power in the employer-work relationship' (Trades Union Congress, 2008, p. 3).

The rise in precarious work is associated with a common pattern seen in industrialised countries where employment has moved away from the 'traditional' forms of full-time, permanent work towards a wider variety of working arrangements including part-time work, temporary employment and contract employment or 'gig' work (Kalleberg, 2000; Van den Heuvel & Wooden, 1997). As well as the variation in working hours, another trend is the increasing number of workers now classified as 'casual'. A casual employee does not have a firm commitment in advance from an employer about how long they will be employed, or the days (or hours) they will work. A casual employee also usually works irregular hours and does not get paid sick or annual leave (Fair Work Ombudsman, 2018).

The relevance of this discussion of worker well-being and precarious work to HRM in the services sector is that a key feature of service work is that it is dominated by a casual workforce, a group of workers who are described by Burgess, Connell, and Winterton (2013), as employed in precarious work arrangements. Gilfillan (2018), in an overview of the characteristics and use of casual workers in Australia, identified that the accommodation and food services group has the highest percentage of casual workers. The concentration of casual workers in the service industries of hospitality, for example, is 79% of workers in that group.

The increase in the number of casual workers is occurring for several reasons. A generalised erosion of the traditional employment contract, typically thought to be based on lifetime employment for dedicated service, is evident. Employers therefore no longer guarantee job security for their employees. As well as the impact of changing employment expectations there are considerable benefits to employers in adopting more flexible employment arrangements. Many companies have reduced the number of full-time employees in order to lower the associated labour costs and to give the organisation the flexibility to contract for skills when needed. Casual work can also be attractive from the worker's perspective as the work arrangements often allow employees to fit in child care responsibilities as well as other interests and employment opportunities (Burgess & Connell, 2006).

Despite the benefits of flexibility offered by alternative forms of work in the services sector, the arrangements create numerous challenges both for employees and for organisations. For the employee, casual work is closely associated with poor work conditions including low hourly rates of pay, low and irregular earnings, reduced employment security, lack of access to notice and severance pay, reduced access to unfair dismissal rights, vulnerability to changes in schedules, loss of skill and age-related pay increments, and lack of representational rights (Australian Council of Trade Unions (ACTU), 2011; Pocock, Buchanan, & Campbell, 2004). For casual employees, unpredictable and fluctuating pay makes it difficult to predict earnings and to borrow money. The reduced control over working arrangements and hours also presents particular difficulty for workers with caring responsibilities (ACTU, 2011).

For the employer, although there is the flexibility and often reduced costs associated with this category of worker, the arrangement also has potentially negative ramifications (Buultjens, 2001). For example, casual workers, due to the transient nature of the terms of employment, are less likely to identify strongly with the organisation (Hall, 2006) and as a result may not absorb and display appropriate organisational values and behaviours.

The limited organisational investment in casuals also means that these employees may have less opportunity to develop necessary skills, and the contribution that they make may be limited to generic industry tasks rather than tasks that add real value as expected by some service providers. Lowry's (2001) investigation of the work arrangements for casual employees in Australia indicated that casuals are employed on a primarily transactional basis, with an underinvestment in employee development (Buultjens, 2001; Lowry, 2001). Over three quarters of Lowry's (2001) research sample reported that they had received some training, but the standard of the training was questionable and mainly consisted of ad hoc on-the-job training related to the immediate task. Furthermore, although over a half of the casual workers reported the availability of promotion opportunities, only a third of workers were progressing their careers. This is possibly because they were not willing to engage in, or commit to, the organisation. Respondents were also extremely critical of the lack of feedback and recognition for the work performed, and this had ramifications for the development of task skills and further detracted from the casual employees' willingness to commit to organisational needs.

The impact of an underinvestment in HRM activities such as training and feedback has ramifications for the quality of the service delivery provided by casuals. Lowry's (2001) findings, for example, indicated that some employees were so dissatisfied with the lack of feedback and recognition that they made a conscious decision *not* to provide quality service. This finding is consistent with the previous research by Schneider, White, and Paul (1998), who established a relationship between HRM practices, including training and supportive supervision, and the service climate.

The outcomes associated with a lack of organisational value alignment and the under-development of skills within the casual workforce is not only a problem in the hospitality industry but may affect other areas of service delivery as well. Using Mills and Margulies' (1980) distinctions, as outlined above, when a service position involves dispensing a product (maintenance-interactive service organisation), problems can occur when the delivery of the product is accompanied by an inappropriate customer interaction style. An example of this would be in specialty retail stores that differentiate themselves on the basis of superior product knowledge and a required approach to customers. Alternatively, where the service is the entire product (personal-interactive service organisations) it becomes even more important that the employee has the appropriate skill base and that their behaviour aligns with the expectations of the organisation. In a university setting, for example, where casual staff are employed to take tutorials, problems can occur when these employees are not briefed appropriately on expected standards. With respect to HR's role in these circumstances, casual teaching staff may be asked to attend appropriate induction training programmes and may also require close mentoring when first on the job. These systems have been activated in a number of leading universities in Australia where casual staff are required to attend training sessions before they are eligible to conduct tutorials. Casual teaching staff are usually also eligible to request student feedback through the formal central university teaching evaluation process. Performance feedback from other academics, however, is usually not formalised and relies on the willingness of other colleagues to provide appropriate mentoring.

Before leaving this discussion of the challenges associated with flexible work arrangements, it is important to consider the increasing presence of agency workers in service work. These workers are spread across a wide range of service industries, for example, nursing, hospital support work, teaching and sales assistant work, and are defined as employees whose wages and labour costs are paid by an agency but who work for a host/client on a fixed-term basis (Hall, 2006, p. 159). The problem noted above of organisational value alignment within the casual workforce similarly exists with agency workers. This is especially the case with companies that require high-involvement and high-performance work practices. A hospital, for example, that differentiates itself in the market through particularly high levels of pastoral care for patients and achieves this through a high-performance work culture would usually allow considerable employee autonomy and empowerment. The success of this approach, however, relies on the employee's alignment with, and understanding of, the organisation's culture. It may not be possible to achieve these goals when using a high number of agency workers.

This last example highlights the strategic HRM challenge for service industry companies that access these peripheral workers. In particular, strategic decisions have to be made about the nature of the tasks assigned to agency workers. There is evidence that companies are using these workers to suit business needs. Hall (2006) has found that the workers are generally employed on a short-term basis, and they report that agency workers are less likely to be learning new skills and less likely to be doing work that is complex or difficult. The suggestion is, then, that companies that are using these workers are making the strategic decision to use them for less central tasks. Following on, Hall (2006) makes the point that the absence of intrinsically challenging work as a motivator for temporary agency workers requires that HR may have to apply higher levels of supervision, surveillance and direct authoritarian control than may be necessary for core, intrinsically motivated employees who are secure and committed.

In summary, the flexible work arrangements that characterise much of the service industry present challenges for employees and employers. When using casuals, HR can make a contribution by reviewing the level of training and mentoring provided to ensure that these workers are clear about what is expected of them in their interaction with customers. Socialisation programmes and ongoing mentoring may help to diminish the fragmented approach to the work that can occur when an organisation draws from a large pool of casuals. When commitment to the organisation is a priority, the prospect of being able to transfer to permanent status or of gaining a promotion can also act as a motivator to casuals to align their behaviour with cultural expectations (Atkinson & Rick, 1996). This is a process often employed in call centres when successful customer service operators are offered promotions to team leadership positions (Holman, 2002). The problems of cultural fit and organisational commitment experienced with casual workers are similarly encountered with the use of agency workers (Geary, 1992). Unlike casual workers, however, who may be employed on an ongoing basis with the company, agency workers are normally only employed for a limited term – and this presents even greater complexity for HR. In response, companies seem to be applying greater discretion about the type of tasks assigned and the autonomy given to these workers within their period of employment.

Managing the Consequences of Services Sector Work

Another major challenge experienced by those HR professionals working with employees in the service industry is managing the employee stress related to the nature of service work itself. A fundamental element of service work is the face-to-face or voice-to-voice interaction with customers (Macdonald & Sirianni, 1996). These interactions involve high levels of emotional labour or 'the management of feeling to create a publicly observable facial and bodily display' (Hochschild, 1983, p. 7). Often emotional labour involves the management of differences between real and expected organisational displayed emotions and this is very much a feature of a service interaction. HR in service-oriented organisations can play a role in paying attention to clearly stated organisational expectations and ensuring employee fit through careful recruitment, selection and training. HR can also assist employees in the management of emotionally charged interactions with customers. The following section highlights the contribution that HR can make in these situations.

Undertakers, health professionals and counsellors take on their professions in the knowledge that they will often be dealing with people who are vulnerable and in distress. Accordingly, training and mentoring activities prepare these professionals for the emotional work that will be part of their job. Consideration may also often be given to a person's temperamental ability to deal with the intensity of the array of emotionally charged situations that occur within the profession. It can be argued, however, that any service interaction has the potential to be characterised by high levels of emotional intensity that may be outside the expected scope of the position. This can often occur in the low paid front-line 'emotional proletariat' work described by Macdonald and Sirianni (1996), who distinguish between these jobs and the services provided by white collar professionals.

The intensity of these potentially emotional encounters in front-line work is highlighted in O'Donohue and Turnley's (2006) research that considered the compassion needed by newspaper employees who dealt with bereaved customers who contacted the newspaper to place *In Memoriam* notices on the anniversary of a close family member's death. The research reviews the sophisticated level of emotional interaction that can sometimes occur in seemingly mundane service exchanges in lower paid organisational positions. Newspaper employees could be consoling a distraught bereaved customer one moment and dealing with a routine classified advertisement in the next. Of particular interest in the research was the exploration of the factors that assisted these employees in coping with the emotional rollercoaster that their work involved. Using Korczynski's (2003) 'communities of coping' explanation, O'Donohue and Turnley (2006) note that the staff, who were mainly women, relied on each other to debrief about traumatic incidents or stories, and it was the collective support within the work environment that allowed the staff to cope with the potential distress of these situations.

Despite the emotional concentration of jobs where service workers are required to demonstrate care and compassion when dealing with customers, interactions with customers can also be an important source of pleasure and satisfaction. Workers who feel they are helping someone often find this interpersonal connection to be an intrinsically satisfying part of the job (Frenkel, Korczynski, Shire, & Tam, 1999). Unfortunately, dealing with distressed customers does not always result in positive outcomes for customer service staff. An increasing amount of stress is generated in front-line service roles by irate, and sometimes violent, customers. This interaction can be particularly distressing for service workers who start out with strong pro-customer attitudes. In these cases, the ongoing need to deal with difficult interactions may be a critical factor in 'burnout' of front-line workers (Korczynski, 2002).

An industry in which customer service operators can often face abusive clients is in call centres. There is actually more potential for abuse in these situations because of the removal of the face-to-face component of the service interaction. Telephone conversations create a social distance and the feeling that the customer service representative is a disembodied voice against which it is appropriate to vent one's rage (Korczynski, 2002). The placement of some call centres offshore to countries such as India has exacerbated this level of abuse as customers incorporate racist abuse into existing complaints against the company (O'Malley, 2006).

Unfortunately in some situations, interactions with customers can escalate into more serious incidents that involve occupational violence and aggression (OVA), defined here as '…any incident where an employee is abused, threatened or assaulted in circumstances arising out of, or in the course of, their employment' (Department of Health, 2011, p. 8). A report of the Victorian Auditor General's Office (2015) in Australia explains that although there are reports of increasing acts of OVA in hospitals, the true extent of OVA is unknown. This is partly because there is significant under-reporting of occupational violence incidents.

Shea, Sheehan, Donohue, Cooper, and De Cieri's (2017) research has provided some insight into the extent and sources of OVA in hospitals in Australia. The outcomes of the research indicate that 67% of respondents reported experiencing OVA in the preceding 12 months with nearly 20% experiencing OVA on a weekly or daily basis. Patients (79%) or relatives of patients (48%) were the main source of violence and aggression. Interestingly midwives were less likely to experience OVA and when it did occur it was likely to come from relatives of patients and patient visitors than the patients themselves. With respect to gender, male nurses were more likely to report having been exposed to OVA in the past 12 months compared to women and nurses working in public hospitals and aged care facilities experienced OVA at greater rates than those in private hospitals, general practice clinics, local government and community settings. One possible explanation is that the public sector hospital may be more likely to deal with higher levels of patient acuity that raises emotional distress levels. In terms of managing OVA incidents, the research found that individual factors such as nurse willingness to comply with safety procedures reduced the likelihood of experiencing OVA. At the workplace level safety factors such as prioritisation of employee safety, supervisors' support for safety and leading indicators of occupational health and safety (OHS) were strongly associated with a reduction in OVA incidents. Leading indicators of OHS include a workplace focus on proactively committing to a safe working environment by implementing positive OHS policies and practices that allow organisations to predict safety concerns and potentially reduce the likelihood of an OHS incident occurring (Shea, De Cieri, Donohue, Cooper, & Sheehan, 2016). Such environments ensure, among other features, that everyone in the workplace values ongoing safety improvement, workers and supervisors have the information they need to work safely and are always involved in decisions affecting their health and safety.

Overall service work can lead to emotionally intense interactions with customers that potentially place employees at risk. It becomes the responsibility of HR therefore, to ensure that these interactions are minimised and that potential danger is averted. OHS legislation in most AMEs ensures that organisations are legally responsible to provide a safe workplace and adopt a 'duty of care' with respect to both employees and customers. As suggested in Shea et al.'s (2016, 2017) leading indicator research, HR can take a role in creating and maintaining a workplace that is committed to a safe working environment by implementing positive OHS policies and practices that ensure that safety improvement is valued, workers and supervisors have the information they need to work safely and they are involved in OHS decision-making. In terms of other practical infrastructure changes, HR can take a role in ensuring appropriate video surveillance of customer behaviour, access to employee assistance programmes for employees to receive counselling, and closer communication with the security department to plan personal reaction strategies.

HR also has the responsibility for designing and communicating the organisation's policy on the prevention of occupational violence in the workplace. Effective policy development usually involves employees in the policy design process. The finalised policy clearly defines the range of violent interactions and the identification of risks, and reminds employees of common warning signs. An explanation is also provided of the employee's responsibilities for recognising signs and reporting them. Guidelines are usually provided about who to notify and what to do in various situations and training is set up on what policies and procedures actually involve. A confidential reporting system supports the effective operationalisation of the policy.

As well as these HRM policy initiatives, Korczynski (2003) emphasises the need to encourage and develop 'communities of coping', or the empathetic dynamic between colleagues that provides support in emotionally stressful service positions. This dynamic often arises informally and can be crucial to survival in the job. HR can assist in the creation of this coping mechanism by developing team structures that acknowledge the natural support mechanisms that often emerge among service workers. A necessary part of the success of these team structures is the design of HRM performance evaluation processes. Research has shown, for example, that performance-based pay in call centres works best when it is constructed on a team-basis rather than when it is developed as an individual reward (Fernie & Metcalf, 1999; Korczynski, 2002). Coupled with the importance of team dynamics, other research has reinforced the important role that the team leader has on employee well-being (Holman, 2002; Rudewicz, 2004). Care should be taken in the selection and training of team leaders to ensure that they are equipped to provide appropriate support. This can be especially important in call centres where customer service operators are often promoted to team leadership roles for their technical competency and may be relatively ill-equipped to cope with the emotional coordination of the team (Holman, 2002).

Conclusions

The rise of service work has increased levels of interpersonal task delivery. The nature of service work is quite different from the previously dominant style of work in manufacturing that involved the production of a tangible, fixed product. Service work spans a wide range of possible interactions, but the essential component across all of these events is that the product is either partly or entirely associated with an interpersonal interaction between the provider and the customer. The management of employees, therefore, in the delivery of the organisation's business, is critical. The extent of the personal interaction between the provider and the customer means that the quality of the customer experience is heavily influenced by the employee who is delivering the service. It becomes essential therefore that employees working within the service industry are clear about their organisation's expectations and provide a service that aligns with the organisation's strategic focus.

There are, however, a number of HR challenges that service work presents. With respect to HRM planning, the interaction cannot really occur unless the customer is present. Staff have to be available when the customer is there and are often redundant when the customer is absent, thus the employment of casual and agency staff becomes a necessity. The benefits of flexibility offered by this workforce are often outweighed by loyalty and skill deficiencies, and accordingly HR has to make strategic decisions about the types of tasks these employees are given and the return on investment in training and development initiatives.

The personal nature of the 'product' can also present unexpected emotional intensity that HR has to manage for both the employee and the customer. Duty of care responsibilities, as well as the maximisation of company performance, may depend on how well HR attends to structural and policy design. At the broader level, the rise of the service sector has intensified the focus that is already being given to the impact HR can make in organisations. The more that human capital emerges as a key resource base, the more important is the strategic impact of HR.

References

AlphaBeta. (2017). The automation advantage. Retrieved from https://www.alphabeta.com/wp-content/uploads/2017/08/The-Automation-Advantage.pdf. Accessed on October 16, 2018.

Atkinson, J., & Rick, J. (1996). *Temporary work and the labour market*. Report No. 311. Institute of Employment Studies, London.

Australian Council of Trade Unions (ACTU). (2011). *The future of work in Australia: dealing with insecurity and risk*. An ACTU options paper on measures to promote job and income security. ACTU, Melbourne.

Burgess, J., & Connell, J. (2006). Temporary work and human resource management: Issues, challenges and responses. *Personnel Review, 35*(2), 125–140.

Burgess, J., Connell, J., & Winterton, J. (2013). Vulnerable workers, precarious work and the role of trade unions and HRM. *The International Journal of Human Resource Management, 24*(22), 4083–4093.

Buultjens, J. (2001). Casual employment: A problematic strategy for the registered clubs sector in New South Wales. *The Journal of Industrial Relations, 43*(4), 470–477.

Department of Health. (2011). *Preventing occupational violence: A policy framework including principles for managing weapons in Victorian health services*. Melbourne, Australia: Department of Health.

Fair Work Ombudsman. (2018). Casual employees. Retrieved from https://www.fairwork.gov.au/employee-entitlements/types-of-employees/casual-part-time-and-full-time/casual-employees. Accessed on October 18, 2018.

Fernie, S., & Metcalf, D. (1999). *(Not) hanging on the telephone: Payment systems in the new sweatshops*. Centre for Economic Performance Paper. London School of Economics, London.

Frenkel, S., Korczynski, M., Shire, K., & Tam, M. (1999). *On the FrontLline: Work organization in the service economy.* Ithaca, NY: ILR/Cornell University Press.

Geary, J. (1992). Employment flexibility and human resource management. *Work, Employment and Society, 6*(2), 251–270.

Gilfillan, G. (2018). *Characteristics and use of casual employees in Australia.* Research Paper Series, 2017–18. Parliament of Australia, AUstralia.

Guest, D. (2017). Human resource management and employee well-being: Towards a new analytic framework. *Human Resource Management Journal, 27*(1), 22–38.

Hall, R. (2006). Temporary agency work and HRM in Australia "Cooperation, specialization and satisfaction for the good of all?" *Personnel Review, 35*(2), 158–174.

Hochschild, A. R. (1983). *The managed heart: Commercialization of human feeling.* Berkeley, CA: University of California Press.

Holman, D. (2002). Employee wellbeing in call centres. *Human Resource Management Journal, 12*(4), 35–50.

International Labour Organisation (ILO). (2018). *World employment social outlook: Trends 2018.* Geneva: ILO.

Kalleberg, A. (2000). Nonstandard employment relations: Part-time, temporary and contract work. *Annual Review of Sociology, 26*, 341–365.

Korczynski, M. (2002). *Human resource management in service work.* Hampshire: Palgrave.

Korczynski, M. (2003). Communities of coping: Collective emotional labour in service work. *Organization, 10*(1), 55–79.

Lovelock, P., & Wirtz, J. (2015). *Services marketing: An Asia Pacific and Australian perspective* (6th ed.)., Melbourne, Australia: Pearson.

Lowry, D. (2001). The casual management of casual work: Casual workers' perceptions of HRM practices in the highly casualised firm. *Asia Pacific Journal of Human Resources, 39*(1), 42–62.

Macdonald, C., & Sirianni, C. (1996). The service society and the changing experience of work. In C. Macdonald & C. Sirianni (Eds.), *Working in the service society* (pp. 1–26). Philadelphia, PA: The University Press.

Mills, P., & Margulies, N. (1980). Towards a core typology of service organisations. *Academy of Management Review, 5*(2), 255–265.

Noon, M., & Blyton, P. (2002)., *The realities of work* (2nd ed.). Hampshire: Palgrave.

O'Donohue, S., & Turnley, D. (2006). Compassion at the counter: Service providers and bereave consumers. *Human Relations, 59*(10), 1429–1448.

O'Malley, N. (2006). Indian call centre staff fed up with racist abuse. *The Age*, March 20, p. 5.

Pocock, B., Buchanan, J., & Campbell, I. (2004). Meeting the challenge of casual work in Australia: Evidence, past treatment and future policy. *Australian Bulletin of Labour, 30*(1), 16–32.

Rudewicz, F. (2004). The road to rage. *Security Management, 48*(2), 40–46.

Schneider, B., White, S., & Paul, M. (1998). Linking service climate and customer perceptions of service quality: Test of a causal model. *Journal of Applied Psychology, 8*(2), 150–163.

Shea, T., De Cieri, H., Donohue, R., Cooper, B., & Sheehan, C. (2016). Leading indicators of occupational health and safety: An employee and workplace level validation study. *Safety Science, 85*, 293–304.

Shea, T., Sheehan, C., Donohue, R., Cooper, B., & De Cieri, H. (2017). Occupational violence and aggression experienced by nursing and caring professionals. *Journal of Nursing Scholarship, 49*(2), 236–243.

Trades Union Congress. (2008). *Hard work, hidden lives*. Full Report of the Commission on Vulnerable Employment. Trades Union Congress, London.

Van den Heuvel, A., & Wooden, M. (1997). Self-employed contractors and job satisfaction. *Journal of Small Business Management, 35*(3), 11–20.

Victorian Auditor General's Office. (2015). *Occupational violence against healthcare workers*. Melbourne, Australia: Victorian Auditor-General's Office.

Wilson, J., & Daugherty, P. R. (2018). Collaborative intelligence: Humans and AI are joining forces. *Harvard Business Review*, July-August 114–123.

Section II

Case Studies

(1) Psychological Contracts
(2) Career Management
(3) HRM and the Service Sector

(1) Psychological Contracts
Should I Stay or Should I Go?

Jack Jones was a senior IT analyst for a leading national food company. Jack had been with the company for over 30 years, beginning work at the company initially as a summer casual whilst completing his university degree. On completion of his biology degree he took up a full-time position with the organisation head office, working initially in the food hygiene section. However, over the years Jack undertook a variety of positions as he moved up through the organisation. With little experience in the area, Jack joined the IT section as it expanded and rose to the position of senior analyst quickly. As a result of his skills and knowledge of the company's new IT systems, and his communication skills, he was approached by senior management to help set up the system in other states where they were still working on manual arrangements that relied on the tacit knowledge of the senior logistics people. Whilst this worked at a local level the increasing need to manage the systems and logistics nationally meant that the local systems had to be integrated into the new system.

An initial discussion with the consultants who helped design and install the current system indicated that they would charge over $250,000 to train and develop the staff in the other states. The company bulked at the cost and in a meeting of senior management it was suggested that Jack to be seconded to the other two plants and spend a week in each helping train the logistic and IT staff in the new system. The senior logistics manager called Jack to his office to ask him to undertake the role, pointing out that it would provide an opportunity to broaden his skill base and would reflect well in his next performance appraisal. In addition, the senior logistics manager indicated that his work would be reflected in his end-of-year bonus 10% of the saving (estimated at $150,000) the company could make that year with the successful implementation of the system.

Jack readily took the opportunity and in the two weeks successfully implemented the system despite the initial resistance at the two sites. His success was attributed to his communication skills and knowledge of the system from an operator's perspective. These attributes gave him standing with the IT people that this wasn't just another consultant pushing their product. Jack worked 13 hours/day to ensure he worked across both shifts at the plants. On his return his manager said little but pointed to the backlog of work that had accrued whilst he was away. However, he knew with the new systems in place the backlog and integration problems would be quickly eliminated, and after all he had his bonus to look forward to.

At the end of the year Jack sat down with his manager to undertake his performance appraisal. As the meeting progressed to its conclusion, Jack was increasingly concerned that the issue of his interstate work was not raised and when he raised it, his manager said that the work he did was not his concern. When Jack asked about the cost saving and his bonus, his manager said that his agreeing to go interstate and help had in fact caused major problems and backlogs in his home plant and he should be happy he was getting the same bonus as everyone else, considering the problems he had caused.

Jack left the meeting stunned; he had expected to be commended for his work and get some indication of this in his bonus. Jack went back to his office and thought about the situation. That night he updated his CV and the next day sent it to three recruitment agencies specialising in IT work. As he waited for the recruitment companies to respond to him, he worked his required hours rather than the hours of unpaid overtime he used to undertake and spent that time networking for a new position.

Written by Peter Holland and James Wood

Questions

(1) What type of psychological contract did Jack have with his organisation prior to the performance management? Explain.
(2) What type of psychological contract did Jack have with his organisation after the performance management? Explain.
(3) Would you describe this as a breach or violation of Jack's psychological contract? Why?
(4) What lessons can be learned from this experience?

(2) Career Management
Banking on Change
David had been working for Global Bank for 20 years and had risen steadily through the ranks. He was initially employed in a general customer service role, but after demonstrating some flare had been promoted into the lending area. Over the years, David was promoted up through the ranks of personal and commercial lending and was now a senior lending manager. David had witnessed and been a part of many changes throughout his banking career and had embraced and adjusted to these changes well. However, during a merger with Commercial Bank, his work situation changed dramatically. David was now reporting to a new manager (from Commercial Bank) who

was completely restructuring the way things worked, with little opportunity for staff to be involved. The new manager was extremely sales focussed and set stringent targets for his lenders to meet. David had great difficulty adjusting to this new style and was concerned that his customer relationships were suffering with the new aggressive sales approach. David was now also working long hours just to get everything done and was not being remunerated or even recognised for the extra hours he was working. He also felt that he was constantly monitored having to provide endless statistics on new leads and activity to generate them, as well as sales results. David was increasingly unhappy in this new work situation and his work began to suffer. What was once a rewarding and fulfilling position now became a chore and David lost interest in his work. Eventually as staff cuts were made to incorporate the new employees from Commercial Bank, David was made redundant and was referred to a recruitment agency for outplacement services.

Although David's career had plateaued somewhat, he was devastated that his career was over with Global Bank and was extremely concerned about his future employment options. He believed that although he had developed sound skills in banking, particularly in lending, he would be very limited in new career opportunities outside of those areas. However, after several consulting sessions with the outplacement service, David realised that he had indeed developed many skills throughout his career that were in fact transferable to other work contexts.

Similarly, during David's banking career he had established quite a network of contacts and it was through these contacts that David was soon offered a position as an insurance broker with the firm Secure. Secure had an excellent reputation in the industry and placed strong emphasis on induction and training of new staff, as well as professional development of existing staff. Having completed the induction programme, David embarked on his new career armed with his company car and new laptop. David enjoyed much success in his new role and was an instant hit with his new clients, as they were impressed with his knowledge and experience. Secure offered flexible work arrangements, such as variable work schedules, to their employees to accommodate both their brokers' needs, as well as clients' needs. David enjoyed the option of working from home on certain days to avoid distractions and was even able to structure his time so that he could collect his children from school each day. In addition, David found that he could manage his time more effectively by being able to complete all of his processing work early in the morning, which was when he worked best. In terms of remuneration, David was now receiving a similar base salary to his previous role; however, in his current role as an insurance broker he was also eligible for commission on each sale that he made. This was indeed a rewarding incentive to increase his sales that he had not previously enjoyed. In his previous role David had avoided training and development programmes, as he thought as well as being a bit of a waste of time that he was too old to learn new skills and he had already risen to a fairly senior level within the organisation and he was comfortable at that level. David now regularly attends professional development programmes and industry conferences in his new role, seeing them as valuable opportunities to further develop and refine his skills, as well as a chance to establish important networking contacts.

After three fulfilling and successful years in the role of insurance broker, David became aware of a fantastic new opportunity for a sales training manager with a new company establishing a finance and insurance business. With such an excellent sales and customer service record, well-developed presentation skills and strong previous management experience, he succeeded in securing the role. David couldn't believe what a difference a change in career had made to his life and how much he now enjoyed his work. Having originally worked in an organisation that he thought he would be with for life with a very rigid organisational structure and fairly traditional values, he was now in a position that he loved with flexible working arrangements in a progressive and dynamic industry.

Written by Ross Donohue

Questions

(1) What aspects of David's experience suggest that he is following a protean or boundaryless career?
(2) What HRM initiatives could be introduced at the new finance and insurance organisation that David has joined to assist his career development?

(3) HRM Service Sector

Managing Risk in Hospital Settings

Occupational violence against healthcare workers is increasingly recognised as a significant issue globally and involves an unnecessary and preventable level of risk in regards to occupational violence. Using the content from the chapter on HRM in the service sector, review the following scenario and analyse possible causes for such an issue and the HR approach that could be taken in response.

Jeremy is a 24-year-old, recently qualified, registered midwife. Two months ago he started work in the maternity ward of a rural public hospital. So far he is enjoying the work. One area of concern for him, however, is that although he gets on quite well with the midwifery nursing team he does not feel that he has as yet developed a good rapport with his supervisor, the clinical midwife, or the clinical midwifery manager. The lack of communication has been exacerbated by recent very heavy workloads for everyone.

Last week Jeremy was on duty when a female patient arrived on the maternity ward in the early stages of labour. The woman was distressed and anxious as the birth was early and she was a first-time mother. Shortly after the patient arrived her husband also appeared on the ward and it was clear that he was agitated. The husband's erratic speech and body language actually suggested to Jeremy that the husband may have been a recent drug user.

Whilst the patient was being admitted onto the ward it became clear that due to higher than normal patient arrivals she was not going to be immediately taken into one of the birthing suites. The husband's reaction was one of anger that his wife could not be sent into one of the birthing areas without delay. His aggressive behaviour escalated. He yelled at the staff and eventually threw a chair through a window.

Jeremy registered the danger posed by the patient's husband to others in the maternity ward. His immediate priority was to contain the situation and keep bystanders safe.

Rather than wait for assistance, Jeremy stepped in to physically restrain the husband. In response the husband became enraged, grabbed some of the glass from the smashed window and injured Jeremy.

Written and adapted by Cathy Sheehan

Source: Victorian Auditor General's Office (2015). Occupational violence against healthcare workers, Victorian Auditor-General's Office: Melbourne, Victoria.

Questions

(1) What are the features of the work of a nurse that identify this role as a service role?
(2) With reference to the chapter content, identify the individual and workplace risk factors that may have contributed to Jeremy's injury.
(3) What is HR's responsibility with respect to these sorts of interactions and what steps can an HR professional take to minimise the likelihood of such incidents?

Section III

Managing the Issues at Work

Chapter 6

Risk and Crisis Management

Cathy Sheehan

Introduction

Unfortunate and largely unexpected events will occur in the life of any organisation. Globalisation and the associated increase in more complex communications and employee movement, along with changing social values have, however, created a context for an increase in the likelihood of unforeseen events. In response, risk and crisis management are now a common part of business strategy and implementation.

Financial risk management has been a long standing organisational priority. The Global Financial Crisis (GFC), however, increased sensitivity to financial risk exposure in the first decade of the twenty-first century. The second decade has been additionally characterised by increasing political instability that has had an impact on business continuity. The decision by the United Kingdom to leave the European Community, commonly referred to as Brexit, for example, has highlighted sensitivity to uncertainty (Hopkin, 2018).

Along with increased financial risk awareness, broader events have consolidated a sense of risk exposure both for organisations and the public in general. Terrorist events have featured in the news; terrorist attacks in the UK in 2017 following a concert by Ariana Grande and attacks in France in 2016 and 2017. Earthquakes and extreme weather events have also heightened the sense of risk exposure, with an earthquake in Iran in 2017 killing more than 400 people, and the combined effects of an earthquake and tsunami in Indonesia leading to the deaths of at least 2,100 people in 2018.

In short, the global management community has become cautious and sensitised to the need to be prepared in the face of unexpected occurrences whether they be financial, terrorist-related or environmental. The focus of this chapter is to consider the strategic human resource management (HRM) response to these disasters as part of an overall approach to risk management.

The definition of risk, offered by the International Standardization Organization (ISO), in the relevant standard, ISO 31000:2018 is the effect of uncertainty on objectives. The definition is further extended in the standard to explain that risk is usually expressed in terms of risk sources, potential events, their consequences and their likelihood (Institute of Risk Management, 2018, p. 4). Hopkin (2018, p. 16), writing about the impact of risk with respect to organisations, provides a further definition of risk as 'An event with the ability to impact (inhibit, enhance or cause doubt about) the effectiveness and efficiency of the core processes of an organization'. Importantly the increasing level of exposure to risk has been accompanied by risk management, the coordinated activities to direct and control an organisation with regard to risk (ISO, 2018).

The risk management process is designed to identify potential events that, if they occur, will impact on the entity. At times, however, disasters come in unexpected forms as sudden, devastating events that pose serious threats to business continuity. These crisis events require a rapid response and force organisations to engage in crisis management.

This chapter reviews the steps taken within both risk and crisis management approaches, and the challenges and ramifications for HRM. The chapter objectives are: to review the risk management process, to consider different approaches to understanding risk and the ramifications for HRM, and to define crisis management and review the implications for HRM in response to specific crisis management issues.

The Process for Managing Risk

The international risk management standard, ISO 31000:2018, provides an overview for the management of risk in a systematic and transparent manner across a range of contexts.

A detailed overview of the individual aspects of the three key areas of the standard is beyond the scope of this chapter. Overall, however, the risk management principles outline what must be achieved and the risk management framework provides information on how to achieve the required integration (Institute of Risk Management (IRM), 2018). Of note is the key role played by leadership and communication within the framework that activates the proposed principles. The risk management process reinforces the principles and framework by providing the steps that need to be taken in order to assess and treat risk (IRM, 2018).

From an HRM perspective, risk management is closely tied to occupational health and safety (OH&S), an area that focuses on the duty of care that an organisation has to the safety, health and welfare of employees. Hofmann, Burke, and Zohar (2017) have explained that although much progress has been made in the area of workplace safety and risk, there is still much to be done in order to understand and improve levels of workplace risk and associated injury, fatality and occurrences of occupational disease. The ISO 31000 guidelines provide important advice and direction for organisations yet despite the logic and rational advice provided there are a variety of approaches to risk that may impact on an organisation's risk management in practice. The following section considers these approaches to risk, including the technical, economic, cultural and psychometric, and the contribution that these approaches make to understanding the role that HRM can play in the ongoing management of risk.

Approaches to Risk

The technical approach to risk has its origins in engineering and the hard sciences, and adopts an objective assessment that helps to identify and eliminate hazards. An established and popular approach in the design of OH&S standards, this approach measures risk as $Risk = Probability \times Magnitude$. Objective scientific sources of evidence are used to identify, estimate, analyse, evaluate and communicate risk issues associated with the likelihood and impact of any risk. For example, according to a *Wall Street Journal* analysis of US Federal accident records, oil industry platforms that are 20 years old or more accounted for more than 60% of fires and nearly 60% of serious injuries aboard platforms in 2009. These platforms are subject to extreme ocean currents, corrosive salt water and frequent hurricanes, and age has become a determinant in platform safety. Such information suggests that there is an infrastructure issue confronting the industry that needs to be addressed (Casselman, 2010). A primary focus in the approach, there-fore, is to identify the relevant hazard, rank the risk according to consequences, assess the probably of the event, and then impose managerial control. The process ties in with regulatory frameworks including legislative and compliance requirements. Inter-nal company mechanisms can also be used to reinforce company policy and ongoing measurement, and feedback can include inspection checklists, safety audits and risk assessments (Glendon, Clarke, & McKenna, 2006). Within the field of OH&S, much time is spent in the development of appropriate work safety standards, and there is a concentration on worker behaviour modification to follow patterns of behaviour in order to reduce accidents and increase productivity.

In contrast to the technical approach that is focused on the elimination of harm, the economic approach considers the benefits of risks, and uses mathematical and statistical techniques to view the elements of risk, bringing the future into the pres-ent and making it calculable (Rose, 1999). Tools and techniques can include cost benefit analysis and expressing benefits and 'disbenefits' as monetary values. This approach depends on all relevant consequences being valued and on determining process and probabilities objectively to estimate tolerable levels of risk (Glendon, Clarke, & McKenna, 2006).

Both the technical and economic approaches adopt a rational perspective and assume that people are risk averse and act to prevent harm. Herbert Simon has proposed, how-ever, that people, rather than being perfectly rational, engage in satisficing behaviour (Simon, 1963). Satisficing, or bounded rationality, involves looking for an outcome that is *good enough*, rather than the absolute best, and this makes sense in a world where information is costly, incomplete and rapidly changing. For individuals work-ing in complex organisations faced by competing demands and pressures to produce results quickly, even when clear guidelines for risk management may be thought through, other perspectives help to explain how reduced risk sensitivity may impact on rational decision-making.

In healthcare, for example, medical staff are expected to follow strict guidelines to ensure the reduction of personal injury and the transfer of disease between patients. Yet in a report on nurse behaviour in South Africa, despite a range of policies aimed at reducing the risk of accidental HIV needle-sticks or other exposures to blood, nurses reported a resistance to wearing gloves because they created a physical barrier between nurse and patient and an impression that patients were 'untouchable' (Zelnick & O'Donnell, 2005). Risk management in these settings sometimes needs to go beyond policy and rules to address cultural pressures. In response, a cultural theory approach recognises how groups in society interpret danger, and how emergent values impact on the interpretation of safety expectations.

The value of cultural theory is in understanding that key social groups' attitudes and values can translate into behaviours that impact on the established order. In a large organisation, uniform risk management standards may be challenged when applied not only across country borders but also across workplaces that have sub-cultures that have developed different perceptions of risk (Hallowell, 2010). Sinclair (2010), in a review of safety culture in an Australian coal mining company, identified substantial and persistent differences across five mine sites in OH&S performance. Reasons given for the development of a site-led 'bottom-up' safety culture as opposed to a management-led 'top down' safety culture include the geographical remoteness of the mine sites and the longevity and insularity of the workforce. Mine workers are physically remote from both corporate management and from localised mine site management. A lack of computer access at underground work sites also means that workers are, effectively, isolated from a key source of management communication. Another relevant feature in the development of a bottom-up safety culture in a mine is the longevity and insularity of the workforce. The average age of workers was 50, and many of the workers had spent their entire working lives at a single mine, or at a very small number of mines. This means that many of these workers had worked side-by-side with a common set of colleagues, often in small team environments, in very confined spaces for the majority of their working lives. The shared experience in relatively remote locations created an emergent set of expectations about how things were to be done (Sinclair, 2010).

The commercial shipping industry is similarly characterised by operational sites distanced from corporate offices where crews work in close proximity to one another for long periods. In response, the shipping industry has recognised the importance of fostering a positive safety culture on individual ships rather than across the fleet as a whole. The development of site-specific responses to risk raises important HRM policy implications. It seems that corporate-driven policy and expectations are likely to be reinterpreted when individual sites are isolated or form close shared communal expectations. These findings present a strong case for focusing on a range of bottom-up, site-specific HRM risk management approaches that take into account historical and cultural factors rather than reliance on corporate-level risk management directives.

A final perspective on risk is the psychometric approach. This view of risk includes the impact of individual factors on risk perception as a subjective cognitive (within the head) phenomenon. Risk perceptions, among other factors, can be impacted by voluntariness, familiarity, novelty, degree of control, chronic-catastrophic potential, immediacy of effect, and the severity of the consequences (Glendon et al., 2006). The ramifications of this perspective require a shifting of perceptions of risk away from statistics and towards personalising the impact. An organisation may have very clear guidelines about appropriate management of hazardous waste, for example, but unless an individual has had some personal experience of the impact of the risk, the rules may be seen as burdensome controls that hinder getting the job done rather than as parameters that protect workers from danger.

Overall, the risk management process, as described above (ISO 31000:2018), provides an important overview for the management of approaches to risk control. The standard outlines a combination of underlying principles and a framework that prioritises leadership and commitment along with a risk management process that outlines the steps in identifying, analysing and treating risks supported with ongoing monitoring and communication. An exploration of some of the perspectives on risk have shown, however, that the process is far from simple and, despite the development of clear company policy and guidelines, cultural and individual factors can impact on the implementation of risk directives. Glendon et al. (2006) advises that, from an HRM perspective, underlying priorities in the risk management process include an active and personal involvement from senior management on a routine basis, open communication links between workers and management, a stable workforce with good industrial relations procedures, workforce empowerment to take responsibility for safety, a strong emphasis on training, and the ongoing collection of safety data. These recommendations not only incorporate a top down approach (as suggested by the Australian Risk Roundtable, 2008), but also reinforce the importance of bottom-up involvement and an organisation-wide understanding of the priority given to any risk management initiative.

Crisis Management

Liou and Lin (2008) characterise a crisis event as one that: possesses high ambiguity with unknown causes and effects, has a low probability of occurring, requires a rapid response, poses a serious threat to the survival of the organisation and its stakeholders, and presents a dilemma necessitating a decision that will result in positive or negative change. Examples of crises that impact on a business include major accidents and destructive natural events, health and environmental disasters, technological break-down, economic and market failures, or the actions of rogue employees (*Harvard Business Essentials*, 2004). Crisis management models generally include before, during and after phases. Campbell's model classifies the identification stage as one that occurs before the crisis occurs (Campbell, 1999). Preparation, response and recovery occur during the crisis period, and then learning can be consolidated in the wake of the event. Heath's (1998) crisis management model similarly includes a 'before' stage, and he refers to this as prevention.

Liou and Lin (2008) recognise the interactive nature of these models and the impor-tance of the opportunity for learning. But, as they point out, September 11 showed that the crisis management process actually often begins with the response phase and, because by definition a crisis is an unexpected event, crisis managers must often solve complex events without the information they require. Nevertheless, Lockwood (2005) has argued that the devastating impact of the September 11 terrorist attacks warrants a generalised increase in disaster preparedness plans and has argued that the HRM func-tion has a key strategic role to play in the management of crisis awareness. During such times, the HRM function has the opportunity to offer substantial leadership before dur-ing, and after the crisis. During a crisis there is a tendency to focus on systems, opera-tions, infrastructure and public relations – with people last on the list. Consistent with the ongoing priority now being given to employee wellbeing as a source of competi-tive advantage (Guest, 2017), organisations should prioritise the management of their people's safety during a period of unexpected threat. To ensure that this is promoted, HR can make the business case for the link between a focus on people within the crisis management plan, and performance indicators and critical success factors that rely on personnel deliverables.

As well as emphasising the strategic imperative of a crisis management plan, HRM can be active in the development of leadership qualities through the senior workforce to ensure that they are capable of handling the communication and integrity issues necessary during a crisis. During a crisis event managers with crisis management and leadership talents are extremely valuable, as these people are used to operating in circumstances where there is little time to gather necessary information to make informed decisions (Sayegh, Anthony, & Perrewe, 2004). Lockwood (2005) has used the classic example of Johnson & Johnson's sound leadership in the handling of the Tylenol crisis. In October of 1982, Tylenol, the leading paracetamol pain-killer medicine in the United States at the time, was taken off the shelves when an unknown suspect replaced Tylenol capsules with cyanide capsules, resulting in the deaths of seven people (Effective Crisis Management, 1982). In line with the company's strategic priority of protecting people first and property second, the leadership group of McNeil Consumer Products, a subsidiary of Johnson & Johnson, immediately released media information and recalled about 31 million bottles with an associated loss of more than $100 million dollars.[1] In such situations, it is the CEO who communicates and represents the message of corporate involvement and honesty. When the CEO is less prepared to deal with such a crisis event, the result can be a loss of faith in the good intentions of the company. Tony Hayward, CEO of BP, for example, was thrust into a media spotlight following a rig explosion that killed 11 workers and caused the worst oil spill in US history. The BP CEO made a number of ill-considered remarks in the confusion that followed the event, including, 'I'd like my life back'. The public and media reaction to his comments was negative and, on 27 October 2010, BP announced that Robert Dudley would replace Haywood as CEO (BP, n.d.).[2]

In view of the pivotal role played by senior management in a crisis situation, Sayegh et al. (2004) propose that HRM managers should become more aware of the role that emotions play in rapid decision-making, and should provide awareness training for senior managers. For example, in a crisis event, how do managers react? Is the event perceived as a threat, a challenge or a loss? Managers can be trained to become aware of how such perceptions influence subsequent decisions and to become skilled in reframing an event using more constructive interpretations.

Coupled with the strategic prioritisation of crisis management and the readiness of the leadership team to assume responsibility for its actions, Lockwood (2005) suggests the establishment of a crisis management team and the key positioning of the HR Director on that team. The HR role in the crisis management team is to provide support through important logistics and information. For example, the HR team through access to personnel records, can assist information officers to reach affected individuals and their families, and work to resolve personal issues created by the crisis. The HR role is also to ensure that required talent and succession planning is in place to enable the organisation to continue business.

Another issue that arises during a crisis situation is the influx of volunteer assistance (Alfes, Antunes, & Shantz, 2017). Rodsutti (2005), using the example of the tsunami experience in Thailand in December 2004, has explained that, in the aftermath of the tsunami, hundreds of volunteers, both from other parts of Thailand and from overseas, arrived to assist. Unfortunately, because of the lack of experience in the management of

---

[1] http://iml.jou.ufl.edu/projects/Fall02/Susi/tylenol.htm. Accessed on January 7, 2011.
[2] http://www.bp.com/genericarticle.do?categoryId=2012968&contentId=7063976. Accessed on January 7, 2011.

a volunteer workforce, many of the volunteers were not effectively deployed. Effective HR approaches in these situations can assist. For example, HR professionals can liaise with the mass media to ensure effective and targeted recruitment of key professional groups. A well-designed online application form works as an efficient selection tool and can also be used to determine job allocation. The form can be used, for example, to distinguish those people who have had previous volunteer experience, those who may be useful in supervisory roles, and also the length of time that volunteers are available. In terms of jobs to be performed, HR will also have a role in judging immediate and longer-term responsibilities, and creating project sign-up sheets that cover daily tasks as well as longer-term responsibilities. An orientation system also needs to be set up so that volunteers have appropriate expectations and preparation for the possible mental stress that the work might require, and also for the cross-cultural requirements of working with people who can be from quite different cultural backgrounds. If possible, the preparation of a volunteer manual assists in orienting staff. HR can also be involved in co-ordinating basic accommodation and food to sustain current volunteers and attract new ones (Rodsutti, 2005).

A key HR issue following a crisis is the loss of key talent and organisational knowledge due to low morale, fear, physical relocation and the death of co-workers. HR needs, therefore, to be involved in the crisis recovery plan, to ensure accessibility to the workplace and the organisation's resources and infrastructure, and to assist employees in regaining a sense of normalcy. HR can identify key personnel who are essential to the recovery effort, along with places to work and communication options. The following sections consider the specific roles that HR can take to assist in the crisis management process and in recovery in two crisis situations: terrorist-created events and the management of a pandemic.

Terrorism

Alexander, Carlton, and Wilkinson (1979, p. 4) have defined terrorism as 'the threat or actual use of force or violence to attain a political goal through fear, coercion or intimidation'. Cinkota, Knight, Liesch, and Steen (2010, p. 828) have refined the definition to include broader objectives as follows: 'Terrorism is the premeditated, systematic threat or use of violence by sub-national groups to attain a political, religious or ideological objective through intimidation of a large audience'. Reasons given for the increase in terrorism since the 1980s include the globalisation of commerce, travel and information transfer. These developments have highlighted the difference between groups, and also provided collaborators with the capacity to communicate and move between nations more readily. There has also been an ascent in religious fundamentalism and its militant capacity (Crandell, Parnell, & Spillan, 2010). And finally, there has been an increase in the availability and capacity of weapons that can create deadly outcomes (Cinkota et al., 2010).

As well as the devastating personal loss that is part of terrorist action, such conflict has a substantial impact on business activity that has to be strategically managed (Bader & Berg, 2014; Henisz, Mansfield, & Von Glinow, 2010). Bader and Berg (2014) also highlight the need for organisations to consider their employees in the event of a terrorist attack. Embassies or military facilities that may previously have been primary targets are now better protected and as a result private business institutions are seen as softer targets; employees are therefore at the forefront of the risk.

In terms of which organisational functions should be involved Mankin and Perry (2004) have observed that many areas consider the responsibility to be outside of their purview. In the government sector, for example, departments have considered that the relevant governmental emergency agency should assume responsibility. More broadly, the SHRM 2005 Disaster Survey Report indicated that, as a result of the September 11 terrorist attacks, 56% of organisations created or revised their disaster preparedness plan, but special note was made that 45% of organisations did not. Lockwood (2005) raised concern about the lack of preparedness of these organisations, and reinforced the important role that the HR department plays in the event of a disaster that impact organisations. More recently Bader and Berg (2014) have similarly emphasised the role to be played by the HRM department.

Minimising injuries to staff and personnel relocation is a key HRM priority during a terrorist attack. During the attack on the World Trade Centre, Morgan Stanley was able to show the benefits of a plan for relocation that had been effectively communicated to staff prior to the event. Morgan Stanley was one of the organisations that had been affected by the previous 1993 bomb attack and had, in response, designed and practised floor-by-floor evacuations of staff. After the first plane crashed into the North Tower in 2001, Morgan Stanley staff quickly and efficiently evacuated their 22 floors (53rd to 74th) of the South Tower. By the time the second plane hit the South Tower, evacuation was under way (Liou & Lin, 2008).

An additional aspect of relocation is a plan to ensure business continuity. Terrorist attacks often result in building and structural damage that threaten both employees and business operations (Perry & Mankin, 2005). Merrill Lynch was another organisation that was effective in the design and implementation of a previously thought through response to the 9/11 terrorist attack, and was able to relocate business roles immediately. When the disaster occurred, the company activated its disaster recovery plan within minutes, and immediately began transferring business critical functions to its command centre in New Jersey. The New Jersey facility had been predesigned as a corporate disaster response area, and all personnel had been previously briefed on how to enact the transfer of information (Stephens, 2003). The reality of a terrorist attack is that there is the very real possibility of personnel shortage due to injury and loss. Transferring operations to another site will assist with the coverage of employee loss at the affected site but the area that absorbs the increase in work then needs to be properly staffed to manage the increased load.

A further important aspect of employee welfare is communication with employees and their families, and Merrill Lynch had also devised a plan to use a telemarketing service along with the company's public internet site to communicate with displaced workers and their families (Stephens, 2003). As part of the communication with staff, HR can be invaluable in providing accurate accounting of employee location to enable search and rescue activity and to keep families informed about employee welfare. In the time following the event, the HRM department must also co-ordinate the counselling of employees and their families, and may have established counsellor networks in place to assist with the recovery effort.

Along with the management of staff following a terrorist attack in an organisation's home country base, Bader and Berg (2014) have considered the issues that companies face when operating overseas in high risk countries. The authors argue that there is a pressing need to carefully manage the physical and mental well-being of their expatriate staff as terrorists are shifting their focus to businesses. A company can provide organisational support to expatriates by ensuring that effective communication channels are established. On-site mentoring using combinations of staff who have already lived in an endangered environment also assist newcomers. Bader and Berg (2014) also highlight the importance of training the expatriate for his or her assignment but note that in the last 25 years there has been very limited research into corporate terrorism threat management in overseas sites. Earlier Harvey (1993) found that companies prioritised the protection of physical assets rather than expatriate safety. More active preparation of expatriates could include measures such as training in self-defence skills, weapon handling, defensive driving and work route alteration strategies as well as behavioural rules in case of an attack. Such training would increase the expatriate's self-confidence and sense of security.

Overall, HRM can be active in advance terrorist scenario planning through the training and education of staff in emergency preparedness. As noted in the previous section on general crisis management, the HR function can also assist with the procurement and allocation of voluntary helpers who come to the affected area to assist in the recovery efforts. HRM can also be invaluable in a relocation plan for business continuity, including predesigned role definition and plans for extended hours of operation and additional staff. In terms of assisting employees with managing the confusion of the event, HRM also has an important role in developing clear communication channels and providing up-to-date records of employee activity and location to assist emergency services and provide feedback to families about employee safety. Finally, HRM needs to provide and ensure appropriate psychological support for employees who are recovering from the disaster.

Pandemics
Pandemics are different from other threats and crises. Threats associated with bombs, or natural disasters such as fires, earthquakes and tsunamis, are over once the event has occurred. While the effects can be devastating and have long-term consequences, recovery can begin. A pandemic, on the other hand, is an unfolding global event that comes in waves that can sweep across the globe in a matter of weeks, and may take up to three months to manage (Staples, 2006). Furthermore, the effects are mainly felt by people rather than by the infrastructure, and for that reason the potential inoperability of the workforce makes the disaster one in which HRM function will have to take a lead management role. Very high levels of absenteeism in the workforce could result from either the workers themselves becoming sick, or from indirect impacts such as the need to care for others or if a quarantine were to be enacted (Orsi & Santos, 2010).

A pandemic is an infection that can spread globally and affect large populations (Orsi & Santos, 2010). There has been an increase in the rise of new infections, including avian, swine and other zoonotic influenza viruses (World Health Organisation, 2018a) as well as the ongoing threat of bioterrorism. In response, experts believe that a pandemic is imminent and threatening. An influenza pandemic is particularly dangerous as it may mutate, overcome vaccines, or migrate rapidly (Orsi & Santas, 2010). The following sections review previous influenza responses, along with a discussion of how HR can respond in such situations.

The severe acute respiratory syndrome (SARS) pandemic of 2003 demonstrated the economic ramifications of an influenza outbreak and the importance of ensuring the health and safety of workers. Economists have estimated $2 billion losses in tourism, retail sales and productivity, and $1 billion losses each in Japan, Hong Kong, Taiwan and Singapore. In Toronto, a major centre of the outbreak, the financial impact was estimated at $30 million a day at the height of the crisis. The workforce was significantly reduced because of illness and precautionary measures. Service areas such as tourism, transportation (airlines) and retailing were hard hit as the public went into 'demand shock' and simply stopped shopping and going out (Tan & Enderwick, 2006). Twenty-five restaurants in Hong Kong, for example, were closed in the first two weeks of April, leading to the unemployment of 1,600 restaurant staff (Lee & Warner, 2005). The HR responses in the Hong Kong hotel industry were reasonably well handled, and mass layoffs and redundancies were avoided. Staff were requested to take accumulated leave or 'no pay' leave. Pregnant women in one hotel were given 'special leave' with full pay when their annual leave was cleared. In terms of preventative mechanisms, staff were requested to take their body temperature before going to work, and were required to wear masks. Public areas were constantly cleaned, and lift-buttons, for example, were treated every two hours with diluted bleach. With respect to communication, there were repeated emails reminding employees of the importance of rest, good personal hygiene and staying at home if unwell (Lee & Warner, 2005).

The World Health Organisation (2018b) advises a number of preparedness and response recommendations: planning and co-ordination, situation monitoring and assessment, reducing the spread of the disease, continuity of healthcare provision and communications. The HR function has an active role in all of these responsibilities. Specifically, the HR group is responsible for appropriate leadership selection and training to assist with the planning and co-ordination of a response. HR also plays a critical information role in registering absences and possible areas of infection spread. With respect to the reduction in the spread of the disease, HR will need to assist with measures that allow social distance between staff and also with customers. Advice on hygiene and decisions about reduced employee travel and who should be placed on leave and how leave arrangements can best be utilised will primarily fall within the ambit of the HR function. The management of the health of workers will also require thought to be given to whether the organisation will provide immunisation when available, and how that procedure will be co-ordinated. Finally, HR has a critical role in communicating with employees, with their families and also with the public about how they are managing disease spread and social distancing requirements. The World Health Organisation 2018 publication *A checklist for pandemic influenza risk and impact management: building capacity for pandemic response: 2018 update* provides a useful guide to the steps that should be taken within each of the pandemic phases identified above.

Before leaving the discussion of the management of a pandemic special recognition needs to be given to the care of 'first responder', that group of professionals who have initial contact with people affected by the disease. Sectors such as hospitals and ambulatory care services, for example, will likely play a large role in containing any disease outbreak, as well as minimising the number of infections and mortalities (Orsi & Santos, 2010). Employers of workers in these sectors therefore need to be particularly mindful of the psychological and physical impact on their staff. There are psychosocial implications of perceived risk and consequences due to occupational exposure. Quarantine, personal infection and the risk of unknowingly transmitting infection to loved ones and colleagues represents a serious need to focus on the health and well-being of healthcare workers. In a Toronto hospital, for example, one diagnosis of SARS resulted in twenty-four members of the unit team being put into quarantine. As well as their physical removal, these workers carried stigmatisation by the public and friends (CCH, 2005). Training therefore has to prepare healthcare workers who, in disaster scenarios, are exposed to significant psychosocial stress as a result of their role in implementing triage procedures. Effectively they have to make decisions about the allocation of scarce resources for multiple patients and address other practical strategies involving vaccine programmes which rely on stockpile supplies of vaccines and anti-virals (CCH, 2005).

Conclusions

The increasing interest in risk and crisis management has developed in response to a number of unexpected but devastating events that have presented serious threats to business continuity over the past 20 years. As most risks and crises have the potential for major ramifications for employees, the HRM function has a key role to play in both the strategic design of relevant programmes as well as in the delivery of immediate assistance during and following any event. Material in the chapter has included a number of resources that can be used in business to assist in the design of an appropriate risk and crisis management approach, as well as issues that need to be addressed by the HRM function. Along with involvement in strategic planning for an event, HRM can assist in the recruitment and selection of leaders who are capable and flexible during a crisis. The HRM role also extends to workforce disaster management training and expectations about possible changed roles during work flow disruptions including communication roles and responsibilities. The management and deployment of a volunteer workforce may also need to be given some pre-planning. During an event, the HRM function is invaluable in providing up-to-date information about the location of staff who may be missing and the gaps in duties that need to be filled. Information also has to be disseminated to staff to inform them of unfolding company policy and advice about how to handle situations such as social distancing in the event of a pandemic. There are also relationships with other stakeholders including employee families, the media and emergency services in which HRM will play a role. Following an event, there is the necessary reallocation of tasks and assistance in getting staff back to health and assisting families with management of affected workers. All of these tasks fall within the HRM responsibilities of protecting the human resource within an organisation, providing a safe and healthy workplace for workers, and ensuring an ongoing positive view of the organisation as an employer of choice.

References

Alexander, Y., Carlton, D., & Wilkinson, P. (1979). *Terrorism: Theory and practice*. Boulder, CA: Westview Press.

Alfes, K., Antunes, B., & Shantz, A. (2017). The management of volunteers: What can human resources do? A review and research agenda. *The International Journal of Human Resource Management, 28*(1), 62–97. http://dx.doi.org/10.1080/09585192.2016.1242508

Australian Risk Roundtable. (2008). Melbourne, Australia: Risk Thinkers Pty Ltd.

Bader, B., & Berg, N. (2014). The influence of terrorism on expatriate performance: A conceptual approach. *International Journal of Human Resource Management, 25*(4), 539–557.

BP (n.d.). BP CEO Tony Haywood to step down and be replaced by Robert Dudley. Retrieved from http://www.bp.com/genericarticle.do?categoryId=2012968&content Id=7063976 Accessed on January 7, 2011.

Campbell, R. (1999). *Crisis control: Preventing and managing corporate crisis.* Wollongong, Australia: Prentice Hall.

Casselman, B. (2010, December 15). Aging oil rigs, pipelines expose Gulf to accidents. *Wall Street Journal,* 1. Retrieved from https://www.wsj.com/articles/SB100014240527 48704584804575644463302701660. Accessed on June 7, 2019.

Cinkota, M., Knight, G., Liesch, P., & Steen, J. (2010). Terrorism and international business: A research agenda. *Journal of International Business Studies, 41,* 826–843.

Crandell, W., Parnell, J. A., & Spillan, J. E. (2010). *Crisis management in the new strategy landscape.* Thousand Oaks, CA: Sage.

Effective Crisis Management. (1982). The Tylenol scandal and crisis management. Retrieved from http://iml.jou.ufl.edu/projects/Fall02/Susi/tylenol.htm. Accessed on January 7, 2011.

Glendon, A. I., Clarke, S. G., & McKenna, E. (2006). *Human safety and risk management* (2nd ed.). Boca Raton, FL: Taylor Francis Group.

Guest, D. (2017). Human resource management and employee well-being: towards a new analytic framework. *Human Resource Management Journal, 27*(1), 22–38.

Hallowell, M. (2010). Safety risk perception in construction companies in the Pacific Northwest of the USA. *Construction Management and Economics, 28*(4), 403–413.

Harvard Business Essentials. (2004). *Crisis management: Master the skills to prevent disasters.* Boston, MA: Harvard Business School Press.

Harvey, M. (1993). A survey of corporate programs for managing terrorist threats. *Journal of International Business Studies, 24*(3), 465–478.

Heath, R. (1998). Dealing with complete crisis: The crisis management shell structure. *Safety Science, 30,* 139–150.

Henisz, W., Mansfield, E., & Von Glinow, A. (2010). Conflict, security and political risk: International business in challenging times. *Journal of International Business Studies, 41,* 759–764.

Hofmann, D. A., Burke, M. J., & Zohar, D. (2017). 100 years of occupational safety research: From basic protections and work analysis to a multilevel view of workplace safety and risk. *Journal of Applied Psychology, 102*(3), 375–388.

Hopkin, P. (2018). *Fundamentals of risk management* (5th ed.). London: The Institute of Risk Management.

Institute of Risk Management (IRM). (2018). *A risk practitioners guide to ISO 31000:-2018.* London: IRM. Retrieved from https://www.theirm.org/media-centre/latest-news-and-views/standard-deviations-a-risk-practitioner-guide-to-iso-31000.aspx. Accessed on October 30, 2018.

International Standardization Organization (ISO). (2018). ISO 31000:2018 Guidelines. Retrieved from https://www.iso.org/obp/ui/#iso:std:iso:31000:ed-2:v1:en:term:3.1. Accessed on October 30, 2018.

Lee, G. O. M., & Warner, M. (2005). Epidemics, labour markets and unemployment: The impact of SARS on human resource management in the Hong Kong service sector. *International Journal of Human Resource Management, 16*(5), 752–771.

Liou, D., & Lin, C. (2008). HRP on terrorism and crises in the Asia Pacific region: Cross-national challenge, reconsideration and proposition from western experiences. *Human Resource Management, 47*(1), 49–72.

Lockwood, N. (2005). Crisis management in today's business environment: HR's strategic role. *SHRM Research Quarterly, 4*(4), 1–9.

Mankin, L., & Perry, R. W. (2004). Commentary: Terrorism challenges for human resource management. *Review of Public Personnel Administration*, *24*(1), 3–17.

Orsi, M., & Santos, J. (2010). Probabilistic modelling of work-based disruptions and input–output analysis of independent ripple effects. *Economic Systems Research*, *22*(1), 3–18.

Perry, R. W., & Mankin, L. D. (2005). Preparing for the unthinkable: Managers, terrorism and the HRM function. *Public Personnel Management*, *34*(2), 175–193.

Rodsutti, M. (2005). How HR can help in the aftermath of disaster. *Human Resource Management International Digest*, *13*(5), 18–20.

Rose, N. (1999). *Powers of freedom: Reframing political thought*. Cambridge: Cambridge University Press.

Sayegh, L., Anthony, W. P., & Perrewe, P. L. (2004). Managerial decision-making under crisis: The role of emotion in an intuitive decision process. *Human Resource Management Review*, *14*, 179–199.

Simon, H. (1963). Economics and psychology. In S. Koch (Ed.), *Psychology: A study of a science* (Vol. 6, pp. 685–723). New York, NY: McGraw-Hill.

Sinclair, D. (2010). The origins of safety culture in coalmining: 'Top-down' versus 'bottom-up.' *Journal of Health, Safety and Environment*, *26*(3), 249–259.

Staples, J. (2006, May). A new type of threat. *Harvard Business Review*, *84*(5), 20–22.

Stephens, D. O. (2003). Protecting records. *Information Management Journal*, *37*(1), 33–40.

Tan, W., & Enderwick, P. (2006). Managing threats in the global era: The impact and response to SARS. *Thunderbird International Business Review*, *48*(4), 515–536.

World Health Organisation (WHO). (2018a). Influenza (Avian and other zoonotic). Retrieved from http://www.who.int/en/news-room/fact-sheets/detail/influenza-(avian-and-other-zoonotic). Accessed on November 2, 2018.

World Health Organisation (WHO). (2018b). A checklist for pandemic influenza risk and impact management: Building capacity for pandemic response. 2018 update. Retrieved from http://www.who.int/influenza/preparedness/pande mic/influenza_risk_management_checklist_2018/en/. Accessed on November 2, 2018.

Zelnick, J., & O'Donnell, M. (2005). The impact of the HIV/AIDS epidemic on hospital nurses in KwaZulu Natal, South Africa: Nurses' perspectives and implications for health policy. *Journal of Public Health Policy*, *26*(2), 163–187.

Chapter 7

Mental Health and Well-being at Work

Hannah Meacham, Jillian Cavanagh, Timothy
Bartram and Katharina Spaeth

Introduction

Mental health and well-being has become an increasingly important issue across countries and within organisations. Over 4.4% (300 million) of the world's population suffer from a mental illness such as depression. Whilst support for managing mental health issues is growing, it depends entirely on location. Mental health support organisations are present in only 49% of low-income countries, compared with 83% of high-income countries (Roberts, 2018). The inclusion of mental health in the Sustainable Development Agenda adopted at the United Nations General Assembly in September 2015 has shown that world leaders recognise the promotion of mental health and well-being as a world priority (World Health Organisation, 2018). Organisations that promote mental health and well-being encourage productivity and positive workplace cultures. Providing employees with tools that support mental health not only assists their individual well-being but also the effectiveness of the organisation. Employees are healthier, motivated and engaged, resulting in a more productive workforce. This chapter will discuss the concepts regarding mental health, in the context of importance of well-being and possible solutions to support the mental health of employees. To explore these issues in action, a detailed example of nurses and the healthcare sector is given in the second half of the chapter.

Employee Well-being

Employee well-being is a multidimensional construct (Veld & Alfes, 2017) defined by Warr (1987) as the quality of experience and functioning of employees in their workplace. Having a qualitatively low experience can lead to job-related anxiety and emotional exhaustion (De Jonge & Schaufeli, 1998) that may have a negative impact on mental health (Burke, Ng, & Fiksenbaum, 2009). There are three key tenants of well-being: physical, psychological and social all of which can have an impact on employee mental health (Grant, Christianson, & Price, 2007; Van De Voorde, Paauwe, & Van Veldhoven, 2012). Before each tenant is discussed, there are two major philosophical traditions that inform well-being – hedonia and eudaimonia. Hedonic view is the pursuit of pleasure, comfort and instant gratification whilst eudaimonia means that 'an individual strives to be better by developing themselves through their talents and use of virtues, and by generating meaning from the resulting personal growth' (Lambert, Passmore, & Holder, 2015, p. 313).

Physical Well-being/Health

Physical well-being considers individuals' functioning and bodily health (Grant et al., 2007). Physical health can be influenced by work stressors and strains (Veld & Alfes, 2017), for example, stress can promote headaches, sickness and the inability to sleep. Stressors, such as a high workload can lead to employees feeling run down and in poor health. High pressure work environments, issues with shift work and high cognitive and physical workload can lead to physical exhaustion particularly if employees are exposed to these stressors for a long period of time without adequate job resources and recovery time (Demerouti, Bakker, Nachreiner, & Schaufeli, 2000).

Physical well-being can be affected by individual experiences; as such employees react to stressors in different ways. Some may be more physically susceptible to stress than others. What is common is the need for recovery (Veld & Alfes, 2017). The need for recovery from work-related fatigue, which is characterised by feelings of overload, social withdrawal, lack of energy, irritability and reduced performance (Han, Trinkoff, & Geiger-Brown, 2014; Winwood, Winefield, & Lushington, 2006) can be hard to come by for employees due to the increasing nature of work intensification.

An increased need for recovery is a sign of increased job strain, which can result in adverse health outcomes which reciprocally result in a heightened need to recover and can in the long term result in severe illnesses (Veld & Alfes, 2017). These physical issues may also affect the mental health of employees, adding to possible anxiety if physical health is weakened. Workplace conditions and job demands can increase the risk of employees developing health issues and illnesses such as back pain, exhaustion and high blood pressure or cardiovascular disease. If left untreated, health issues can worsen and impair employees' ability to complete their job roles. Low physical well-being can result in higher amounts of workplace accidents (Grant et al., 2007), creating a snowball effect negatively influencing employee mental health.

Psychological/Mental Well-being

Psychological well-being is concerned with the mental state of employees (Brunetto et al., 2018). Stress, anxiety, depression and post-traumatic stress disorder can all effect employees' mental health. Depression for example has been on the increase worldwide, with an estimated prevalence of 18% in developed nations (Lim et al., 2018). **Table 7.1** shows the percentage of population diagnosed with depression across nations.

Psychological well-being is associated with happiness and thus with employees' individual and subjective experience (Veld & Alfes, 2017). Subjective well-being is often used interchangeably with happiness referring to the levels of positive affect and degree of job and life satisfaction in general (Lambert et al., 2015). Job satisfaction is defined in terms of employees' subjective judgment about their work situation related to fulfilment and realising individual potential. The component of happiness is the experiences of pleasure balancing out negative and positive thoughts and feelings (Grant et al., 2007). Happiness considers an individual's experiences and functioning

Table 7.1 Percentage of Population Diagnosed with Depression per Country.

Country	Percentage
United States of America	5.17
Sweden	4.97
Australia	4.95
New Zealand	4.77
United Kingdom	4.34
Russia	4.06
Canada	4.0
India	3.85
China	3.68
Saudi Arabia	3.66

Source: Global Burden of Disease Collaborative Network (2017).

at work regarding their satisfaction and commitment (Van De Voorde et al., 2012). Thus, the focus is on attitudes and behaviour. Moreover, happiness comprises subjective feelings of fulfilment and purpose by employees and can be operationalised, that is, measured through affective commitment (Veld & Alfes, 2017). As it is subject to emotions, some researchers call it emotional well-being (Fredrickson & Joiner, 2002; Ziegler, Merker, Schmid, & Puhan, 2017).

Social Well-being
Social well-being is a more recent concept (Van De Voorde et al., 2012). It focuses on the quality of interrelationships at work. Here, literature draws a distinction between the relationships with colleagues, supervisors and the organisation itself. The social approach to well-being considers an individual's functioning and relational experience. It is characterised in terms of social support, trust, cooperation, coordination, leader–member exchange and integration (Grant et al., 2007). These characteristics can then influence an individual's perception of social interactions, organisational structure and feelings of happiness (Law, Steinwender, & Leclair, 1998).

Presenteeism
Many employees go to work despite being ill or mentally unfit to work. Presenteeism is where employees are physically at work but unfocused, not paying attention to their tasks (Karimi, Cheng, Bartram, Leggat, & Sarkeshik, 2015). Presenteeism can also be associated with burnout (emotional exhaustion). It has been reported that up to 67% of all employees who experience burnout have considered leaving their profession (Stern, 2012). Not only does presenteeism have an effect on turnover rates, but also affects productivity costs for employers (Evans-Lacko & Knapp, 2016). **Fig. 7.1** outlines associated productivity costs per country. Presenteeism can also have a negative effect on colleagues' mental health. It has been reported that employees don't want to let their equally stressed colleagues down by taking a sick day (Szymczak et al., 2015), nor do they want to be ostracised for having a day off. When a presentee employee fails to complete their normal duties, the burden falls to colleagues, who may then resent the extra work they have to complete, impacting the mental health of all employees.

Fig. 7.1 Productivity Costs per Country.

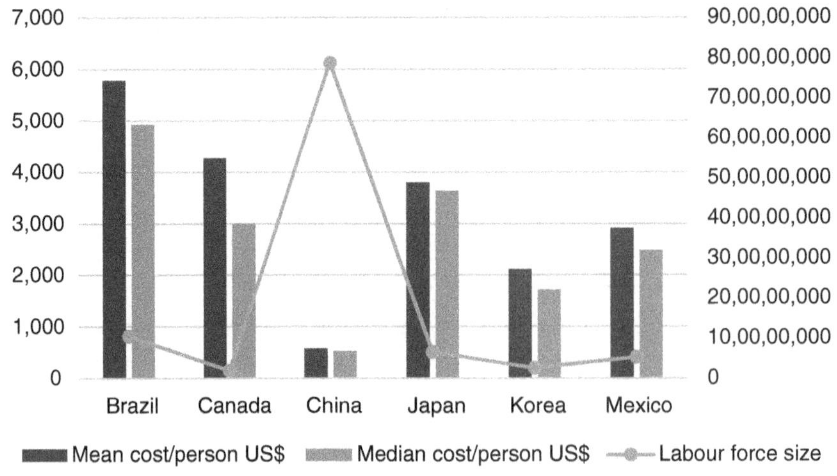

Source: Adapted from Evans-Lacko and Knapp (2016).

Emotional Labour

Emotional labour is labour that involves dealing with people's feelings (Phillips, 1996) and includes emotional display rules, meaning a specific expression is necessary for a situation even though it might not be the natural reaction. This can leave a dissonance between displayed and felt emotions (Schaubroeck & Jones, 2000). Emotional labour may have negative impact on employees' mental health when emotional expressions are not authentic. Being inauthentic in your emotions can be stressful (Schaubroeck & Jones, 2000). Emotional labour can also be connected to burnout through emotional dissonance (Cheng, Bartram, Karimi, & Leggat, 2013).

The Importance of Good Mental Health

Positive organisational outcomes such as improved performance, decreased turnover and higher employee engagement have been linked to employee well-being and positive mental health (Brunetto et al., 2018; Karimi et al., 2015). Any diminished well-being is likely to result in loss of employee performance and increase in absenteeism (Grant et al., 2007; Karimi et al., 2015; O'Brien-Pallas & Baumann, 2000) thus putting more pressure and stress on colleagues. Continuous stress can lead to a diverse range of pathological outcomes such as mental health issues, for example, depression or diseases including coronary heart disease (Karimi et al., 2015). Depression, for example, is particularly important to address as, other than the suffering it can cause employees, it can also affect the quality of employee performance and the workload of fellow colleagues. The stigma of mental illness may stop employees from disclosing due to perceptions from managers of being less capable to do their job role.

Resilience

Building resilience can be an important aspect in dealing with the negative mental health effects on employees. Resilience occurs when an individual recovers swiftly and effortlessly from obstructions that may occur in or out of work (Zautra, Hall, & Murray, 2010). Resilience can be seen as a personality trait (Campbell-Sills, Cohan, &

Stein, 2006) and also a process to support mental health and well-being (Luthar, Saw-yer, & Brown, 2006). Resilient individuals are said to be able to continue in the face of challenging setbacks. Personal resilience can be seen as the capacity to endure sig-nificant interruption to normal life (Schetter & Dolbier, 2011). Key traits can include: self-assurance; self-confidence; ingenuity; optimism; flexibility and a positive outlook (Jackson, Firtko, & Edenborough, 2007). Resilience as an individual characteristic can assist in coping with low levels of staff support, lack of autonomy and diminish-ing health and workability (Gillespie, Chaboyer, Wallis, & Grimbeek, 2007; Lundman et al., 2010). Therefore we see an increase in organisations developing HR practices focussed on increasing the resilience of employees (Shin, Taylor, & Seo, 2012).

Traditional methods have been focussed on resilience training, such as face-to-face training (Waite & Richardson, 2004) psychological capital training interventions (Luthans, Avey, Avolio, & Peterson, 2010). To enhance resilience in employees, organ-isations need to utilise multiple HR practices. Bardoel, Pettit, De Cieri, and McMillan (2014) identify eight main HR practices as outlined in **Table 7.2**.

Table 7.2 HR Practices to Enhance Employee Resilience.

HR Practice	Example
Development of social support.	Clearly defined teams.
Work-life balance practices.	Parental leave packages.
Employee development programmes.	Specific resilience training.
Flexible work arrangements.	Working from home/change in shift work.
Occupational health and safety systems.	Mental health support officers.
Risk and crisis management systems.	Clearly defined and practiced crisis plans.
Diversity management.	Hiring and integrating a diverse workforce.
Employee assistance programmes.	Counselling availability.

Solutions and Support Mechanisms to Improve Mental Health and Well-being

Human resource management (HRM) can be utilised to increase physical, psychological and social well-being (Veld & Alfes, 2017) to achieve positive mental health outcomes. This is important for both the organisation and employees themselves. HRM practices such as training, mentorship and mindfulness workshops can have a positive effect on employee well-being and organisational performance. Management needs to be aware of possible trade-offs between the different types of well-being (Van De Voorde et al., 2012) ensuring that one does not negatively affect the other – deadly combinations of HR practices. For example, social well-being strategies such as buddy systems may negatively impact psychological well-being if the two 'buddies' do not get along, thus negatively impacting the mental health of both participants. Generally, HRM positively affects employee well-being if it creates a climate for supportive well-being (Veld & Alfes, 2017). For example, in the UK, the Health and Safety Executive is currently trying to encourage the National Health Service (NHS) to comply with its work-related stress management standards. This includes providing health boards with tools to assess work-related stress and a range of recommendations to improve implementation of stress assessment protocols.

Organisational climate has a mediating role to employee well-being (Caricati et al., 2014). Organisational climate is the shared perception of the organisation, what is it is like to work for, its policies, practices, routines and structures (Bowen & Ostroff, 2004). Establishing a supportive working environment promoting job satisfaction and reducing stress (O'Brien-Pallas & Baumann, 2000; Pahlevan Sharif, Ahadzadeh, & Sharif Nia, 2018) can assist employee mental health. A supportive work environment has adequate staffing, provides support, and relationships are rewarding and trustworthy (Karimi et al., 2015). Work environment interventions, such as team work, autonomous decision-making and training, need to be internally consistent practices with supporting policies (Bartram, Stanton, Leggat, Casimir, & Fraser, 2007). The design of HR systems should be distinctive, consistent and have an overall consensus (Bowen & Ostroff, 2004). Furthermore, it should be visible and include consistent HR messages. Ambiguous or mixed messages negatively affect performance and organisational outcomes.

A positive work environment can be assisted through job crafting, where employees can customise their jobs. There is a positive relationship between job crafting and well-being, meaning that management and particularly HR can influence well-being on an individual level through the organisation of work (Yepes-Baldó, Romeo, Westerberg, & Nordin, 2018). Therefore, middle and line management play a critical role in job crafting and successfully implementing HRM practices (Stanton, Young, Bartram, & Leggat, 2010); for example, customising the location of a job, such as employees working from home, or amended hours, can support the mental health of employees. Close interaction between CEO, senior management and HR managers enables a consistent formulation and implementation of HR practices (Bartram et al., 2007). Moreover, supervisors are a source of emotional support, thus directly influencing employee well-being (Laschinger & Fida, 2013). Another way job crafting can positively influence well-being is by managing work load and improving participation in decision-making (Demerouti et al., 2000).

High-performance work systems (HPWS) can also influence the working environment. Components of HPWS, including selective hiring, use of teams, training and trans-formational leadership (Bartram, Casimir, Djurkovic, Leggat, & Stanton, 2012), can positively influence the organisational climate to support employees' mental health. HPWS are bundles of interrelated HRM practices such as the above that together recruit, select, develop, motivate and retain employees (Boxall & Macky, 2009), having a positive effect on both employees and organisations.

The design of organisational interventions to support employees such as training, performance management, role clarity and work–life balance arrangements (Veld & Alfes, 2017) can provide additional support for employee mental health. For example, training on emotional intelligence and resilience may assist employees to control the effects of emotional labour. Such training could include participants understanding key dimensions, and learning effective strategies and exercises to be able to develop emotional intelligence skills. Emotional intelligence tools within the recruitment and selection process can also be utilised to ascertain the level of training and support required for employee emotional labour (Karimi et al., 2015). The following section explores the issues and context of mental health in the nursing profession.

Mental Health and Well-being: A Case Study of the Nursing Profession

Nurses are the largest sector of the health workforce and its frontline in most advanced market economies (AMEs) and a highly skilled workforce, which works in a highly dynamic and challenging work environment (Holland, Allen, & Cooper, 2013). The nature of the work and the environment can impact on their mental health. In the last few decades, the healthcare industry in AMEs has been subject to heavy budget cuts and demographic changes such as ageing which have impacted hospital organisations (Feo & Kitson, 2016; Halldorsdottir, Einarsdottir, & Edvardsson, 2018). Additionally, high turnover and increased casual nursing contracts (O'Brien-Pallas & Baumann, 2000) put additional strain on full-time nurses (Bruyneel, Thoelen, Adriaenssens, & Sermeus, 2017; Mantler, Godin, Cameron, & Horsburgh, 2015). Expectations for high-quality healthcare remains, increasing pressure on the healthcare systems and its workforce in AMEs (Holland, Allen, & Cooper, 2013). As one NHS nurse from the UK detailed to a national newspaper

> It was only the beginning of the shift and I already felt like I was so far up shit creek without a paddle that I was off the map. Everyone is busy and I feel like I'm drowning. (Ward, 2015)

The healthcare working environment has become more complex from increasing patient age, high patient turnaround demand, and increasing workload due to patient movements between care units (Duffield & O'Brien-Pallas, 2003). Moreover, healthcare providers have experienced an increase in verbal and emotional abuse from patients and amongst staff (Duncan et al., 2016). In this instance, the mental health and well-being of nurses becomes essential for their retention and the quality patient care they give (Cheng et al., 2013; Duffield & O'Brien-Pallas, 2003).

In AMEs nurses have migrated from public to the private sector leaving the public health sector deprived of skilled nurses (Brunetto et al., 2018). There has been an increase in patient throughput but not an increase in staffing numbers, and an increasing workload due to fewer available nurses and resources (Leiter & Laschinger, 2006). This has left an inadequate number of trained nurses, who have limited influence on policies, poor working conditions and career opportunities (O'Brien-Pallas & Baumann, 2000). Nursing can be physically and psychologically demanding, and highly emotionally challenging (Holland, Tham, & Gill, 2018). For example, intensive care units have a high workload and high mortality rate. The increased workload and increased number of patients (Jakob & Rothen, 1997) has led to a critical nurse shortage (Karimi et al., 2015) and a higher perception of the NHS having insufficient resources (Brunetto et al., 2018). To be able to decrease a nursing shortage and improve nurses' experiences at work, organisations are looking to employee well-being strategies as a way to mitigate the effects of perceived stress on the mental health of nurses (Brennan, 2017).

Support, from management and the community is seen as critical for the nursing profession (Rahimaghaee, Nayeri, & Mohammadi, 2010). Research has indicated that nurses expect support from the community in which they work, as well as their managers, organisation and colleagues (Taheri, Ghasemi, Negarandeh, Janani, & Mirbazegh, 2018). Furthermore, nurses' concern about a lack of respect from the community can influence their intention to leave the nursing profession altogether (Varaei, Vaismoradi, Jasper, & Faghihzadeh, 2012). This low level of support not only affects nurses' mental health but may also affect how they complete their job tasks, possibly threatening patient health (Burke, Moodie, Dolan, & Fiksenbaum, 2012). Factors that may decrease social support include poor work conditions and organisational climate and a lack of management assistance (Abualrub, 2004). One such example comes from an NHS trust in the UK, where a nurse manager was recognised with a CEO award after providing support to her colleague Scott who suffered clinical depression. In an interview with the University Hospitals of North Midlands, Scott said

> *The trust I have been able to establish with her makes everything easier and less daunting. She is the most caring member of staff I have ever had the pleasure to work with. (NHS Trust, 2015)*

What Affects Nurses' Well-being?

There are various reasons affecting nurses' physical and psychological well-being. An interaction between employees and their work environment where the interaction is perceived as demanding or threatening, may exceed their capabilities and existing resources. This can lead to job stress, negatively affecting well-being (Karimi et al., 2015).

Work environments, such as the hospital and ward in which nurses work can impact their stress levels, resulting in negative mental health implications. A positive work environment promotes nursing competencies and skills, resulting in higher job satisfaction and nurses providing higher quality of care. Moreover, the working environment is a combination of conditions characterised by job demands and job resources (Demerouti et al., 2000). Job demands in the nursing work environment can be time pressure, demanding patient contact but also the introduction of new medical technologies, lack of time to plan and prepare work, frequent interruptions and little work autonomy. These demands, if not counteracted with job resources, such as adequate staffing and management support can negatively influence the stress and anxiety of nurses, thus impacting their mental health.

The culture of nursing can itself be detrimental to nurses' mental health. There have been incidences of a 'culture of survival' where doctors and ward managers actively run difficult work environments. Some nurses thrive with job stress, however, employees who struggle can feel a sense of failure, leading to an experience of depression. In the course of a shift, nurses may encounter violent and abusive patients who do not appreciate the care they provide. Nurses may also be faced with situations out of their control, such as patients who become sicker or lose their lives, which can be very difficult to cope with. Nurses experiencing a good level of well-being are more likely to illustrate a high quality of care (Pahlevan Sharif et al., 2018). As nurses' efforts at work decreases, the increasing workload possibly puts patients and other staff members at risk (Holland et al., 2018). Nurses may find it difficult to concentrate on job tasks, making them more prone to mistakes, such as incorrect drug doses. Unfortunately, due to poor cultural climates it can be difficult for nurses to seek treatment (Lampert, 2017). It is seen as normal to work double shifts that are usually 12–14 hours long as is. This is on top of the norm to work night or rotating shifts, which can disrupt well-being and increase mental health issues if continued for a long period of time (Dall'Ora, Ball, Recio-Saucedo, & Griffiths, 2016; Ferri et al., 2016). Even though it is purported that registered nurses in the US enjoy apparently one of the best careers in the country (Rhodan, 2017), American nurses have been shown to experience depression at twice the rate of the population; 18% for nurses, compared to 9% for the general population (Peckham, 2015). Depression-related suicide in the UK for nurses outpaces other professions by 25% (Windsor-Shellard, 2017). Depression often has a higher prevalence in females, twice that of males. Due to the make-up of the nursing workforce (e.g. 89% female in Australia), depression may have a greater hold in the nursing profession and should be a major concern of the healthcare industry. Limited psychological well-being can lead to irrational choices and lower effort (Pahlevan Sharif et al., 2018) which can directly affect patient outcomes.

The job demands of nursing, such as organisational change, staff shortages, patient violence and a lack of management support, can affect nurses' stress, anxiety and burnout (McDonald, Jackson, Wilkes, & Vickers, 2013), intensifying the need for nurses to obtain the characteristics associated with resilience. A more personal individual trait to influence well-being is emotional intelligence, or resilience, as it moderates the relationship between stress and psychological health (Karimi et al., 2015). Research has identified the need for resilience training programmes tailored to nurses working in heightened stress environments (Akerjordet & Severinsson, 2008; Mayes & Schott-Baer, 2010). These training programmes may include ways to build key relationships, in this case with work colleagues, meditation, journal writing and change management coaching. Resilience strategies that are utilised whilst dealing with patients and difficult situations (Kemeny, Boettcher, DeShon, & Stevens, 2006; McDonald et al., 2013) may decrease the negative impact on their mental health (Gillespie et al., 2007). Emotional labour is a considerable part of work in healthcare (Phillips, 1996). The better nurses are prepared for the emotional demanding side of the job, the better they can cope (Bartram et al., 2012). Nurses have to work harder with increased emotional labour meaning they cannot show their real feelings. Nurses may exhibit surface acting and deep acting. Surface acting occurs when the nurse's underlying feelings are not altered but their expression is altered to fit the situation. Deep acting occurs when a nurse's inner feelings are adjusted to match the outward expression (Cheng, Bartram, Karimi, & Leggat, 2013). Using surface acting intensifies the risk of exhaustion more than deep acting (Kim, 2008). Therefore emotional labour can pose a risk to a nurse's overall health (Bartram et al., 2012).

Presenteeism can affect nurses' attention to detail, they can become slow in dealing with patients and exhibit low productivity (Karimi et al., 2015). However, presenteeism is not only bad for productivity, it can also prove to be fatal for vulnerable patients. Unclear thinking and poor attention to detail can play a part in the risk to patients. A Robert Wood Johnson Foundation survey reported that nurses with high levels of presenteeism were more likely to report medical errors and poor judgement of patient care (Levak, Ruhm, & Gupta, 2013). A further paediatric nurse study found that 83% of nurses surveyed admitted to attending work when they were unfit to do so, even though 95% knew this could pose a danger to patients (Szymczak et al., 2015). A US survey of presenteeism habits found that 75% of nurses continued to go to work, even when feeling unfit to do so (Levak et al., 2013). In the UK, a Royal College of Nursing questionnaire found that 82% nurses attended work whilst ill. More than half cited work-related stress as being amongst the causes of their illnesses (Royal College of Nursing, 2013). The same percentage was found in Ireland, suggesting that presenteeism is a worldwide issue (Sprinks, 2015) that can affect the mental health of nurses. As this case study illustrates, the management of mental health and well-being is a multifaceted issue and needs to be managed and resourced effectively.

Conclusion

The chapter has detailed the importance of mental health support for employees, giving an in-depth example of nurses and the healthcare industry as a whole. Mental health issues such as anxiety and depression are not easy to detect, support and recover from due to the individualistic effect they have on each person. Additionally, the workplace environment for nurses especially can be hazardous due to high workload, violence and the emotional toll of caring for sick patients. Building employee well-being and resilience are two ways in which organisations can prevent and support mental health issues. Thus, increasing job satisfaction, retention and performance outcomes.

References

Abualrub, R. F. (2004). Job stress, job performance, and social support among hospital nurses. *Journal of Nursing Scholarship, 36*(1), 73–78.

Akerjordet, K., & Severinsson, E. (2008). Emotionally intelligent nurse leadership: A literature review study. *Journal of Nursing Management, 16*(5), 565–577.

Bardoel, E. A., Pettit, T. M., De Cieri, H., & McMillan, L. (2014). Employee resilience: An emerging challenge for HRM. *Asia Pacific Journal of Human Resources, 52*(3), 279–297. doi:10.1111/1744-7941.12033

Bartram, T., Casimir, G., Djurkovic, N., Leggat, S. G., & Stanton, P. (2012). Do perceived high performance work systems influence the relationship between emotional labour, burnout and intention to leave? A study of Australian nurses. *Journal of Advanced Nursing, 68*(7), 1567–1578.

Bartram, T., Stanton, P., Leggat, S., Casimir, G., & Fraser, B. (2007). Lost in translation: Exploring the link between HRM and performance in healthcare. *Human Resource Management Journal, 17*(1), 21–41.

Bowen, D. E., & Ostroff, C. (2004). Understanding HRM–firm performance linkages: The role of the "strength" of the HRM system. *Academy of Management Review, 29*(2), 203–221.

Boxall, P., & Macky, K. (2009). Research and theory on high-performance work systems: Progressing the high-involvement stream. *Human Resource Management Journal, 19*(1), 3–23.

Brennan, E. J. (2017). Towards resilience and wellbeing in nurses. *British Journal of Nursing, 26*(1), 43–47.

Brunetto, Y., Xerri, M., Trinchero, E., Beattie, R., Shacklock, K., Farr-Wharton, R., & Borgonovi, E. (2018). Comparing the impact of management on public and private sector nurses in the UK, Italy, and Australia. *Public Management Review, 20*(4), 525–544.

Bruyneel, L., Thoelen, T., Adriaenssens, J., & Sermeus, W. (2017). Emergency room nurses' pathway to turnover intention: A moderated serial mediation analysis. *Journal of Advanced Nursing, 73*(4), 930–942.

Burke, R., Moodie, S., Dolan, S., & Fiksenbaum, L. (2012). Job demands, social support, work satisfaction and psychological well-being among nurses in Spain, Working Paper. https://pdfs.semanticscholar.org/deab/950dbf89feddb44cae4bea0366fa4e980421.pdf.

Burke, R., Ng, E., & Fiksenbaum, L. (2009). Virtues, work satisfactions and psychological wellbeing among nurses. *International Journal of Workplace Health Management, 2*(3), 202–219.

Campbell-Sills, L., Cohan, S. L., & Stein, M. B. (2006). Relationship of resilience to personality, coping, and psychiatric symptoms in young adults. *Behaviour Research and Therapy, 44*(4), 585–599.

Caricati, L., Sala, R. L., Marletta, G., Pelosi, G., Ampollini, M., Fabbri, A., … Mancini, T. (2014). Work climate, work values and professional commitment as predictors of job satisfaction in nurses. *Journal of Nursing Management, 22*(8), 984–994.

Cheng, C., Bartram, T., Karimi, L., & Leggat, S. G. (2013). The role of team climate in the management of emotional labour: Implications for nurse retention. *Journal of Advanced Nursing, 69*(12), 2812–2825.

Dall'Ora, C., Ball, J., Recio-Saucedo, A., & Griffiths, P. (2016). Characteristics of shift work and their impact on employee performance and wellbeing: A literature review. *International Journal of Nursing Studies, 57*, 12–27.

De Jonge, J., & Schaufeli, W. B. (1998). Job characteristics and employee well-being: A test of Warr's Vitamin Model in health care workers using structural equation modelling. *Journal of Organizational Behavior: The International Journal of Industrial, Occupational and Organizational Psychology and Behavior, 19*(4), 387–407.

Demerouti, E., Bakker, A. B., Nachreiner, F., & Schaufeli, W. B. (2000). A model of burnout and life satisfaction amongst nurses. *Journal of Advanced Nursing, 32*(2), 454–464.

Duffield, C., & O'Brien-Pallas, L. (2003). The causes and consequences of nursing shortages: A helicopter view of the research. *Australian Health Review, 26*(1), 186–193.

Duncan, S. M., Hyndamn, K., Estabrooks, C. A., Hesketh, K., Humphrey, C. K., Wong, J. S., … Giovannetti, P. (2016). Nurses' experience of violence in Alberta and British Columbia hospitals. *Canadian Journal of Nursing Research Archive, 32*(4), 57–78.

Evans-Lacko, S., & Knapp, M. (2016). Global patterns of workplace productivity for people with depression: Absenteeism and presenteeism costs across eight diverse countries. *Social Psychiatry and Psychiatric Epidemiology, 51*(11), 1525–1537.

Feo, R., & Kitson, A. (2016). Promoting patient-centred fundamental care in acute healthcare systems. *International Journal of Nursing Studies, 57*, 1–11.

Ferri, P., Guadi, M., Marcheselli, L., Balduzzi, S., Magnani, D., & Di Lorenzo, R. (2016). The impact of shift work on the psychological and physical health of nurses in a general hospital: A comparison between rotating night shifts and day shifts. *Risk Management and Healthcare Policy, 9*, 203.

Fredrickson, B. L., & Joiner, T. (2002). Positive emotions trigger upward spirals toward emotional well-being. *Psychological Science, 13*(2), 172–175.

Gillespie, B. M., Chaboyer, W., Wallis, M., & Grimbeek, P. (2007). Resilience in the operating room: Developing and testing of a resilience model. *Journal of Advanced Nursing, 59*(4), 427–438.

Global Burden of Disease Collaborative Network. (2017). Global Burden of Disease Study 2016 from Institute for Health Metrics and Evaluation. Retrieved from http://ghdx.healthdata.org/gbd-results-tool

Grant, A. M., Christianson, M. K., & Price, R. H. (2007). Happiness, health, or relationships? Managerial practices and employee well-being tradeoffs. *Academy of Management Perspectives, 21*(3), 51–63.

Halldorsdottir, S., Einarsdottir, E. J., & Edvardsson, I. R. (2018). Effects of cutbacks on motivating factors among nurses in primary health care. *Scandinavian Journal of Caring Sciences, 32*(1), 397–406.

Han, K., Trinkoff, A. M., & Geiger-Brown, J. (2014). Factors associated with work-related fatigue and recovery in hospital nurses working 12-hour shifts. *Workplace Health & Safety, 62*(10), 409–414.

Holland, P. J., Tham, T. L., & Gill, F. J. (2018). What nurses and midwives want: Findings from the national survey on workplace climate and well-being. *International Journal of Nursing Practice, 24*(3), e12630.

Jackson, D., Firtko, A., & Edenborough, M. (2007). Personal resilience as a strategy for surviving and thriving in the face of workplace adversity: A literature review. *Journal of Advanced Nursing, 60*(1), 1–9.

Jakob, S., & Rothen, H. U. (1997). Intensive care 1980–1995: Change in patient characteristics, nursing workload and outcome. *Intensive Care Medicine, 23*(11), 1165–1170.

Karimi, L., Cheng, C., Bartram, T., Leggat, S. G., & Sarkeshik, S. (2015). The effects of emotional intelligence and stress-related presenteeism on nurses well-being. *Asia Pacific Journal of Human Resources, 53*(3), 296–310.

Kemeny, B., Boettcher, I. F., DeShon, R. P., & Stevens, A. B. (2006). Using experiential techniques for staff development. *Journal of Gerontological Nursing, 32*(8), 9.

Lambert, L., Passmore, H.-A., & Holder, M. D. (2015). Foundational frameworks of positive psychology: Mapping well-being orientations. *Canadian Psychology/Psychologie Canadienne, 56*(3), 311.

Lampert, L. (Producer). (2017). Depression in nurses: The unspoken epidemic. Retrieved from http://minoritynurse.com/depression-in-nurses-the-unspoken-epidemic

Law, M., Steinwender, S., & Leclair, L. (1998). Occupation, health and well-being. *Canadian Journal of Occupational Therapy, 65*(2), 81–91.

Levak, S., Ruhm, C., & Gupta, S. (2013). The effects of nurse presenteeism on quality of care and patient safety. Retrieved from http://www.rwjf.org/en/library/research/2013/08/the-effects-of-nurse-presenteeism-on-quality-of-care-and-patient.html

Lim, G. Y., Tam, W. W., Lu, Y., Ho, C. S., Zhang, M. W., & Ho, R. C. (2018). Prevalence of depression in the community from 30 countries between 1994 and 2014. *Scientific reports, 8*(1), 2861.

Lundman, B., Aléx, L., Jonsén, E., Norberg, A., Nygren, B., Fischer, R. S., & Strandberg, G. (2010). Inner strength: A theoretical analysis of salutogenic concepts. *International Journal of Nursing Studies, 47*(2), 251–260.

Luthans, F., Avey, J. B., Avolio, B. J., & Peterson, S. J. (2010). The development and resulting performance impact of positive psychological capital. *Human Resource Development Quarterly, 21*(1), 41–67.

Luthar, S. S., Sawyer, J. A., & Brown, P. J. (2006). Conceptual issues in studies of resilience. *Annals of the New York Academy of Sciences, 1094*(1), 105–115.

Mantler, J., Godin, J., Cameron, S. J., & Horsburgh, M. E. (2015). Cynicism in hospital staff nurses: The effect of intention to leave and job change over time. *Journal of Nursing Management, 23*(5), 577–587.

Mayes, P., & Schott-Baer, D. (2010). Professional development for night shift nurses. *The Journal of Continuing Education in Nursing, 41*(1), 17–22.

McDonald, G., Jackson, D., Wilkes, L., & Vickers, M. (2013). Personal resilience in nurses and midwives: Effects of a work-based educational intervention. *Contemporary Nurse, 45*(1), 134–143.

NHS Trust. (2015). Nurse recognised for exceptional support of staff. Retrieved from http://www.uhnm.nhs.uk/news/Pages/Nurse-wins-CEO-Award-for-giving-exceptional-support-to-colleague.aspx

O'Brien-Pallas, L., & Baumann, A. (2000). Toward evidence-based policy decisions: A case study of nursing health human resources in Ontario, Canada. *Nursing Inquiry, 7*(4), 248–257.

Pahlevan Sharif, S., Ahadzadeh, A. S., & Sharif Nia, H. (2018). Mediating role of psychological well-being in the relationship between organizational support and nursesiating role of psyc-sectional study. *Journal of Advanced Nursing, 74*(4), 887–899.

Peckham, C. (Producer). (2015). Nurses tell all: Benefits, salaries, and whether they'd do it again. Retrieved from https://www.medscape.com/viewarticle/854372_6

Phillips, S. (1996). Labouring the emotions: Expanding the remit of nursing work? *Journal of Advanced Nursing, 24*(1), 139–143.

Rahimaghaee, F., Nayeri, N. D., & Mohammadi, E. (2010). Managers' roles in the professional growth of Iranian clinical nurses. *Nursing & health sciences*, *12*(4), 470–476.

Rhodan, M. (Producer). (2017). This is the best job in America. Retrieved from http://time.com/3935051/best-job-america/

Roberts, S. (2018). Mental Illness is a global porblem: We need a global response. Retrieved from https://www.healthpovertyaction.org/news-events/mental-health-world-health-day-2017/

Royal College of Nursing. (2013). *Beyond breaking point?: A survey report of RCN members on health, wellbeing and stress*. London: Royal College of Nursing.

Schaubroeck, J., & Jones, J. R. (2000). Antecedents of workplace emotional labor dimensions and moderators of their effects on physical symptoms. *Journal of Organizational Behavior: The International Journal of Industrial, Occupational and Organizational Psychology and Behavior*, *21*(2), 163–183.

Schetter, C. D., & Dolbier, C. (2011). Resilience in the context of chronic stress and health in adults. *Social and Personality Psychology Compass*, *5*(9), 634–652.

Shin, J., Taylor, M. S., & Seo, M.-G. (2012). Resources for change: The relationships of organizational inducements and psychological resilience to employees' attitudes and behaviors toward organizational change. *Academy of Management Journal*, *55*(3), 727–748.

Sprinks, J. (2015). District nursing reaches crisis point in Northern Ireland. *Primary Health Care (2014+)*, *25*(3), 8.

Stanton, P., Young, S., Bartram, T., & Leggat, S. G. (2010). Singing the same song: Translating HRM messages across management hierarchies in Australian hospitals. *The International Journal of Human Resource Management*, *21*(4), 567–581.

Stern, G. (2012, May 21). Employee burnout: Around the corner? Already here? *Fortune*. https://fortune.com/2012/05/21/employee-burnout-around-the-corner-already-here/.

Szymczak, J. E., Smathers, S., Hoegg, C., Klieger, S., Coffin, S. E., & Sammons, J. S. (2015). Reasons why physicians and advanced practice clinicians work while sick: A mixed-methods analysis. *JAMA Pediatrics*, *169*(9), 815–821.

Taheri, M., Ghasemi, E., Negarandeh, R., Janani, L., & Mirbazegh, F. (2018). Social wellbeing among Iranian caregivers. *Social Indicators Research*.

Van De Voorde, K., Paauwe, J., & Van Veldhoven, M. (2012). Employee well-being and the HRM–organizational performance relationship: A review of quantitative studies. *International Journal of Management Reviews*, *14*(4), 391–407.

Varaei, S., Vaismoradi, M., Jasper, M., & Faghihzadeh, S. (2012). Iranian nurses self-perception, Vaismoradiluencing nursing image. *Journal of Nursing Management*, *20*(4), 551–560.

Veld, M., & Alfes, K. (2017). HRM, climate and employee well-being: Comparing an optimistic and critical perspective. *The International Journal of Human Resource Management*, *28*(16), 2299–2318.

Waite, P. J., & Richardson, G. E. (2004). Determining the efficacy of resiliency training in the work site. *Journal of Allied Health*, *33*(3), 178–183.

Ward, P. (2015). Night shift from hell: My mistake almost cost someone their life. *The Guardian*. Retrieved from https://www.theguardian.com/healthcare-network/2015/sep/17/night-shift-from-hell-my-mistake-almost-cost-someone-their-life

Windsor-Shellard, B. (2017). *Suicide by occupation, England: 2011 to 2015*. England. Retrieved from https://www.ons.gov.uk/peoplepopulationandcommunity/birthsdeathsandmarriages/deaths/articles/suicidebyoccupation/england2011to2015

Winwood, P. C., Winefield, A. H., & Lushington, K. (2006). Work-related fatigue and recovery: The contribution of age, domestic responsibilities and shiftwork. *Journal of Advanced Nursing*, *56*(4), 438–449.

World Health Organisation. (2018). Mental health. Retrieved from https://www.who.int/mental_health/en/

Yepes-Baldó, M., Romeo, M., Westerberg, K., & Nordin, M. (2018). Job crafting, employee well-being, and quality of care. *Western Journal of Nursing Research*, *40*(1), 52–66.

Zautra, A. J., Hall, J. S., & Murray, K. E. (2010). Resilience: A new definition of health for people and communities. In J. R. Reich, A. J. Zautra, & J. S. Hall (Eds.), *Handbook of adult resilience* (pp. 3–30). New York, NY: Guilford.

Ziegler, S., Merker, H., Schmid, M., & Puhan, M. A. (2017). The impact of the inpatient practice of continuous deep sedation until death on healthcare professionals' emotional well-being: A systematic review. *BMC Palliative Care*, *16*(1), 30.

Chapter 8

The Dark Side of Work

Peter Holland and Ross Donohue

Introduction

The main focus of human resource management has been to develop principles, policies and practices that facilitate competitive advantage through people. Much of the focus is to develop a strategic fit between all aspects of HR. In developing such an approach, it is expected to lead to an organisation where people are satisfied and motivated to remain and that is attractive to potential employees. However, this focus can neglect the context aspect of work and, in particular, what we term the 'dark side' of work, where a 'deadly combination' of increased pressure to perform through work intensification, a longer-hours work culture, the threat of job loss, or simple bad management and systems create a climate of fear and discontent, which can potentially erupt into violence. This chapter explores some of these features of the dark side of workplace behaviours to better understand why these occur, how they occur, and what can be done to mitigate these issues.

Towards a Definition

In discussing the issue of workplace violence, it is useful to start with a definition and, whilst workplace violence is increasingly being researched, its definition has remained contested (Furnham & Taylor, 2011). Much of this debate relates to the difficult and contentious issue of actions, boundaries and subjectivity in how an individual assesses and interprets the acts of others (Gill, Fisher, & Bowie, 2002). We take a holistic view, similar to Furnham and Taylor (2011), in which we see workplace violence as a broad spectrum of activities, from verbal to emotional and psychological abuse through to workplace homicide. Gill, Fisher, and Bowie (2002, p. 4), have detailed from the research other aspects we can include to help develop an understanding of the scope or boundaries of these issues. These characteristics include:

- *Target*: Whom is the violence aimed at?
- *Source*: Where is the violence coming from?
- *Perception of the act*: Do the target(s) perceive it as a violent act?
- *Work related*: The violence occurs whilst undertaking work-related duties.

These features help build the boundaries and reflect the key aspects of workplace violence. It also allow for the inclusion of contemporary issues such as cyber-work and the associated issues of cyber-bullying, criminal and terrorist acts, and consumer/client/ patient violence (Gill et al., 2002). In addition, a typology of violence by Californian Occupational Safety and Health (CAL/OSHA, 1995), which has subsequently been further developed by Howard (1996) and Gill et al. (2002), helps to articulate the types of violence that can be experienced at work. The typologies in **Table 8.1** identify four distinct types.

Table 8.1 Expanded Typology of Workplace Violence.

Type	Description
(1) Intrusive violence Criminal intent by strangers. Terrorist act. Mental illness and drug-related aggression. Protest violence.	The perpetrator has no legitimate relationship with the business or its employees, and the act of violence is usually related to an act of criminal intent. Crimes typically include robbery and terrorism, and account for the vast majority of workplace homicides.
(2) Consumer-related violence Customer/client/patients against staff. Vicarious trauma to staff. Staff violence to clients/customers.	The perpetrator has a legitimate relationship with the business and becomes violent whilst being served by the business; typical victims include health care workers and authority figures such as police/prison staff and teachers.
(3) Relationship violence Staff-on-staff violence. Domestic violence at work.	The perpetrator is an employee or past employee of the business who attacks, threatens or harasses an employee in the workplace.
(4) Organisational violence Organisational violence against staff. Organisational violence against clients, customers or patient.	The perpetrator is, by default, the organisation itself which, through its structures, systems and response, causes or prolongs violence against employees.

Sources: CAL/OSHA (1995), Howard (1996), Gill et al. (2002) and NIOSH (2004).

Exploring the Dark Workplace: The HR Perspective

The concept of the dark side of work covers a variety of issues, from fraud, which can bring down a whole company, through to homicide. The systems, issues or triggers that cause this can be wide and varied, and it is not within the scope of this chapter to provide a detailed analysis of these issues; rather, this chapter serves as an overview of the topic, with a particular focus on violence at work for those who need to understand and manage these issues. From a workplace perspective, the triggers for such acts can broadly be set out in terms of organisational factors and personal factors. These are explored further below.

Whilst the extreme outburst of workplace violence, such as homicides, often leads news bulletins, the concept of workplace violence itself is a less well developed area of research in the field of human resource management. According to the US Bureau of Statistics, over two million employees are injured each year through workplace assaults, with workplace violence accounting for 18% of violent crime in the US (Bureau of Justice). This gives some perspective on the significance of these issues.

Increasingly, the challenge is for management and, in particular, HR professionals to understand the issues and problems, and to develop the right set of policies and practices to mitigate these increasingly frequent events.

From an HR perspective, this is important because such issues are to the detriment of the whole organisation. From a strategic fit perspective, they show a lack of alignment between HR policies which are developed to enhance the overall organisation and benefit its employees. These misalignments are identified in the human resources literature as deadly combinations (Becker, Huselid, Pickus, & Spratt, 1997). Deadly combinations have the potential to develop when human resource policies and practices actively work against each other and therefore sustained organisational effectiveness (Becker et al., 1997; Boxall & Purcell, 2016). For example, having policies on flexible work and work–life balance but having a culture of long working hours. The development of deadly combinations can occur for a variety of reasons, but is often because of the organisational culture and/or the piecemeal adoption of human resource practices. The result of such deadly combinations is likely to be negative on both individuals and the organisation (Guest, Paauwe & Wright, 2012).

When these events occur, if not dealt with appropriately, they can undermine the bedrock of good human resource management practice. In addition, there is the long-term impact on the morale of the workforce, whilst the organisation's ability to attract and retain talent can also be significantly damaged. Talented people are unlikely to remain in an environment where workplace violence occurs, is accepted and/or is endemic. Such a culture doesn't sit well with developing a winning employee value proposition based on intrinsic satisfaction, values and ethics to fulfil employee expectations and aspirations. This is reinforced in Mayhew et al. (2004, p. 130), who argue:

> The negative organisational consequences may be visible through higher turnover, poor organisational reputation, and increased cost of product delivery, or even prosecution and common law claims.

Other manifestations of a culture of workplace violence may see employees undertaking less obvious withdrawal behaviour such as organisational citizenship behviours. As noted in Chapter 1, given the dynamic and reciprocal nature of the employment relationship, the actions of management are continually evaluated and assessed by employees and their representatives (Costigan, Ilter, & Berman, 1998). Actions that violate this relationship can create an atmosphere in which employees may be less willing to develop a committed relationship with management and/or with the organisation, which can lead to withdrawal behaviour, higher turnover or deviant behaviour. As such, the impact of organisational principles, policies and practices as a catalyst for such behaviour needs to be investigated and more fully understood.

A focus on organisational learning is a key and often underexplored aspect of workplace violence, and is explored more fully later in this chapter. In this context, the culture of the organisation is critical in influencing management attitudes to their workforce and to issues of workplace violence. This is because employees are continually appraising multiple sources of information and evidence to inform their impression of the overall nature and effectiveness of management.

The Organisation as a 'Dark Satanic Mill'[1]

As Gill et al. (2002) note, early research on workplace violence focussed on anger management and self-defence training as a response to the perceived shortfall in employees' ability to deal with these issues. This conveniently neglected the way organisations are structured, their culture, and how they are managed as a primary aspect of the manifestation of workplace violence.

In this context, it is important to note that the nature of the workplace has changed. Over the past three decades, economic instability and increased competition on a global scale have seen the workplace become more intensified, insecure and transient, with the fear of outsourcing and offshoring of both blue and white collar jobs ever apparent. These factors can give rise to increased anxiety, anger, frustration and stress and, if left unchecked, can result in increasingly negative effects on work and on the attitudes of employees (Hoel, Sparks, & Cooper, 2001). As a result, the pressure can give rise to a dysfunctional culture, despite the best efforts of human resource managers. As Bowie (1998) argues, because of poor management where a climate of systemic violence and institutional abuse is knowingly allowed to develop and thrive – including the threat of layoffs, increased work intensification, and where longer hours are expected and the employees are blamed for problems – the seeds of a dysfunctional organisation are planted. In such an environment, Mayhew (2002) argues, fear and violence can grow unchecked. Furnham and Taylor (2004) have identified a list of key issues that they describe as danger signals for the growth of malcontents in the workplace as a result of a poorly managed organisation. The list, whilst not exhaustive, provides a good indication of the signs and factors that need to be managed by the organisation, and includes:

- an 'us vs. them' feel to the management–employee relationship;
- a feeling or assumption that loyalty and commitment is one-way, where employees show unquestioning loyalty and where management does not feel the need to reciprocate;
- having poor or rigged grievance procedures which lack employee input;
- a culture of growing (and excessive) use of surveillance and suspicion, and of little trust;
- hypocritical messages where managers say one thing and do another;
- where sticks are preferred to carrots to motivate, and where top management get the 'carrot method';
- where management is reactive, not proactive, and have a short-term view of everything;
- where people are promoted (and rewarded) by nepotism;
- where corruption and ingratiation are rewarded rather than ability and effort;
- where the focus of work is extrinsic satisfaction only – there can be no joy in work itself;
- where communication channels are poor and information is lost or presented too late to be acted upon;
- where employees feel alienated from top management and staff do not identify with the company or its products; and
- where it is commonplace to overtly or covertly break rules and legal requirements. (*Source:* Adapted from Furhman & Taylor, 2004.)

---

[1] A reference to William Blake's 'dark satanic mills' of the industrial revolution.

In the environments noted above, the corporate culture may be such that workplace violence might go undetected until a tragic event occurs. This can be due to a variety of issues, including: a lack of awareness of the issues, a lack of understanding of the issues and how to deal with them, or simply a lack of reporting. When considering these issues and workplace violence, Braverman (2002, p. 114), makes the point: 'Every act of violence is the outcome of a series of events. Every situation, threat or act of violence is preceded by early signs of trouble'. This situation is often related to a further point addressed by Frost (2003), who links these poor management systems and poor work environments to the incompetence of managers in terms of management ability and (poor) people skills. This is often linked to poor training and development in these areas of key management skills.

Underlying many of the issues raised in the list developed by Furhman and Taylor (2004) are the themes of trust, justice and equity – the key themes which underpin this book. This is further supported by the work of Karlsson (2012), who argues that employees need dignity and autonomy at work. Where these are denied, there is often a link with bad management, which, he notes, usually lacks inherent trust in employees. This situation can then provide fertile ground for resistance and misbehaviour at work. Indeed, some high-profile workplace shootings in the United States have previously been linked to perceived unjust treatment. As Gill et al. (2002) point out in this context, these violent actions, which are initially seen as the action of an unstable individual, may in fact have their origin in organisational culture.

Corporate Psychopaths

Whilst discussing issues of workplace violence, it is important to put the research in context, as the vast majority of workers are reliable, trustworthy and loyal corporate citizens who contribute and are committed to their organisations. Some workers, however, can be manipulative, self-serving and deceitful; they damage working relationships and are potentially destructive to their organisations. As such it is up to management to create and manage these negative behviours and support a safe workplace where staff are engaged. A key aspect of this process is understanding employees in this second category who may have a psychopathic personality disorder. Unlike criminal psychopaths, these individuals operate below the radar of the law, as their psychopathic behaviour is not usually florid enough to result in criminal prosecution, and they are referred to as sub-criminal psychopaths or as corporate psychopaths in the work context (Boddy, 2011, 2014a, 2014b). Gao and Raine (2010) reviewed extant brain functioning studies involving criminal and sub-criminal psychopath populations and concluded that sub-criminal psychopaths do not demonstrate the neurological impairment to the areas of the brain (amygdala, hippocampus or prefrontal cortex) that their criminal counterparts do. A characteristic of both groups is a lack of empathy. It would appear, however, that whilst sub-criminal psychopaths understand empathy at a conceptual/intellectual level, they are incapable of experiencing this emotion. Indeed, according to Wellons (2012), the capacity of sub-criminal psychopaths to use their understanding of empathy for their own instrumental needs may explain why they are able to avoid illegal behaviour and criminal prosecution. In terms of their other characteristics, corporate psychopaths (this label is used throughout the rest of this chapter) are impulsive, callous, narcissistic (i.e. lack the self-control required to inhibit self-serving negative behaviours), calculating, duplicitous, grandiose and aggressive.

Leadership and Corporate Psychopaths

Given the recent prevalence of fraud, corruption, embezzlement, large-scale Ponzi schemes and corporate collapses in the twenty-first century, many commentators on ethical business practices have begun to question the behaviour of organisational leaders (Babiak, Neuman, & Hare, 2010). While the incidence of psychopathy in the general population is believed to be approximately 1%, experts (Babiak & Hare, 2006; Boddy, 2011) estimate that amongst organisational leaders the rate is likely to be considerably higher. It is the case that, in recent years, business has become hypercompetitive and activities such as corporate takeovers, acquisitions and downsizings have become more prevalent. As a result, organisations have strived to become leaner, more flexible and increasingly focussed on radical and innovative solutions to survive (Babiak & Hare, 2006). Therefore, it is perhaps not surprising that those employees who are bold, risk-takers, fearless, low in anxiety, cunning, polished, willing to ignore organisational rules, and who believe 'the end justifies the means' (all features of corporate psychopaths) might be promoted to leadership positions. Corporate psychopaths invariably possess an inordinate sense of entitlement and are driven by the trappings that come with leadership: power, prestige and the capacity to control and influence others (Wexler, 2008).

Corporate psychopaths also tend to present very well during job interviews, as they are superficially charming, confident, strong, calm, adept at cultivating power networks, and skilled in social manipulation. As Furnham (2015) notes, once inside organisations psychopaths identify support networks to help them establish themselves and ascend through the organisation. However, the characteristics and behaviours of corporate psychopaths are more closely associated with superior impression management skills than they are with strong job performance (Hare, 1999). Thus, whilst corporate psychopaths may present themselves ostensibly as being competent and effective leaders, eventually their reckless actions, lack of behavioural control and proclivity to lie about their abilities and manipulate their colleagues, often result in dysfunctional and destructive leadership. Empirical evidence supports this view; Babiak et al. (2010), in a study involving managers and executives, found that psychopathy was positively related to charisma/presentation skills (i.e. to creativity, and to good communication and strategic-thinking skills). However, this study also found that leaders' psychopathy was negatively related to their responsibility/performance (i.e. to being a team player, to supervision skills and to overall performance). Boddy (2010) also found in a study of Australian senior employees a strong positive association between the presence of corporate psychopaths in the workplace and employee perceptions of bullying and unfair supervision.

Corporate Psychopaths in Teams

Teamwork is becoming increasingly prevalent in organisations (Cohen & Bailey, 1997). Clearly, effective team functioning is critical for organisational success; however, team performance can be compromised by a team member with a psychopathic personality disorder. Recent research examining the role of psychopathy in workgroup or team settings (Baysinger, Scherer, & LeBreton, 2014) indicates that groups characterised by higher levels of psychopathy were more likely to encounter greater levels of dysfunctional interactions, and that members held more negative perceptions of the group than teams characterised by lower levels of psychopathy. This study also found that psychopathy led to higher levels of negative socio-emotional behaviour by members which, in turn, engendered lower levels of team performance.

According to a leading expert on psychopathy (Hare, 1999), psychopaths working in teams are capable of irreparably damaging the morale and emotional well-being of their colleagues. They may abuse, ridicule, sexually harass, bully and blame others for their own mistakes (Boddy, 2011). Corporate psychopaths are motivated by what they observe to be their victims' vulnerabilities. Due to their blunted human emotions (lack of empathy for others and diminished capacity for guilt and remorse for their own actions), corporate psychopaths obtain a perverse pleasure from abusing their targets within workgroups (Babiak & O'Toole, 2012). Consequently, corporate psychopaths can cause victims of their behaviour within teams to become stressed and feel helpless, and can undermine their self-confidence. Corporate psychopaths are also likely to tell lies and to start malicious rumours about colleagues in order to deliberately orchestrate conflict and intense competition between team members (Clarke, 2005). Aside from the devastating personal consequences, there are also human resource management implications that arise from the presence of corporate psychopaths in work groups. Team members who are subject to their victimisation are likely to reduce their commitment and performance, and to ultimately leave the organisation and/or file actions against the organisation. Given the 'war for talent' that is currently being waged in the business sector, corporate psychopaths have the capacity to undermine the competitive advantage and organisational brand that arises from a firm's capacity to retain valued employees.

Corporate Psychopaths and Human Resource Management's Role

Due to the close association between leadership and desirable organisational outcomes such as good governance and corporate social responsibility (Boddy, 2013; Singh, 2008) – see Chapter 13 – experts have advocated that senior executives should be screened for psychopathy and integrity. Once identified, these corporate psychopaths can be removed from their leadership roles and exited from their organisations. However, there are ethical, legal and practical constraints on the capability of organisations to screen for corporate psychopaths. While there is a reliable and valid clinical instrument (Hare Psychopathy Checklist-Revised) which can detect psychopaths in criminal and psychiatric contexts, this instrument requires repeated observation and review of an inmate's criminal history, and should be administered by a trained clinical psychologist.

At present there is no generally accepted and psychometrically sound self-report measure of psychopathy that could be applied in an organisational setting (Wellons, 2012). Indeed, as corporate psychopaths are gifted liars, they are invariably capable of scoring favourably on any paper-and-pencil test. Nonetheless, advances are being made in this area and, as recruiters and human resource managers become more aware of the characteristics and behaviours of corporate psychopaths, the likelihood of them being identified is increasing. The use of structured behavioural interviewing, requiring interviewees to recount how they behaved when confronted with previous organisational problems, may provide some insight into whether candidates are corporate psychopaths (Babiak & Hare, 2006). Exercising due diligence in terms of verifying applicants' qualifications and employment history, and the careful scrutinising of referees may also help to identify corporate psychopaths.

Langbert (2010) has provided a number of recommendations that human resource managers can implement to detect corporate psychopaths. He suggests instituting a monitoring system for employees to anonymously report abusive/bullying behaviour. In addition, he advocates including assessments of integrity and teamwork behaviour in performance appraisals. Finally, Langbert (2010) suggests encouraging interaction between workgroups and departments to constrain the capacity of corporate psychopaths to start false rumours or to manipulate their colleagues.

The Cost of Workplace Violence

The cost to the organisation of workplace violence and psychological damage can be seen from a variety of perspectives, including the moral and economic impacts on the individual, on colleagues, and on the organisation and society as a whole. The economic impact, as noted, is wide and varied, and is succinctly summed up in **Fig. 8.1** where, using research by the World Health Organisation (WHO), the economic costs are categorised into direct and indirect costs.

Fig. 8.1 The Costs of Workplace Violence.

Direct costs
Legal services
Medical costs
Perpetrator control costs
Costs of policing

Workplace violence

Indirect costs
Lost earning and time
Lost human capital investment
Productivity
Psychological costs

Source: WHO (2004).

Whilst by no means exhaustive, the impact, both in the short and long term, of covert and overt forms of workplace violence can be identified. Some studies have attempted to quantify the damage workplace violence does. For example, a study (Paoli, 2000) in the European Union identified an absenteeism rate of 35% for those affected by workplace violence compared to 23% for those not impacted by workplace violence. Mayhew et al. (2004) also note the impact on interpersonal and workplace relationships – both inside and outside of the workplace. Internationally, the International Labour Organization (ILO) estimates workplace violence and associated issues costs at between 1.0% and 3.5% of GDP.

Workplace Violence Intervention

A central pillar in the development of a framework to manage workplace violence is a clear and articulated policy. The key aspects of a good policy, as Paludi, Nydegger, and Paludi (2006) note, must be more than just a compliance document, and must proactively focus both on preventing workplace violence and on remedying any violations of that policy.

In terms of a frame of reference, Chappell and DeMartino (1998) argue in **Table 8.2** what a policy needs to focus on.

Table 8.2 Policy Development of Workplace Violence.

Prevention	The emphasis is on the employer to deal with the causes of workplace violence.
Targeted	The policy needs to address appropriate action for the type and level of violence.
Multiple	The development of a combination of responses to deal with what are often complex issues and problems is required.
Immediate	Delays can cause chain reactions, and thus instances of workplace violence need to be responded to quickly and effectively.
Participatory	Policy and programmes must have employees' and/or their representatives' input to be accepted and relevant.
Long term	Ensure issues are addressed immediately and then followed-up, and that policies are reviewed regularly.

Equally, the principles upon which a good policy is based are essential if the policy is to have legitimacy at all levels in the workplace. Paludi, Nydegger and Pauldi (2006) propose the following principles of a quality preventative programme:

- it must have top management support;
- the policy needs to cover all employees of the organisation;
- the focus should be proactive and not reactive;
- the policy should be cognisant of workplace culture;
- it needs to ensure a variety of expertise is available to deal with the various issues and incidences;
- management should take a proactive role in communicating the policy;
- the policy should be practical; and
- the policy should be regularly reviewed.

From this position, the types of behaviour that are unacceptable in the workplace can then be addressed, and the consequences or sanctions for such behaviour can be administered. The OSHA in the United States has identified the following as essential components of an effective policy:

- employees should be educated on unacceptable behaviour;
- employees should not be put or put themselves in a situation where they are at risk of violence;
- where required, employees (dealing with the public) should be trained to deal with potentially violent situations;
- potentially violent clients are to be managed appropriately, and staff provided with appropriate support;
- backup and support are to be provided to employees as and when required;
- employees are encouraged to report all events and threats associated with workplace violence;

- all events should be investigated;
- management should provide full assistance and support to employees; and
- management should apply and enforce rules fairly and consistently. *(Source:* OSHA, 2000, cited in Paludi, Nydegger, & Paudi, 2006.)

Violence at Work and the Learning Organisation

As noted, central to the development of a quality prevention programme is that management plays a central role through tacit development, support and review of the principles, policies and practices upon which workplace violence interventions and recoveries are based. This, we would argue, requires more than simple policies; it also requires an organisation that constantly reviews and tests its system – what we would term organisation learning (Senge, 1990). Ellis and Shipelberg (2003, p. 1,237) define organisational learning as 'the process through which organisation members develop shared knowledge based on analysis of data gathered from or provided by multiple sources'. At its core, the organisation learning approach identifies the organisation as a system of interconnected parts, where every action has an effect on the organisation (Braverman, 2002), and the focus is on the integration of continual learning with business objectives at the individual, group and organisational levels. Its significance lies in unlocking the potential knowledge throughout the organisation and in allowing this information to flow (Walton, 1999). The rhetoric of most organisations is that they would see themselves as just such a learning organisation – which from a passive perspective is true, in that learning is embedded in all organisations. However, it is only through planned and supportive approaches by management that such a culture can develop and extract this (quality) knowledge. This is because it takes resources and because it requires management to be open to knowledge and ideas from all areas of the organisation, to accept they may be wrong in their approach, and to be able to take criticism and review their systems. Only through this approach can progress be made on understanding why things have gone wrong (Braverman, 2002).

To highlight the relationship between effective workplace violence strategies and organisational learning, we use the framework developed by Argris and Schon (1978) of single, double and triple loop learning. This approach allows a more effective understanding of the nature and impact of learning within the organisation.

Single Loop Learning

The focus here is on correcting problems to enable the organisation to continue. Significantly, this reactive approach never examines the actual core of the problem, so there is a likelihood that it will be continually repeated as the core issue is never addressed. As Burgoyne (1995) notes, a strong emphasis on this approach can inhibit future learning and change. In a workplace violence context, this can be seen, for example, in the blaming of an employee for an incidence or letting the incidence escalate, thereby denying any responsibility by management.

Double Loop Learning

The focus of double loop learning is to look deeper into how the problem occurred in the first place. The key here, as Hartel, Strybosch and Blyth (2006) note, is that management separates the symptoms from the causes. In this way, the focus of resources is effectively directed toward the real problem. As Walton (1999) notes, the issue here is challenging the accepted orthodoxies, as this approach addresses the nature of the system(s) at work and not just the issue itself. In the context of workplace violence, this may mean accepting that a solution to an issue is outside the knowledge and skills of management, and management therefore seeks a range of external expertise to deal with the issues and incidence.

Triple Loop Learning

At this level, the focus is on a strategic approach to issues to identify what can be done to eliminate problems from within the organisation. This can mean reviewing and reflecting on previous learning experiences to form the basis for new learning and insights (Walton, 1999). A key point Burgoyne (1995) makes in this context is that this level of learning enables organisations to maintain core values, as it is continually taking a proactive rather than reactive approach to issues. In this context of workplace violence, it may be a process of testing the policies and systems, and of reviewing these continually.

Conclusion

It is clear that workplace violence is an increasingly significant issue. Whilst its manifestations are varied and complex, it is an increasingly important area of HR and it needs to be managed and reviewed through the development of appropriate policies and practices. As noted, the development of a learning organisation culture can be a critical factor in the successful management of workplace violence.

References

Argris, C., & Schon, D. (1978). *Organisational learning: A theory of action perspectives*. Reading, MA: Addison-Wesley.

Babiak, P., & Hare, R. D. (2006). *Snakes in suits: When psychopaths go to work*. New York, NY: Regan Books.

Babiak, P., Neumann, C. S., & Hare, R. D. (2010). Corporate psychopathy: Talking the walk. *Behavioral Sciences and the Law, 28*, 174–193.

Babiak, P., & O'Toole, M. E. (2012, November). The corporate psychopath. *FBI Law Enforcement Bulletin, 81*(11), 7–11.

Baysinger, M. A., Scherer, K. T., & LeBreton, J. M. (2014). Exploring the disruptive effects of psychopathy and aggression on group processes and group effectiveness. *Journal of Applied Psychology, 99*, 48–65.

Becker, B., Huselid, M., Pickus, P., & Spratt, M. (1997). HR as a source of shareholder value: Research and recommendations. *Human Resource Management, 36*(1), 39–47.

Boddy, C. R. (2010). Corporate psychopaths, bullying and unfair supervision in the workplace. *Journal of Business Ethics, 100*, 367–379.

Boddy, C. R. (2011). *Corporate psychopaths: Organisational destroyers*. New York, NY: Palgrave Macmillan.

Boddy, C. R. (2013). Corporate psychopaths: Uncaring citizens, irresponsible leaders. *Journal of Corporate Citizenship, 49*, 8–16.

Boddy, C. R. (2014a). Corporate psychopaths: Conflict, employee affective well-being and counterproductive work behaviour. *Journal of Business Ethics, 121*, 107–121.

Boddy, C. R. (2014b). Extreme managers, extreme workplaces: Capitalism, organizations and corporate psychopaths. *Organization, 22*(4), 530–551.

Boxall, P., & Purcell, J. (2016). *Strategy and human resource management* (4th ed.). Basingstoke: Palgrave Macmillan.

Bowie, V. (1998). Workplace violence. Paper presented at the Australian institute of criminology conference, Melbourne.

Braverman, M. (2002). Prevention of violence affecting workers: A systems perspective. In M. Gill, B. Fisher, & V. Bowie (Eds.), *Violence at work: Cause, patterns and prevention* (pp. 114–131). Devon: Willan Publishing.

Burgoyne, J. (1995, September). Feeding minds to grow the business. *People Management, 1*(22), 7–15.

CAL/OSHA. (1995). *CAL/OSHA guidelines for workplace security*. Sacramento, CA: California Occupational Safety and Health Administration.

Chappell, D., & DeMartino, V. (1998). *Violence at work*. Geneva: ILO.

Clarke, J. (2005). *Working with monsters: How to identify and protect yourself from the workplace psychopath*. Sydney, Australia: Random House.

Cohen, S. G., & Bailey, D. E. (1997). What makes teams work: Group effectiveness research from the shop floor to the executive suite. *Journal of Management, 23*, 239–290.

Costigan, R., Ilter, S., & Berman, J. (1998). A multi-dimensional study of trust inorganizations. *Journal of Managerial Issues, 10*, 303–317.

Ellis, S., & Shpielberg, N. (2003). Organisational learning: Mechanicians and managers' percieved uncertainty. *Human Relations, 56*(10), 1233–1254.

Frost, P. (2003). *Toxic emotions at work*. Boston, MA: Harvard Business School Press.

Furnham, A. (2011). *Backstabbers and bullies: How to cope with the dark side of people at work*. London: Bloomsbury.

Furnham, A., & Talyor, J. (2004). *The dark side of behaviour at work*. Hampshire: Palgrave-Macmillian.

Furnham, A., & Taylor, J. (2011). *Bad apples: Identify, prevent & manage negative behaviour at work*. Hampshire: Palgrave-Macmillian.

Gao, Y. & Raine, A. (2010). Successful and unsuccessful psychopaths: a neurobiological model. *Behavioral Science Law, 28*(2), 194–210.

Gill, M., Fisher, B., & Bowie, V. (2002). *Violence at work: Cause, patterns and prevention*. Devon: Willan Publishing.

Guest, D., Paauwe, J., & Wright, P. (2012). HRM and performance: Achievements and challenges. In D. Guest, J. Paauwe, P. Wright (Eds.), *What do we know and where do we go?* (pp. 1–18). London: John Wiley & Son.

Hare, R. (1999). *Without conscience: The disturbing world of the psychopaths among us*. New York, NY: Guilford Press.

Hartel, C., Strybosch, V., & Blyth, A. (2006). The learning organisation. In P. Holland & H. DeCieri (Eds.), *Contemporary issues in human resource development: An Australian perspective* (pp. 289–304). Melbourne, Australia: Pearson.

Hoel, H., Sparks, K., & Cooper, C. (2001). The cost of violence/stress at work and the benefits of a violence/stress free working environment. Report Commissioned by the ILO, Geneva.

Howard, J. (1996). State and local regulatory approaches to preventing WPV. *Occupational Medicine, 11*(2), 26–35.

Karlsson, J. (2012). *Organizational misbehaviour in the workplace*. Hampshire: Palgrave-Macmillian.

Langbert, B. M. (2010). Managing psychopathic employees. *Cornell HR review*. Retrieved from http://digitalcommons.ilr.cornell.edu/chrr/1. Accessed on March 30, 2014.

Mayhew, C. (2002). Occupational violence in industrialised countries: Types incidence patterns and 'at risk' groups of workers. Affecting workers In M. Gill, B. Fisher, & V. Bowie (Eds.), *Violence at work: Cause, patterns and prevention* (pp. 21–40). Devon: Willan Publishing.

Mayhew, C., McCarthy, P., Chappell, D., Quinlan, M., Barker, M., & Sheehan, M. (2004). Measuring the extant and impact from occupational violence and bullying on traumatised workers. *Employee Responsibilities and Rights Journal, 16*(3), 117–134.

National Institute for Occupational Safety and Health (NIOSH). (2004). *Workplace violence prevention strategies and research needs.* Baltimore MD: NIOSH.

Paoli, P. (2000). *Violence at work in European Union recent findings.* Dublin: European Foundation for the Improvement of Living and Working Conditions.

Paludi, M., Nydegger, R., & Paludi, C. (2006). *Understanding workplace violence.* Westport, CT: Praeger.

Senge, P. (1990). *The fifth discipline: The art and practice of the learning organisation.* Australia: Random House.

Singh, J. (2008). Impostors masquerading as leaders: Can the contagion be contained? *Journal of Business Ethics, 82,* 733–745.

Walton, J. (1999). *Strategic human resource development.* Harlow: Financial Times/ Prentice Hall.

Wellons, S. (2012). The devil in the boardroom: Corporate psychopaths and their impact on business. *PURE Insights, 1,* 42–45.

Wexler, M. N. (2008). Conjectures on systemic psychopathy: Reframing the contemporary organisation. *Society and Business Review, 3,* 224–238.

WHO. (2004). *The economic dimensions of workplace violence.* Geneva: WHO.

Section III

Case Studies

(1) Crisis and Risk Management
(2) Mental Health and Wellbeing at Work
(3) The Dark Side of Work

(1) Crisis and Risk Management

Samarco Dam Failure

On 5 November 2015, the devastating collapse of two dams owned by Samarco in Mariana, killed 19 people and flooded the Doce River, an important river for the southeast region of Brazil. The 40 million litres of contaminated water and sediment from iron ore extraction that was released polluted the water supply in the Doce River for hundreds of thousands of people and decimated wildlife. The event has been described as the biggest environmental accident in the history of the state of Minas Gerais in Brazil.

Before the disaster, Samarco, the operator of the Germano iron ore mine and its joint venture owners BHP and Vale, was identified as a Brazilian success story. In 2014, despite falling international iron prices, it declared a net profit of $1.3bn.

In the time since the collapse, the organisations have been the focus of lawsuits with federal prosecutors and civil groups claiming negligence and misleading actions by management in the run-up to the disaster. A central argument against the companies involved is that the failure was connected with a leadership and management approach that focussed on cutting costs and increasing production. In the minutes from a board meeting on August 2015, that were included in the legal proceedings, company directors said: 'Despite the improvements in cost reduction the world is not standing still and further improvements are needed'. According to José Adércio Sampaio, coordinator of a taskforce of federal prosecutors, 'They prioritized profits and left safety in second place'.

Concerns raised in court proceedings following the disaster, revealed that as the event unfolded devices that had been installed to measure liquid pressure and water level were either not working, lacked batteries or had been moved to other dams. Lawyers representing a class action against BHP also argued that safety warning measures in place at the Fundão dam were inadequate; specifically there was not a proper system to warn people living downstream in the event of a dam failure. There was also no warning siren for example. Although these sirens may not be legally required, when the dam broke, residents were warned by telephone calls or in one case by a neighbour on a motorbike shouting: 'The dam has burst!'

There is evidence, however, that safety was important. In August 2012, the board noted Samarco's safety performance urging that the company should 'maintain its focus on eliminating fatal risks'. Indeed since it started operation in 2008, in response to problems with drainage and erosion, Samarco lowered the reservoir and adjusted the drainage system along with associated remedial works. Additionally six months prior the collapse, the company carried out a worst-case assessment of the dam, near Mariana in Minas Gerais state, and were warned of a possible loss from a 'liquification break' with up to 20 deaths, and land, water resources and biodiversity impacts for a 20-year period with an estimated cost of $3.4bn.

In the aftermath of the collapse Samarco, Vale and BHP Billiton have commissioned an investigation by the international law firm Cleary Gottlieb Steen & Hamilton (CGSH). The report published in 2016, described attempts by Samarco to correct drainage problems and highlighted the impact of three small seismic shocks in the area about 90 minutes before the dam failed. The explanation that was provided stated that 'This additional movement is likely to have accelerated the failure process that was already well advanced'.

Following the disaster Samarco has dedicated substantial resources to affected communities and to re-starting operations at the mine that is a huge source of employment for the Mariana district. Between 2011 and 2015, Samarco reportedly contributed more than $3bn in local investment, making up more than half of tax revenues in the city of Mariana. In March 2016 the three companies made a deal with the federal and state governments to carry out repair, restoration and reconstruction programmes and have spent more than $1bn on clean-up and relief operations.

Samarco and its owners are keen to return to production and in statements to *The Guardian*, Samarco, Vale and BHP *Billiton* said that safety was a priority and that the dam complied with Brazilian legislation.

Written by Cathy Sheehan

Sources
Phillips, D., & Brasileiro, D. (2018). Unreported documents show mining company was aware of threat before country's worst environmental disaster but took no action, prosecutors allege. *The Guardian*. Retrieved from https://www.theguardian.com/world/2018/feb/28/brazil-dam-collapse-samarco-fundao-mining

Gray, D. (2018). BHP settles US class action over Samarco dam failure for $67 million. *The Herald Sun*. Retrieved from https://www.smh.com.au/business/companies/bhp-settles-us-class-action-over-samarco-dam-failure-for-67-million-20180809-p4zwel.html

Lo, C. (2018). Samarco dam disaster: dealing with the fallout of a tragedy. Mining Safety, Retrieved from https://www.mining-technology.com/mining-safety/samarco-dam-disaster-dealing-fallout-tragedy

Questions

(1) With respect to the priorities identified in the chapter on crisis and risk management, review what the company had done to prepare for the crisis and how it managed the situation following the disaster.

(2) What does the case information show about the difficulties faced by management when balancing cost and sociopolitical responsibilities?

(3) Identify the responsibilities that would have been taken on by the HRM function during the disaster and following the event.

(2) Mental Health and Wellbeing at Work

Just Managing: Critical Care in Intensive Care Units

Background

HospitalCo intensive care unit (ICU) is a 20-bed level 3 unit (which is the highest and most complex with the sickest patients) with a 90% bed occupancy. Because of the nursing shortage, on most days the rostered number of nurses on a shift is insufficient for the 18 or 19 patients, and continually puts more pressure on staff. The nurse-to-patient ratio for mechanically ventilated patients is 1:1 plus a shift coordinator and an admissions/resource nurse, so for each shift four or five extra nurses are needed.

Casual pool or agency nurses are employed on a shift-by-shift basis. These nurses choose this lifestyle for flexibility, and to suit their family, childcare, travel or study needs. Some nurses are regular extras to the HospitalCo unit, some are unknown to the regular staff, and they can be unfamiliar with the environment. These staff are usually allocated less complex patients, so take a lighter patient load than the regular experienced staff. They often also need supervision and support to safely care for their allocated patient, putting more strain on the workload of core staff.

Last year a 12-hour-shift roster pattern was introduced to the HospitalCo ICU. Advantages to 12-hour shifts are that nurses work less shifts per roster, which can be desirable for some. More than 50% of nurses choose this option, with the remainder preferring to work the traditional 8- or 10-hour shift pattern. Disadvantages to the 12-hour shift pattern are that nurses work 50% of their shifts on nights, the shift is long and can be tiring, and recovery time can take longer. In addition, there is less opportunity for professional development and unit communication. Managing the two roster patterns to ensure that there is always a nurse to care for each patient is complex.

In the last few years, annual turnover of staff in the ICU has been 20%, reflecting the national average for critical care nursing. This has also impacted upon the roster profile, as there are usually five or six graduate nurses and nurses new to the intensive care environment on a given shift – all requiring supervision and support.

Case Profile

Jo is a Clinical Nurse in the ICU and has worked there for seven years, and has held the position for the past four years. Jo completed a postgraduate certificate in intensive care nursing five years ago. For most shifts Jo is the coordinator or admission nurse; these roles are the most senior on the shift and can be stressful. This evening Jo arrived on night duty at 21:00 to find that there were 14 rostered nurses (including three new graduate nurses and two nurses on orientation) to care for the 19 patients in the ICU. This wasn't an unusual situation and the hospital manager was still ringing the nursing agency trying to find more staff to cover the shift. Two of the regular staff on days off had agreed to work an extra shift, and two nurses from the evening shift had agreed to work double shifts, which would be great for that shift, but would mean that they wouldn't be working the next day and so the morning shift would be short – an on-going problem, and further potential source of tension between shift managers. The medical consultant on duty had agreed that the one patient who was not mechanically ventilated could be transferred out to a ward. This would help relieve the ICU staffing problem, but Jo was well aware that transfers out of ICU out of hours are associated with high risk, which was less than ideal.

Finally it looked as if there were enough staff for the patients for the night. Now Jo had to work out how to safely allocate nurses to the patients to factor in the skill mix (capacity of nurse to care for complexity of patient) and the supervision and support required by the inexperienced nurses. As usual the pressure was on the experienced ICU staff to take on their own complex patients with the extra load of supervising the inexperienced staff. In addition Jo needed to have a plan to staff for an unexpected admission during the night. She also needed to be able to attend a code call anywhere in the hospital as the ICU shift coordinator was a member of the resuscitation team.

Jo had allocated one of the graduate nurses, Pam, to a young male patient, Ash, who was physiologically stable, recovering from chest trauma. He had a tracheostomy and was on a ventilation weaning regime. This would be simple enough on its own, but it appeared that Ash was becoming agitated. Pam had no experience in dealing with this type of patient and her support person was busy with her own unstable patient. The support staff member was well known in the unit for not being friendly to junior staff. Once she had reviewed the sickest patients on the shift with the night registrar, Jo had planned to spend some time with Pam to discuss how to assess and manage Ash's agitation. Before she got to Pam and her patient, however, Jo heard the emergency alarm ringing in that direction and so hurried over. Ash had pulled out his tracheostomy tube and tried to get out of bed, but Pam had tried to restrain him, with both of them falling to the floor. Jo called for help and calmly managed the event. Jo's attention then turned to Pam, who had hurt her back and was distressed.

'What a terrible start to a career in ICU' Jo thought, and felt guilty that she had not been able to provide more support to Pam. Jo had many pressures at the beginning of that shift; she had felt unsupported herself and now felt that she had let down Pam. She wouldn't be surprised if Pam didn't want to continue working in the ICU anymore, and wondered if she really needed all this stress herself.

Written by Fenella Gill

Questions

(1) What intervention strategies would you recommend in the short-term?
(2) What intervention strategies would you recommend in the long-term to reduce the turnover rate of 20%?

(3) The Dark Side of Work

A Learning Organisation in Action

The health sector is a place of work that experiences significant workplace violence as research across countries testifies, with patient-focussed violence a particular issue. One of the key areas of risk is the Accident and Emergency Department. Criminal penalties have been used in some jurisdictions to attempt to prevent these issues. A further strategy is to develop guidelines and recommendations. However, research continues to indicate that workplace violence against healthcare workers remains high, and in many cases continues to increase, particularly as drugs like 'ice' create psychotic episodes for those using the drugs.

A study by Gates et al. (2011) in the US explored the development, implementation and subsequent evaluation of a violence intervention programme over a four-year period. The approach used an action learning methodology, which involved addressing a real and complex issue through a problem-solving and learning approach. Following initial action, a process of reflection and review was undertaken (Rigg, 2014) on the complex nature of the issue. The group was comprised of academic researchers, and key stakeholders, that is, hospital employees and administrators. Using focus groups to initially gather information about workplace violence issues, intervention strategies were then developed. Initial findings from the study indicated that the planned interventions strategies were relevant, acceptable, feasible and comprehensive (Gates et al., 2011, p. 38). What was seen as particularly important was agreement from the stakeholders on the best way to address workplace violence.

Written by Peter Holland and Ross Donohue

Questions

(1) What type of learning is focussing on penalties for violence in the hospital system – why?

(2) What type of learning is focussing on guidelines and recommendations – why?

(3) What type of learning is undertaken in the process outlined by Gates et al. (2011) – why?

Section IV

Emerging Issues at Work

Chapter 9

To Test or Not to Test: Drug and Genetic Testing in the 21st Century Workplace

Peter Holland and Tse Leng Tham

Introduction

Whilst the concept of monitoring and surveillance has been part of the workplace for centuries, the advancements in technologies combined with the availability and diminished costs, has created a significant shift in the type and intensity of monitoring and surveillance not least in the sphere of biological testing. The advancement has not only been extensive but also invasive. From a biological perspective, drug testing was once seen as applicable for critical incident professions (such as pilots) and associated with large organisations that had the resources to undertake such operations. However, drug testing is now within the realms of most organisations. In addition, the emerging issues and availability of genetic testing also opens up a further Pandora's Box of ethical, legal and social complexities with regards to the acquisition of information on each individual's make-up in the workplace.

As these issues permeate the workplace, it is often HR who needs to make decisions on the impact of biological monitoring and surveillance. This includes having to weigh the cost and benefits – both tangible (cost) and intangible (employment relationship) – of these decisions such as the impact on trust within the employee–employer relationship – the bedrock of good human resource management (HRM). Other key considerations also include the impact of these decisions on employment relations, privacy and ethics. Issues and debates that surround the implementation of these processes, therefore, need to be more fully understood. They also need to be considered within the context of two distinct paths for management to take – that is, to test or not to test?

Biological Testing: Drug Testing in the Workplace

Substance abuse and the potential dangers it poses in the workplace are well documented in terms of their negative impact from both human and economic perspectives (Bouchery, Harwood, Sacks, Simon, & Brewer, 2011; French, Maclean, Sindelar, &

137

Fang, 2011; Gates, Grove, & Copeland, 2013; Holland, 2016; Roche, Pidd, & Kostadinov, 2016). These issues are often the catalyst for the use of biological forms of monitoring and surveillance in the workplace. For example, a key argument for enacting such testing is the need to provide a safe workplace. Employers are generally subject to legal liability through the actions and/or omissions of their employees regardless of their state of mind. The use of drug testing programmes in both employment and pre-employment testing is argued to help reduce accidents and is potentially an effective way of removing the issue of substance abuse in the workplace (Ames & Bennet, 2011; Flynn, 1999; Holland, Pyman, & Teicher, 2005). These points provide a compelling case for drug testing in the workplace. Firstly, to ensure that the employee is meeting his/her contractual obligations to a satisfactory standard. Secondly, to meet the employer's requirements of duty of care under health and safety legislation (Bohle & Quinlan, 2000; Holland, 2016; Holland et al., 2005). Implicit in these points is the potential that employers who do not have drug testing policies and programmes are maintaining an unsafe workplace (Webb & Festa, 1994).

However, the cost-effectiveness and overall value of drug testing is questionable. As Gip (1999) points out, research has found that most workers who use illicit drugs never use them at work, and when they use drugs on their own time, they do so in a way that does not affect work performance. Further, within the scope of the employment contract, performance is an important and related consideration in the drug testing debate. As DesJardine and McCall (1990, p. 203) point out: 'To what level of performance are employers entitled to?' If an employee's productivity is satisfactory and he/she is meeting contractual obligations, the knowledge of drug use on grounds of productivity is not pertinent. Further, whilst the issue of duty of care is important, not every job has the potential to do harm. DesJardine and McCall (1990) argue that by saying employers can use drug testing to prevent harm is in effect not to say that every employer has the right to know about the drug use of every employee. In this context therefore, less intrusive testing alternatives such as impairment testing to determine fitness for work are likely to be more effective and are less likely to raise privacy, fairness or ethical concerns. These are important considerations for employees and their representatives when drug testing is being considered or implemented in the workplace.

From an employee's perspective, a further consideration is the principal of the right to privacy (Greenwood, Holland, & Choon, 2006). Using Mills' principle of liberty, Bowie and Duska (1990) argue that employees have the right to do whatever they wish as long as it does not harm the employer. In this context, if a person chooses to partake in illicit drugs outside of their work commitments, it is of no concern to the employer so long as it does not impinge on work performance (Bowie & Duska, 1990; Greenwood et al., 2006). In addition, drug testing can suffer from accuracy problems. Typically, drug tests cannot determine whether the effects of illicit drugs, which may remain in the system for days and even weeks, will substantially impair or affect performance. Webb and Festa (1994) also note that the link between drug usage and on-the-job injuries is tenuous at best. If drug use in the private domain of the lives of employees does not impinge on performance at work, would such drug testing at the workplace be akin to Henry Ford's 'sociology department' where investigators monitored the private lives of the workers and their families to ensure that they were leading 'healthy' and 'moral' lifestyles?

Additionally, drug testing may also uncover other medical conditions or the use of over-the-counter or prescribed drugs by employees (such as metabolites of morphine), which have the potential to affect the employment status of workers (Holland, 2016). Employees also have a right to 'informational privacy' (Holland et al., 2005). This supports DesJardine and McCall (1990) and Greenwood et al. (2006), who argue the employee's right to privacy is violated when personal information is harvested which is irrelevant to the job. Therefore, the argument that the innocent has nothing to fear from drug testing is erroneous, because it may violate employee rights – particularly if testing has the potential to provide the employer with generic medical information which is not relevant to the contractual relationship (Cranford, 2001). In addition, mandatory testing may be open to improper or malicious use of procedures to intimidate or target employees who undertake activities that may be unpopular with management, such as union activism (Webb & Festa, 1994). In addition, in this day and age the potential for this information to be 'hacked' is not to be underestimated. Therefore, the use of drug testing within the workplace may create an atmosphere of insecurity, oppression and anxiety in employees, and may actually result in lower performance and higher turnover (Bohle & Quinlan, 2000) Whilst methodological problems remain (see Holland, 2016; Holland et al., 2005), it is also worth noting the internet is replete with tips on how to mask illicit drug use and evade drug tests and detection. Indeed, as can be seen with the recent ban of the Russian team from the 2018 Winter Olympics, such processes can be developed at a very sophisticated level.

Within the larger context of the employment relationship, work culture and the social environment have also been identified as critical and complex factors in the drug testing debate (Frone, 2009). For example, a culture of drug use – both legal and illicit drugs – in geographically isolated locations has been linked to the physical and dangerous nature of the work (see Allsop, Phillips, & Calogero, 2001; Allsop & Pidd, 2001). This leads to other cultural issues in the workplace, with research finding a link between the nature of work in general and associated drug use (Allsop et al., 2001; French et al., 2011). Issues of control, alienation, isolation and stress – linked with individuals' perceptions of their powerlessness – have been identified as factors related to drug use in the workplace (Ames & Grube, 1999; Bohle & Quinlan, 2000; Greenburg & Greenburg, 1995; Roche, Kostadinov, & Fischer, 2017). As Midford (2001, p. 46) argues:

> In the workplace, holding the view that drug use is a problem for the individual worker is functional from the point of view of the employers, because it avoids any exploration of how the workplace may contribute to the problem. However, to gain an understanding of workplace drug problems, one must look at a full range of factors that influence patterns of drug use.

Unions and others argue (Holland et al., 2005; Mansfield, 2001), for the joint development and implementation of drug testing policy by employee representatives, employees and employers, particularly where the misuse of alcohol or illicit drugs are identified as workplace issues (Pidd, Roche, & Buisman-Piljman, 2011; Spicer, Miller, & Smith, 2003). Indeed, any policies dealing with workplace hazards and health and safety should be jointly developed and implemented, with a focus on promoting safety at work through addressing the causes of alcohol or illicit drug misuse in the workplace (Frone, 2016; Schou & Moan, 2016). This necessitates a consultative, educative and rehabilitative approach rather than a punitive approach; and the maintenance of confidentiality at all levels (Holland, 2016; Mansfield, 2001).

This pluralist stance is based upon the argument that it is only when drugs and alcohol are misused to the extent that the user cannot properly and safely carry out regular duties insomuch that a need for control and prevention measures arise. In any consideration of an appropriate response, particularly in workplace, there must be an examination of the broader environmental factors pertaining to the individual workplace or industry (Frone, 2016; Roche et al., 2017). This is because the misuse of alcohol and other drugs may be symptomatic of other problems which are in the control of the employer. For example, shiftwork and longer working hours, monotonous or repetitive work, fatigue, workplace stressors or job insecurity and control (Frone, 2016; Holland, 2016).

This approach is supported by the work of Duffy and Ask (2001) and Hagen, Egan, and Eltringham (1992) who found a link between higher alcohol consumption and work pressure, lack of control and over-work. This is also supported by the work of Phillip (2001), and Roman, Johnson, and Blum (2000) in terms of the relationship between stress at work and increased alcohol consumption. Indeed, the fatigue generated by these factors combined with increased deregulation of the labour market (job insecurity), raises major issues regarding occupational health and safety in the workplace (Holland, 2016; Holland et al., 2005; Nolan, 2000). As Mansfield (2001) notes, if management is truly interested in these issues, a more holistic approach should be adopted. This, for example, should include fatigue monitoring and management systems. This broadens the drug testing debate and raises the critical issue of fitness for duty.

Holistic Approaches and Fitness for Duty

The issue of fitness for duty often raises a more subtle and complex issue of control in the workplace. Employees and unions often see the introduction of measures such as drug testing as management exercising increased authority under the guise of 'managerial prerogative' (Wickham & Holland, 2002), and as a strategy to marginalise the countervailing power of unions, particularly where there is no consultation on the subject (see Holland et al., 2005; Webb & Festa, 1994; Wickham & Holland, 2002). This perspective has come increasingly under review with the emergence of HRM, underpinned by a unitarist philosophy. This can potentially see testing becoming a major issue of conflict between management, employees and their unions (Holland, 2016; Holland et al., 2005). The need to strike a balance between the employer's legal obligations and employees' rights is a complex and sensitive issue in the development of drug policies. Similarly, Nolan (2000) and Holland (2016) have pointed out those legal obligations that are too dogmatically defined can easily clash with industrial relations. This was highlighted by Holland (2016), who noted that in a case which overturned the convention of context in Australia – a zero-tolerance policy overrode the context within which the positive drug test occurred (despite there being no link to work incident) – the consequences of this being that outside work activities now potentially come into the purview of the employer.

The need for a more holistic and pragmatic approach has led to the advocacy of a non-discriminatory testing regime for a wide range of physical and psychological factors which may impair performance (Holland, 2016; Nolan & Nomchong, 2001). Whilst the search for appropriate tests remains problematic, the philosophical underpinning of this approach is that the causes of impairment are not confined to circumstances within the employee's control and may be impacted by workplace conditions which are under the employer's control. Only a holistic approach can address these broader issues.

Biological Testing: Genetic Testing and the Workplace

Genetic testing involves the acquisition of a person's genetic information. This could be done by testing of a small amount of genetic material such as a drop of blood or hair sample to examine a person's deoxyribonucleic acid (DNA), ribonucleic acid (RNA) or similar protein to determine the predisposition to certain inherited disorders (Mainsbridge, 2002). Acquiring an individual's genetic information may also be retrieved via comparatively non-invasive method in the form of detailed medical history. As discussed earlier in this chapter, it is increasingly commonplace for employers to have such information available to them or to conduct a wide range health assessment such as drug testing on employees or potential employees. In view of rapid advancements in genetic technology and the improvements in the accuracy and availability of genetic tests, there is the potential for genetic information to be used in pre-employment screening or as a means of continuing health surveillance for occupational health and safety purposes (Australian Law Reform Commission, 2003; Mainsbridge, 2002). In fact, such practices have already gained traction particularly in the United States, where genetic testing at the workplace has a relatively long history (Duffy, 2010). Elsewhere in Australia (Brandt-Rauf, Borak, & Deubner, 2015), Canada (Godard et al., 2003), and some European countries (Hendriks, 1997; Wedderburn, Rae, Williams, Carey-Heaton, & Miedzybrodzka, 2014), this contention of genetic testing at the workplace is increasingly being cast under the proverbial microscope as it becomes a topic that has raised significant and complex ethical, legal and social issues.

Although it was only in the last decade or so that the complexities around genetic testing in an employment context has received considerably more attention, its application at the workplace can be dated back to the 1930s. In the interest of safeguarding the health and safety of employees, genetic testing was used in pre-employment screening to avoid hiring those who were predisposed to bronchitis in the pottery industry[1] (Brandt-Rauf, Brandt-Rauf, Gershon, & Brandt-Rauf, 2011). Similarly, today much of the focus of using genetic testing at the workplace from the employer's perspective is the emphasis on exercising duty of care as mandated under occupation health and safety regulations (Brandt-Rauf et al., 2015; Mainsbridge, 2002). To this effect, genetic testing may be useful in providing information on an employee or potential employee's genetic predisposition where it may either pose a safety risk to the individual, coworker, or other third parties, or indicate that an individual may have increased susceptibility to certain workplace hazards (Mainsbridge, 2002).

Aside from fulfilling occupational health and safety obligations, employers may also have a vested economic interest in the potential use of genetic testing of employees. This relates closely to maximising the productivity of a workforce and minimising unnecessary expenditure. With such information, employers may be able to exclude individuals who have been identified with predispositions of developing a genetic condition that may impede their future ability to perform requirements of the job, and to do so safely (Otlowski, 2002). This may help reduce potential productivity losses and costs associated with absenteeism, sick leave entitlements, health insurance costs, employing and training temporary or permanent replacements (Mainsbridge, 2002; Miller, 2017; Otlowski, 2002). Arguably, on a more pragmatic level, genetic information

---

[1]It has been well documented that long-term exposure to silica dust and toxic gases such as part of the pottery-making process may cause serious health problems including chronic bronchitis, emphysema and tuberculosis.

may also assist in maximising the selection of the most suitable applicant for the job. Whilst the legal, privacy and ethical considerations and implications of this approach in many advanced market economies (AMEs) is beyond the scope of this chapter, clearly this is where genetic testing could push the employment law boundaries, under the guise of improving health and safety protection for the employer and the employee. Significant concerns around this (mis)use of such information which could adversely impact employees' employability and right to privacy remain. The dilemma is that at one level, workplace genetic testing has the potential to protect the health of employees, but such information used the wrong way can be an agent for discrimination. The subtext to such concerns is the potential use of such genetic information to illegally discriminate against or dismiss employees with predispositions to developing certain genetic conditions (Miller, 2017).

Genetic Discrimination
Genetic discrimination, the differential treatment of an individual on the account of actual or assumed genetic make-up (Geller et al., 1996), is a growing concern in the workplace context as it has capacity for far-reaching implications that is not limited only to the individual involved, but also to the society at large (Duffy, 2010; Otlowski, Taylor, & Barlow-Stewart, 2003). The underlying concern here is whether employers are equipped with sufficient knowledge and expertise in interpreting genetic information appropriately and then applying it in making employee-related decisions *fairly*. For instance, genetic information differs from other forms of health indicators in that it is:

- not an absolute indicator that a genetic disorder will develop;
- limited in what it can predict. Genetic information reveals only possibilities rather than certainties; and
- unable to predict the timing of onset nor the extent to which symptoms will develop as the manifestation of genetic disorders is dependent on the complex interaction between genetics, environmental and lifestyle factors (e.g. stress levels, diet and exercise) (Mainsbridge, 2002).

As such, a potential candidate may have a family history of positive tests for a genetic mutation, for example Huntington's disease, but this only indicates a person's increased susceptibility in developing this disease. When, how and the severity of symptoms likely to develop (and therefore, the extent to which this candidate's ability to perform inherent job requirements may or will be impaired) is not something genetic information alone can conclusively reveal. There is a possibility that this candidate, throughout his or her working life, may never develop symptoms of this genetic disorder. Would this candidate not then be unfairly discriminated against if he or she was refused a job on the account of this genetic information?

Evidence suggests that cases of inappropriate discrimination based on lack of understanding of genetic information in workplaces is a growing concern internationally (Otlowski et al., 2003; Taylor, Treloar, Barlow-Stewart, Stranger, & Otlowski, 2008). An iconic case in Australia illustrates these concerns – a young applicant for a position in the public sector revealed in the final entry requirement medical test that there is a familial history of Huntington's disease, which meant a 50% probability that he has inherited that genetic mutation. A condition of his employment was a negative genetic test for the relevant genetic mutation. However, the applicant refused to take the test as he did not want to be privy to the knowledge of whether he was indeed a carrier of that genotype. He was initially refused the job but upon an appeal process, that decision was reversed. However, conditions of his employment included a reduction in superannuation and other benefits for the first decade of tenure. These would only return to the standard rates in the case where he did not develop the disease (Mainsbridge, 2002; Taylor et al., 2008).

On a macro-perspective, by excluding individuals such as the young applicant in the case above from certain forms of employment, are we, in effect, creating a 'genetic underclass' consisting of individuals who are considered unemployable because of their genetic make-up (Duffy, 2010; Mainsbridge, 2002)? Individuals who happen to be 'asymptomatic ill', where they may test positive for certain genetic disorders but never actually develop the relevant symptoms are essentially denied opportunities of employment and societal contribution (Mainsbridge, 2002). The young applicant in the earlier case has a 50% chance of not carrying the genotype for Huntington's disease. Indeed, he may never, in his 'working life', develop symptoms of this genetic disorder even if he was a carrier. Had the young applicant not appealed the initial rejection on the account of his familial medical history, would we have excluded a potential key talent and his contributions to the organisation and society at large?

Another critical concern highlighted by the issues above is individual privacy. Genetic testing is likely to reveal information that is highly sensitive, such as insights into the future health and life prospects of an individual. Individuals may not want others to be privy to such sensitive information or they themselves may not want to have that information. When such testing is mandated as a condition of employment, are we infringing an individual's 'right to know' and informational privacy? This is a pertinent question especially in contexts of varying levels of legal protection around the world when it comes to privacy laws. In many advanced market economies (AMEs) like Australia, at present, there is no protection for employment records of current and former employees. In other words, if an applicant goes through pre-employment genetic testing and goes on to become an employee with that organisation, such information may be disclosed to other parties, including subsequent employers and insurers. Therefore, this may not only have implications for the individual's future employability, but also potentially, his or her insurability. Additionally, the concerns of privacy here are also compounded considering genetic information is shared and relational in nature wherein it could reveal information about family members as well. In essence, this takes monitoring and surveillance in the workplace to a new level of intrusion, particularly with regard to the issue of informational privacy. As Gilliom and Monahan (2012) point out, managerial control has gone from supervision to 'Super Vision'. Let's also not forget the clear and present danger of these types of records being electronically hacked.

Clearly, the use of genetic testing particularly in the context of employment and the workplace is still one riddled with complexities and challenges. This is also one aspect the law in many AMEs which has not kept pace with the technological advances. For now, much of the onus is placed on employers to recognise the unique ethical, legal and social challenges of applying genetic testing in the workplace and to take steps in ensuring its usage (if actually needed) balances the needs of both the employer's responsibilities to safeguard the health and safety of employees, employees' rights to privacy and equal workplace opportunities. As per the theme of this chapter, these are two roads here – to test or not to test. As Duffy (2010) notes:

Personhood and what it means to be human is being challenged by advances in genetic technology. We must not forget that we are in a prime position to determine the social significance of genetic information. There is a human element to genetic information that is separate and must remain divorced from the science. (p. 158)

The Ethics of Biological Monitoring and Surveillance

It is clear that the intensity and depth of biological monitoring and surveillance in the twenty-first century has moved apace. It is also clear that legal guidelines are struggling to keep pace across the world and across state boundaries. Perhaps it is at this point that we look to ethics to guide us in the development of policies and practices. Taking a Utilitarianism position of considering the greatest good for the greatest number of people affected by the action (Crane & Matten, 2016), it is difficult to see how engaging in blanket biological monitoring and surveillance is the morally preferable action. This is because of the potential negative outcomes identified, including damage to the employment relationship underpinned (see Holland, 2016; Martin, Wellen, & Grimmer, 2016) underpinned by a lack of trust – the antitheses of contemporary HRM objectives. Taking a Deontological approach would also consider such practices to not be in the interest of the individual or organisations. The first principle of universality reflects the fact that management don't generally place themselves under the same level of monitoring and surveillance. Focussing on the second principle of human dignity, the question to ask seems self-evident that employees would be unlikely to freely decide in agreeing to employers undertaking the levels of invasive biological scrutiny described in this chapter without concerns. Hence, the level and intent of these practices are morally questionable under this second principle. Finally, the third principle necessitates the question whether every other rational being, including your family, friends and strangers agree to these levels of scrutiny. It seems unlikely that all other rational human beings would accept the levels of biological monitoring and surveillance described above. However, we need to be realistic and accept that these potential forms of scrutiny will only increase. A key feature therefore, is how we manage them and equally, and the decision can still remain knowing what we know about these issues is – to test or not to test.

Conclusions

This chapter illustrates the problems and complexity surrounding the development of biological monitoring and surveillance in the workplace as it moves apace in the twenty-first century. Appropriate levels of monitoring and surveillance are a vexed question. At what point does the prerogative of the employer's right to protect, manage and run their organisations conflict or infringe upon employees' rights to informational privacy? It is clear from this overview that detailed assessments of both the tangible and intangible costs and benefits can be made in relation to biological monitoring and surveillance in the workplace. First, the issue of managerial prerogative versus employee privacy rights needs to be considered. Second, how monitoring and surveillance mechanisms are introduced (if at all), and how and why the information is being used (and protected) needs to be understood. Third, despite organisations having policies on drug and alcohol testing, and hopefully genetic testing, the issue of trust and commitment within the employment relationship cannot be underestimated.

In other words, the fundamental question in this context is *why* organisations have decided to implement biological monitoring and surveillance programmes? Without consideration of these issues, a breakdown of the employment relationship can occur. Understanding the views of all stakeholders is required to ensure all available options are considered, all available information is consulted, and the practicalities of monitoring and surveillance are fully understood.

References

Allsop, S., Phillips, M., & Calogero, C. (Eds.). (2001). *Drug and work: Responding to alcohol and other drug problems in Australian workplaces*, Melbourne, Australia: IP Communications.

Allsop, S., & Pidd, K. (2001). The nature of drug related harm in the workplace. In S. Allsop, M. Phillips, & C. Calogero (Eds.), *Drug and work: Responding to alcohol and other drug problems in Australian workplaces* (pp. 4–21). Melbourne, Australia: IP Communications.

Ames, G., & Bennett, J. (2011). Prevention interventions of alcohol problems in the workplace: A review and guiding framework. *Alcohol Research and Health, 34*(2), 175–187.

Ames, G., & Grube, J. W. (1999). Alcohol availability and workplace drinking: Mixed method analysis, *Journal of Studies of Alcohol, 60*(3), 383–393.

Australian Law Reform Commission. (2003). Essentially yours: The protection of human genetic information in Australia (Report No. 96). Retrieved from https://www.alrc.gov.au/publications/report-96

Bohle, P., & Quinlan, M. (2000). *Managing health and safety: A multidisciplinary approach* (2nd ed.). Melbourne, Australia: MacMillan.

Bouchery, E., Harwood, H., Sacks, J., Simon, C., & Brewer, R. (2011). Economic costs of excessive alcohol consumption in the US, 2006. *American Journal of Preventative Medicine, 41*(5), 516–524.

Bowie, N. E., & Duska, R. F. (1990). *Business ethics* (2nd ed.). Upper Saddle River, NJ: Prentice Hall.

Brandt-Rauf, P., Borak, J., & Deubner, D. C. (2015). Genetic screening in the workplace. *Journal of Occupational and Environmental Medicine, 57*(3), e17–e18.

Brandt-Rauf, S. I., Brandt-Rauf, E., Gershon, R., & Brandt-Rauf, P. W. (2011). The differing perspectives of workers and occupational medicine physicians on the ethical, legal and social issues of genetic testing in the workplace. *NEW SOLUTIONS: A Journal of Environmental and Occupational Health Policy, 21*(1), 89–102.

Crane, A., & Matten, D. (2016). *Business ethics: Managing corporate citizenship and sustainability in the age of globalization* (4th ed.). Oxford: Oxford University Press.

Cranford, M. (2001). Drug testing and the right to privacy. *Journal of Business Ethics, 17*, 1805–1815.

DesJardine, J. R., & McCall, J. J. (1990). *Contemporary issues in business ethics* (2nd ed.). Belmont, CA: Wadsworth Publishing Company.

Duffy, J. (2010). 12 fingers or one, it's how you play? Genetic discrimination in the Australian workforce. *Alternative Law Journal, 35*(3), 155–158.

Duffy, J., & Ask, A. (2001). Ten ingredients for developing and implementing a drug and alcohol policy in your workplace. *Drugs and work: Responding to alcohol and other drug problems in Australian workplaces*. Melbourne, Australia: IP Communications.

Flynn, G. (1999). How to prescribe drug testing. *Workforce, 78*(1), 107–109.

French, M., Maclean, J., Sindelar, J., & Fang, H. (2011). The morning after: Alcohol misuse and employment problems. *Applied Economics, 43*(21), 2705–2720.

Frone, M. (2009). Does a permissive workplace substance use climate affect employees who do not use alcohol and drugs at work? A US national study. *Psychology of Addictive Behaviors*, *23*(2), 386–390.

Frone, M. (2016). Work stress and alcohol use: Developing and testing a biphasic self-medication model. *Work Stress*, *30*(4), 374–394.

Gates, P., Grove, R., & Copeland, J. (2013). Impact of substance use on the Australian workforce, *Journal of Addiction and Prevention*, *1*(2), 1–9.

Geller, L. N., Alper, J. S., Billings, P. R., Barash, C. I., Beckwith, J., & Natowicz, M. R. (1996). Individual, family, and societal dimensions of genetic discrimination: A case study analysis. *Science and Engineering Ethics*, *2*, 71–88.

Gip, M. A. (1999). Drug testing assailed. *Security Management*, *43*(12), 16.

Gilliom, J., & Monahan T. (2012). *SuperVision*. Chicago, IL: University of Chicago Press.

Godard, B., Raeburn, S., Pembrey, M., Bobrow, M., Farndon, P., & Aymé, S. (2003). Genetic information and testing in insurance and employment: Technical, social and ethical issues. *European Journal of Human Genetics*, *11*(S2), 123–142.

Greenburg, E., & Greenburg, S. (1995). Work alienation and problem alcohol behavior. *Journal of Health and Social Behavior*, *36*(1), 83–102.

Greenwood, M., Holland, P., & Choon, K. (2006). Re-evaluating drug testing: Questions of moral and symbolic control. In J. Deckop, B. Giacalone, & C. Jurkiewicz (Eds.), *Human resource management ethics: In the information age* (pp. 161–180). Greenwich, CT: IAP.

Hagen, R., Egan, D., & Eltringham, A. (1992). Work, drugs and alcohol, *Occupational health and safety commission inquiry into alcohol, drugs and the workplace*. Melbourne, Australia: Victorian Occupational Health and Safety Commission.

Hendriks, A. (1997) Genetics, human rights and employment: American and European perspectives. *Medicine and Law*, *16*, 557–565.

Holland, P. (2016). Drug testing in Australia: Still a contested terrain. *Journal of Industrial Relations*, *58*(5), 688–696.

Holland, P. J., Pyman, A., & Teicher, J. (2005). Negotiating the contested terrain of drug testing in the Australian workplace. *Journal of Industrial Relations*, *47*(3), 326–338.

Mainsbridge, A. (2002). Employers and genetic information: A new frontier for discrimination. *Macquarie Law Journal*, *2*, 61–85.

Mansfield, B. (2001). Impairment of employees: The union view. Retrieved from http://www.actu.asn.au/public/news/1056670370_26248.html

Martin, A. J., Wellen, J. M., & Grimmer, M. R. (2016). An eye on your work: How empowerment affects the relationship between electronic surveillance and counterproductive work behaviours. *The International Journal of Human Resource Management*, *27*(21), 2635–2651.

Midford, R. (2001). The nature and extent of drug related harm in the workplace. In S. Allsop, M. Phillips, & C. Calogero (Eds.), *Drug and work: Responding to alcohol and other drug problems in Australian workplaces* (pp. 42–56). Melbourne, Australia: IP Communications.

Miller, S. (2017). Would proposed law require genetic testing for employees? *HRNews*. Retrieved from https://search-proquest-com.ezproxy.lib.monash.edu.au/docview/18796 40493?accountid=12528

Nolan, J. (2000). Unions stuffed or stoned. *Workers Online*, *71*, 1–5.

Nolan, J., & Nomchong, K. (2001). Fitness for duty: Recent legal developments. ACIRRRT Working Paper No. 69. ACIRRT, University of Sydney, Sydney, Australia.

Otlowski, M. F. (2002). Employers' use of genetic test information: Is there a need for regulation? *Australian Journal of Labour Law*, *15*(1), 1–39.

Otlowski, M. F., Taylor, S. D., & Barlow-Stewart, K. K. (2002). Australian empirical study into genetic discrimination. *Genetics in Medicine*, *4*(5), 392–395.

Otlowski, M. F., Taylor, S. D., & Barlow-Stewart, K. K. (2003). Genetic discrimination: Too few data. *European Journal of Human Genetics, 11*(1), 1–2.

Phillip, M. (2001). The prevalence of drug-use and risk of drug-related harm in the workplace. In S. Allsop, M. Phillips, & C. Calogero (Eds.), (2001). *Drug and work: Responding to alcohol and other drug problems in Australian workplaces* (pp. 20–41). Melbourne, Australia: IP Communications.

Pidd, K., Roche, A., & Buisman-Pijlman, F. (2011). Intoxicated workers: Findings from a national Australian survey. *Addiction, 106*(9), 1623–1633.

Roche, A., Kostadinov, V., & Fischer, J. (2017). Stress and addiction. In C. L. Cooper & J. C. Quick (Eds.), *The handbook of stress and health: A guide to research and practice* (pp. 252–282), Chichester: John Wiley & Sons.

Roche, A., Pidd, K., & Kostadinov, V. (2016). Alcohol- and drug-related absenteeism: A costly problem. *Australian and New Zealand Journal of Public Health, 40*(3), 236–238.

Roman, R. M., Johnson, J. A., & Blum, T. (2000). The workplace, employer and employee. In D. B. Cooper (Ed.), *Alcohol use* (pp. 121–133), Abingdon: Radcliffe Medical Press Ltd.

Schou, L., & Moan, I. S. (2016). Alcohol use–sickness absence association and the moderating role of gender and socioeconomic status: A literature review. *Drug and Alcohol Review, 35*(2), 158–169.

Spicer, R., Miller, T., & Smith, G. (2003). Worker substance use, workplace problems and the risk of occupational injury: A matched case-control study. *Journal of Studies on Alcohol, 64*(4), 570–578.

Taylor, S., Treloar, S., Barlow-Stewart, K., Stranger, M., & Otlowski, M. (2008). Investigating genetic discrimination in Australia: A large-scale survey of clinical genetics clients. *Clinical Genetics, 74*(1), 20–30.

Webb, G., & Festa, J. (1994). Alcohol and other drug problems in the workplace: Is drug testing the appropriate solution, *Journal of Occupational Health and Safety, Australia and New Zealand, 10*(2), 95–106.

Wedderburn, S., Rae, D., Williams, J., Carey-Heaton, R., & Miedzybrodzka, Z. (2014). Genetic discrimination and predictive testing for Huntington's disease and familial cancer in Northern Scotland: The I-Respond-UK Study. *Neurol Neurosurg Psychiatry, 85*, 80.

Wickham, M., & Holland, P. (2002). Drug testing in the workplace: Unravelling the issues. *Journal of Occupational Health and Safety, Australia and New Zealand, 18*(1), 55–59.

Chapter 10

Employer and Employee Vetting: Reputation Management Challenges in the Information Age

Debora Jeske and Peter Holland

Introduction

The technology of the twenty-first century has created a paradigm shift in reputation management, and as such has made it an increasingly prominent issue particularly in recruitment and selection for the employer and job applicants. As traditional forms of information were replaced by electronic documentation and online resources, a new practice called 'cyber-vetting' emerged. Cyber-vetting is the proactive process of gathering online information in the recruitment and selection process (Berkelaar, 2014), facilitated by the presence of social media sites which has increased information gathering opportunities for employers. However, as more and more information about employers becomes available online, employer branding and reputations are increasingly subject to the views of their applicants and employees. Given the important role that employer branding and image plays for the attraction and retention of talent in contemporary research (e.g. Biswas & Suar, 2016; Russell & Brannan, 2016), online reputation management in the age of cyber-vetting and online review sites is becoming a challenge for many organisations.

This chapter therefore highlights the new challenges that arise for reputation management due to new cyber-vetting practices for employers, and most notably, HR professionals (Pabo-Nzaou, Lemieux, Beaupré, & Uwizeyemungu, 2016).

Cyber-vetting Practices and the Link to Reputation Management

Research has shown that much of the information on social media sites and other websites is unreliable, with information gathered being outdated, inaccurate or simply wrong. Many employers are unable to verify the information, rely on inaccurate information or take into account information that they should not consider in their decision-making (e.g. lifestyle choices). This creates a number of legal and ethical issues (Jeske & Shultz, 2016). Applicants and employees applying for promotion are unlikely to have the opportunity for redress, especially if they are not aware of what information is obtained about them online. However, when such situations come to light, employers may face irreparable brand damage and legal redress.

Similarly, applicants and employees can visit review websites such as glassdoor, Vault, LinkedIn, CareerLeak, Hallway and Monster to learn more about how other individuals review their potential or current employers. Glassdoor alone holds 40 million reviews of approximately 700,000 organisations (Heath, 2018). Reviews on these sites capture the experience of employees and applicants within their organisations. Posts may comment on culture, communication and leadership. This means many employees use online information about their organisation to reflect on their employer's brand and image, while applicants use these sites to find out whether the work and culture is a good fit for them (see work by Elving, Westhoff, Meeusen, & Schoonderbeek, 2012; Holland, 2014, chapters 2 and 9), frequently even before they apply for jobs. Indeed as Ranosa (2018) points out, those who use glassdoor to research their target organisation are more likely to stay on with a new employer than those who do not use such information when they apply. Negative reports can hint at a larger issue that needs to be addressed for current as well as future employees (Heath, 2018). Many review sites now allow employers to respond to negative reviews, giving them a voice in the process and a means to reassure employees and applicants.

However, the usefulness and merit of such reviews has its limits – both for employers but also applicants and employees. This is due to the design of such platforms. Unlike social media posts, most reviews on review sites can be submitted anonymously (a trend that has been described as 'Yelpfication' in Heath, 2018). Reviews are considered an individual's perspective, which means platforms do not assess the fidelity of the information. As a result, the review's accuracy and reliability are unknown, a problem for all users of such review sites (particularly employers, see Heath, 2018). Even if the review is unsubstantiated or misrepresents the employer, such posts are unlikely to be removed upon request by an employer. What is more, these developments mean that the management of reputations and expectations now starts well before organisations begin their hiring processes (Mosley, 2015). In response, many organisations now dedicate more and more resources to proactively managing their online presence, brand and image (see work and recommendations by Acikgoz & Bergman, 2016; Breaugh, 2013), as outlined in the next section.

Employer Reputation Management in the Context of Recruitment and Selection

In the context of employer reputation, two HR practices are particularly impacted by the use of cyber-vetting: recruitment and selection. Recruitment is frequently linked to campaigns that anticipate some cyber-vetting activity on the part of the potential employees. Careful branding is used to showcase a particular brand or establish a positive employer reputation. Such campaigns have been shown to have a positive effect on employer attractiveness and brand image (Carpentier et al., 2017) as well as attitudes towards employers across a variety of sectors (Carpentier et al., 2017; Ladkin & Buhalis, 2016; Sharma & Prasad, 2018). This has been particularly acknowledged in the context of talent management with employer branding becoming more and more important for employers who compete for a limited number of candidates (Uen, Ahlstrom, Chen, & Liu, 2015). Selection is the second component heavily influenced by cyber-vetting, most notably by employers (although employees may also use cyber-vetting to decide if they wish to accept an offer from a specific company). As noted, reviews on specialised websites are increasingly viewed by job applicants as outside the employer's control (Wolf, Sims, & Yang, 2015). Such reviewer sites contribute to the concerns about reputation management, as one negative review can lead applicants to ignore positive reviews (reflecting a so-called 'negativity bias', see Kanouse, 1984). This trend towards sharing one's views about employers via different media site is in line with evidence that more and more employees view social media type platforms as ways to express their voice (e.g. Holland, Cooper, & Hecker, 2016, 2018; Martin, Parry, & Flowers, 2015). Many employees have used social media and company review sites to discuss salaries, job conditions and share information with each other, often raising concerns of employers about what information (true or not) reaches the public domain (Ladkin & Buhalis, 2016).

These circumstances – mutual or reciprocal cyber-vetting – result in a significant challenge for employer reputation management. Indeed, more and more employers find themselves in the hot seat for a number of reasons. For example, organisations requesting information from applicants (e.g., about the number of children, marital status or information about the applicant's place of birth and other aspects not relevant to employment) may trigger negative applicant reactions which may even culminate in legal action (García-Izquierdo, Aguinis, & Ramos-Villagrasa, 2010). Such actions undermine not only applicants' trust but also employees' perceptions of procedural justice and the perceived motives and trustworthiness. In addition, procedural justice perceptions have been associated with turnover intention (Ko & Hur, 2014). Accordingly, violations of both procedural justice and perceived trustworthiness during the application process have been shown to reduce satisfaction with the process and intention to pursue employment with a given employer, and result in a posting to one of the websites discussed. Evidence indicates that job applicants are not just monitoring their own online profiles, but monitor their prospective employers' social media content as well (Hurrell, Scholarios, & Richards, 2017). This is particularly the case when employees and employers use social media for employment purposes (Holland et al., 2016; Hurrell et al., 2017). Not surprisingly, this means employers are now under scrutiny from employees and potentially at risk from social media campaigns themselves (Wheatcroft, 2016).

Organisations want to have the right people in the right place at the right time. In addition, they want to ensure person–organisation fit. However, this is where cyber-vetting frequently generates more information – and problems – than traditional approaches in recruitment and selection. Cyber-vetting is unlike conventional information gathering and background checks. These typically source public documents and records generally with the consent of the job applicants, through information provided via their resume. Cyber-vetting tends to be ad hoc and covert and thus without the permission, knowledge and therefore consent of the applicant (Berkelaar & Buzzanel, 2014). This might then lead to several legal liabilities due to the breadth and depth of information that is sourced, which infringe on the individual' s rights (e.g. no consent, privacy violations). Equally, the information sourced through algorithms may be false, misleading or inaccurate and by its covert nature precludes the applicants from either addressing or correcting false, out of date or misleading information. This is why the use of social media by employers and employees has been called a double-edged sword (Wheatcroft, 2016); the information may be wielded by and against current employees, job applicants and employers.

Good Practice for HR Professionals

HR departments are often by default the first department that applicants and new employees interact with. In addition, they are tasked with managing information about and for applicants and employees. As a result, HR professionals are frequently the first port of call for both applicants and employees in the case of negative events and experiences. This makes HR, though not necessarily voluntarily, the 'guardians of employer brand and reputation' (Yancey, 2017). This 'guardianship' leads us to formulate a number of points for HR professionals which they might find useful as starting points for discussions around reputation management:

- Information gathering activities associated with cyber-vetting require ethical, transparent and respectful processes. Corporate reputations may not just be damaged by reviews from customers or employees (see Schulze Horn et al., 2015). Applicants' impressions should be as important as employees' views, both online and offline. Indeed, many applicants are blunt in their critiques of organisational processes on reviewer sites (e.g. when they are ignored or no explanations are provided for rejections). Such reviews and branding disasters can easily put off prospective applicants in turn (Clifford, 2014). Providing at least minimal but timely feedback to applicants is not just a matter of courtesy, but also a wise choice if one wants to retain the reputation as a conscientious and reliable employer.

- While reputation management has been a business priority for some time (Hepburn, 2005), the emergence of employer review platforms has changed the extent and the speed with which employers need to engage with all parties (Hepburn, 2005; Ladkin & Buhalis, 2016). When organisations fail to respond in a timely fashion to negative reviews, they risk compounding the impression that they do not care about the experience of their employees and applicants. For example, a company review suggesting that 'sexual harassment was the norm' is not a good sign and may be a glimpse of a workplace culture that tolerates sexual misconduct (see Heath, 2018). Not responding to such reviews can be the death knell for any diversity initiatives. Having dedicated staff to monitor such review sites and to engage with all reviewers through feedback can reduce the fallout. In addition, such staff ought to inform management immediately about problematic conduct in the company, before these define the image of the company.

- The availability of HR as well as other departmental managers to deal with issues as they arise (and before they become part of the public domain) will be an important step to minimise reputational damage to an organisation. While HR practitioners are frequently sought out by employees when they face difficult times (Daniel, 2017), managers in all areas ought to take action when they become aware of issues that may affect the reputation of the organisation as a whole. Making exit interviews a regular feature and offering means for intraorganisational mediation are two small steps in the right direction. Training and development in understanding and managing these issues should be provided to every member of staff who supervises others within the organisation as well.

- Organisations are increasingly assessed in terms of the values they live and endorse. To succeed in the pursuit of positive employer brand reputations, policies, organisational culture, values and corporate reputation need to come together (Hepburn, 2005; Sivertzen, Ragnhild Nilsen, & Olafsen, 2013). The genuine and lived importance of values (e.g. Sivertzen et al., 2013), growth and development opportunities, as well as considerations for work-life balance have all been shown to influence applicants' intention to join organisations (e.g. Hepburn, 2005; Holliday Wayne & Casper, 2012; Sharma & Prasad, 2018). Asking employees and applicants about the perceived versus lived values may be an important step forward to understand why applicants refuse job offers, do not apply or withdraw from the application process midway.

- The source and valence of information (such as online reviews) that is used by applicants to make critical decisions need more attention. Or in the words of our colleagues, 'understanding the inferences applicants make from reputational information can help HR professionals develop and market their images more effectively' (Holliday Wayne & Casper, 2012, p. 123). This means it is important for HR professionals to engage with applicants in a more in-depth manner than before: connecting with applicants who decide to refuse offers is one way to identify value clashes. This might help internal staff identify which aspects of their processes and communication will need to be corrected, updated or reviewed.

- Several websites and consultancies generate employer-of-the year rankings and comparative lists. Many employers are keen to join these lists and ranks in order to benefit from the publicity that such ranks may generate as external recognition of employer practices has become more important to many prospective applicants (Holliday Wayne & Casper, 2012). Organisations need to consider the effect of both negative and positive press reports via third parties on their reputational capital. Developing social media and reputation policies that consider and keep track of emerging legal or federal legislation (case law) are important tasks for employers (Alaniz, 2016), particularly when social media and thus cyber-vetting is used in recruitment and selection (Ladkin & Buhalis, 2016).

- In the absence of ethical guidance, a few hypothetical arguments may demonstrate the issue of ethics and justice. One option is to take a consequential approach which judges the morality of an issue based on the consequences it generates (Crane & Matten, 2016). Applying this to cyber-vetting, we would argue that the potential negative (legal and moral) impact would be counterproductive and employers would gain little from such practices in the long term, compared to more effective legitimate practices. This point is reinforced by the Utilitarianism position of bringing about the greatest good for the greatest number of people affected by the action (Crane & Matten, 2016). Adopting a utilitarian perspective, however, it is difficult to see how engaging in cyber-vetting is the morally preferable action, because of the potential negative outcomes for both the individual and the organisation. The deontological approach would consider such practices to not be in the interest of the individual or organisations. What is more, based on the first principle of universality, it is unlikely management would place themselves under the same level of scrutiny. In addition, and based on the second principle of human dignity, the question to ask is if employees – if free to decide for themselves – would actually agree to prospective employers trailing through their private online accounts. Hence, such practices are morally questionable under this second principle. Based on the third principle of practical test, the question to ask is if every other rational being, including your family, friends and strangers would condone the action, and apply the same rule. It seems doubtful that all other individuals would accept cyber-vetting as a general principle to follow. As such it is increasingly difficult to see the positives of cyber-vetting on both moral and ethical grounds.

Given the lack of guidance to date, it is encouraging to see that the use of social media information in applicant recruitment – and thus cyber-vetting – has been contemplated in a number of articles (e.g. Chiang & Suen, 2015; Melanthiou, Pavlou, & Constantinou, 2015; Slovensky & Ross, 2012). Further work discusses the pros and cons of using such data as well as the ethical, moral and legal dilemmas (Elefant, 2011; Holland & Jeske, 2017, chapter 11; Jeske & Shultz, 2016; Roth, Bobko, van Iddekinge, & Thatcher, 2016).

Conclusion

While legal jurisdiction and culture may vary, reputational challenges in lieu of cyber-vetting are significant concerns for all HR professionals, especially in a globalised economy with an increasingly global workforce. This is due to the fact that employer vetting is quickly establishing itself as a regular feature in the decision-making process among applicants in numerous countries (particularly when these are highly skilled and have many different options nationally and internationally). This means it is more important than ever before to proactively manage an employer's online profile in order to prevent negative reviews in the first place (rather than ignore these; Lucas, 2016). One approach is to recognise that many different individual groups may participate in review processes, including temporary workers. Organisations further need to monitor HR and managerial compliance to good practice to avoid applicant backlash due to the use of particularly privacy-invasive practices that may undermine trust in the organisation. While new legal frameworks are having a positive impact on workplace practices, too many organisations are still more reactive than proactive in terms of employer and employee vetting.

This chapter thus highlights HR's role in reputation management by reducing or avoiding reputational harm, an issue related to risk management (e.g. Becker & Smidt, 2016; Elving et al., 2012; Holt, 2016; Schulze Horn et al., 2015, see chapter 13). To our knowledge, reputation repair activities are often employed after the fact, implying limited or no concurrent reputation management. To counter these trends, some organisational soul searching may be required. First, all organisations should clarify for themselves to what extent their HR departments are perceived and believed to be responsible for reputation management (rather than Public Relations). Second, it is unclear to what extent HR professionals are knowledgeable about reputation management and the link to cyber-vetting. And third, it is still unknown which variables motivate a proactive (rather than passive) adoption of reputation management in combination with cyber-vetting. As a result, more research is still needed in order to gain a better understanding of effective reputation management approaches in the context of employer and employee cyber-vetting.

References

Acikgoz, Y., & Bergman, S. M. (2016). Social media and employee recruitment: Chasing the runaway bandwagon. In B. R. Landers & G. B. Schmidt (Eds.), *Social media in employee selection and recruitment. Theory, practice, and current challenges* (pp. 175–195). New York, NY: Springer International Publishing.

Alaniz, R. D. (2016, July 14). Are your firm's and clients' social media policies legal? Retrieved from http://www.cpapracticeadvisor.com/article/12226200/are-your-firmsand-clients-social-media-policies-legal. Accessed on July 22, 2018.

Becker, K., & Smidt, M. (2016). A risk perspective on human resource management: A review and directions for future research. *Human Resource Management Review, 26,* 149–165.

Berkelaar, B. (2014). Cybervetting, online information and personnel selection: Employers: New transparency expectations and the emergence of digital social contracts. *Management Communication Quarterly, 28*(4), 479–506.

Berkelaar, B., & Buzzanel, P. (2014). Cybervetting, person-environement fit, and personnel selection: employers' surveillance and sensemaking of job applicants' online information. *Journal of Applied Communication Research, 42*(4), 456–476.

Biswas, M. K., & Suar, D. (2016). Antecedents and consequences of employer branding. *Journal of Business Ethics, 136,* 57–72.

Breaugh, J. A. (2013). Employee recruitment. *Annual Review of Psychology, 64*(January), 389–416.

Carpentier, M., van Hoye, G., Stockman, S., Schollaert, E., van Theemsche, B., & Jacobs, G. (2017). Recruiting nurses through social media: Effects on employer brand and attractiveness. *Journal of Advanced Nursing, 73*(11), 2696–2708.

Chiang, J. K.-H., & Suen, H.-Y. (2015). Self-presentation and hiring recommendations in online communities: Lessons from LinkedIn. *Computers in Human Behavior, 48*(2015), 516–524.

Clifford, S. (2014). A video prank at Domino's damages its brand. *New York Times.* Retrieved from http://www.nytimes.com/2009/04/16/business/media/16dominos.html?_r=0. Accessed on November 20, 2015.

Crane, A., & Matten, D. (2016). *Business ethics: Managing corporate citizenship and sustainability in the age of globalization.* Oxford: Oxford University Press.

Daniel, T. A. (2017). Managing toxic emotions at work: HR's unique role as the organizational shock absorber. *Employment Relations Today, 43*(4), 13–19.

Elefant, C. (2011). The 'power' of social media: Legal issues and best practices for utilities engaging social media. *Energy Law Journal, 32,* 1–56.

Elving, J. L., Westhoff, J. J. C., Meeusen, K., & Schoonderbeek, J.-W. (2012). The war for talent? The relevance of employer branding in job advertisements for becoming an employer of choice. *Journal of Brand Management, 20,* 355–373.

García-Izquierdo, A. L., Aguinis, H., & Ramos-Villagrasa, P. J. (2010). Science practice gap in e-recruitment. *International Journal of Selection and Assessment, 18*(4), 432–438.

Heath, N. (2018). Seek and you shall find. *HRMonthly,* August, pp. 24–27.

Hepburn, S. (2005). Creating a winning employer reputation. *Strategic HR Review, 4*(4), 20–23.

Holland, P., Cooper, B., & Hecker, R. (2016). Use of social media at work: A new form of employee voice? *International Journal of Human Resource Management, 27*(21), 2621–2634.

Holland, P., Cooper, B., & Hecker, R. (2018). Social media at work: A new form of employee voice? In P. Holland, J. Teicher, & J. Donaghey (Eds.), *Employee voice at work* (pp. 73–90). New York, NY: Springer.

Holland, P., & Jeske, D. (2017). The changing role of social media at work: Implications for recruitment and selection. In T. Bondarouk, H. Ruel, & E. Parry (Eds), *Electronic HRM in the smart era* (pp. 287–309). Bingley: Emerald Publishing.

Holland, P. J. (2014). Employers and voice. In A. Wilkinson., T. Dundon., J. Donaghey, & R. Freeman (Eds.), *The handbook of research on employee voice* (pp. 135–154). Cheltenham: Edward Elgar.

Holliday Wayne, J., & Casper, W. J. (2012). Why does firm reputation in human resource policies influence college students? The mechanisms underlying job pursuit intentions. *Human Resource Management, 51*(1), 121–142.

Holt, D. (2016, n.d.). Branding in the age of social media. *Harvard Business Review*. Retrieved from https://hbr.org/2016/03/branding-in-the-age-of-social-media. Accessed on July 22, 2018.

Hurrell, S. A., Scholarios, D., & Richards, J. (2017). 'The kids are alert': Generation Y responses to employer use and monitoring of social networking sites. *New Technology, Work and Employment, 32*(1), 64–83.

Jeske, D., & Shultz, K.S. (2016). Using social media content for screening in recruitment and selection: Pros and cons. *Work, Employment & Society, 30*, 535–546.

Kanouse, D. E. (1984). Explaining negativity biases in evaluation and choice behavior: Theory and research. In T. C. Kinnear (Eds), *Advances in consumer research* (Vol. 11, pp. 703–708). Provo, UT: Association for Consumer Research.

Ko, J., & Hur, S. (2014). The impacts of employee benefits, procedural justice, and managerial trustworthiness on work attitudes: Integrated understanding based on social exchange theory. *Public Administration Review, 74*(2), 176–187.

Ladkin, A., & Buhalis, D. (2016). Online and social media recruitment: Hospitality employer and prospective employee considerations. *International Journal of Contemporary Hospitality Management, 28*(2), 327–345.

Lucas, S. (2016, May 25.). The worst possible response to a bad Glassdoor review. Retrieved from http://www.inc.com/suzanne-lucas/the-worst-possible-response-to-a-bad-glassdoor-review.html. Accessed on July 22, 2018.

Martin, G., Parry, E., & Flowers, P. (2015). Do social media enhance constructive employee voice all of the time or just some of the time? *Human Resource Management Journal, 25*, 541–562.

Melanthiou, Y., Pavlou, F., & Constantinou, E. (2015). The use of social network sites as an e-recruitment tool. *Journal of Transnational Management, 20*, 31–49.

Mosley, R.W. (2015, May 11). CEOs need to pay attention to employer branding. Retrieved from https://hbr.org/2015/05/ceos-need-to-pay-attention-to-employer-branding. Accessed on July 22, 2018.

Pabo-Nzaou, P., Lemieux, N., Beaupré, D., & Uwizeyemungu, S. (2016). Critical challenges associated with the adoption of social media: A Delphi of a panel of Canadian human resources managers. *Journal of Business Research, 69*, 4011–4019.

Ranosa. (2018, August 21). How to use Glassdoor reviews to your advantage. *HRD Tech Newsletter*. Retrieved from https://www.hrtechnologynews.com/news/talent-acquisition/how-to-use-glassdoor-reviews-to-your-advantage/109325. Accessed on July 22, 2018.

Roth, P. L., Bobko, P., van Iddekinge, C. H., & Thatcher, J. B. (2016). Social media in employee-selection-related decisions: A research agenda for uncharted territory. *Journal of Management, 42*, 269–298.

Russell, S., & Brannan, M. J. (2016). "Getting the right people on the bus": Recruitment, selection and integration for the branded organization. *European Management Journal, 34*, 114–124.

Schulze Horn, I., Taros, T., Dirkes, S., Hüer, L., Rose, M., Tietmeyer, R., & Constantinides, E. (2015). Business reputation and social media: A primer on threats and responses. *Journal of Direct, Data and Digital Marketing Practice, 16*(3), 193–208.

Sharma, R., & Prasad, A. (2018). Employer brand and its unexplored impact on intent to join. *International Journal of Organizational Analysis, 26*(3), 536–566.

Sivertzen, A.-M., Ragnhild Nilsen, E., & Olafsen, A. H. (2013). Employer branding: Employer attractiveness and the use of social media. *Journal of Product & Brand Management, 22*(7), 473–483.

Slovensky, R., & Ross, W. H. (2012). Should human resource managers use social media to screen job applicants? Managerial and legal issues in the USA. *Info, 14*, 55–69.

Uen, J. F., Ahlstrom, D., Chen, S., & Liu, J. (2015). Employer brand management, organizational prestige and employees' word-of-mouth referrals in Taiwan. *Asia Pacific Journal of Human Resources, 53*, 104–123.

Westin, A. F. (1967). *Privacy and freedom*. New York, NY: Atheneum Press.

Wheatcroft, J. (2016). Risks and rewards in the world of social media. *Human Resource Management International Digest, 24*(5), 16–18.

Wolf, M., Sims, J., & Yang, H. (2015). Look who's co-creating: Employer branding on social media. *Proceedings of the 23rd European conference on information systems*, Münster, Germany. AIS Electronic Library (AISeL) Paper No. 205. Retrieved from http://aisel.aisnet.org/ecis2015_cr/205. Accessed on June 28, 2016.

Yancey, J. (2017, May 19). Social media's impact on your brand: Every organization now needs a strategic HR function. Retrieved from https://www.hr.com/en/magazines/all_articles/social-media%E2%80%99s-impact-on-your-brand-every-organiza_j2vy6s6m.html. Accessed on July 22, 2018.

Chapter 11

Sustainable HRM: Rhetoric Versus Reality

Renee Paulet

Introduction

Sustainability is emerging as a major theme of life, work and employment in the twenty-first century. As our knowledge about how humans impact on the world increases, so too has our concern about the need to take action. Often, such action brings images of environmental concerns to mind; however, the concept of sustainability refers not only to the environment, but to all aspects of life, including economic development, human development and social development. At a macro level, forward-thinking governments are integrating sustainability principles into their policies and supporting worldwide sustainability initiatives, such as the 2030 Agenda for Sustainable Development Goals (SDGs). At the organisational level, there are numerous examples of organisational decisions being informed by sustainability principles. For some organisations, such as IKEA, Siemens and LEGO, sustainability informs all aspects of the organisation's strategy, policy and actions. Some organisations exist to achieve sustainable outcomes, such as non-profits that provide social support and opportunities for future development. Other organisations enact individual sustainable actions, driven by varied motivation such as genuine sustainable principles, economic gain, positive social reputation, or even a combination of motivations.

In this chapter, the focus is on how organisations can adopt and support sustainability principles through the organisation's human resources. Over the past two decades, human resource management (HRM) theorists and practitioners have been exploring the connections between HRM and sustainability in both a theoretical and practical way, to the extent that there is a specific area of research emerging – sustainable HRM. Kramar (2014, p. 1084) defines sustainable HRM as

> *the patterns of planned or emerging HR strategies and practices intended to enable the achievement of financial, social and ecological goals whilst simultaneously reproducing the HR base over a long term.*

This chapter explores the main issues surrounding sustainable HRM. The first section of the chapter explores the complexity of defining what is meant by sustainable HRM. In doing so, this draws out some of the ambiguities of this topic. The second section builds on these definitional issues to provide a coherent understanding of sustainable HRM, and where sustainability fits in with more traditional HRM theories, notably strategic HRM (SHRM). The third section brings together both theoretical and practical approaches to the development of sustainable HRM. The final section explores the arguments for and against sustainable HRM, teasing out the advantages that can be gained from infusing sustainability principles into and through HRM, as well as the difficulties and realities of doing so.

Defining Sustainable HRM: A Case of Easier Said Than Done

The topic of sustainable HRM is a relatively new concept, and as such a definitive definition of sustainable HRM is yet to be agreed upon by academics and practitioners. One of the difficulties in developing a universally agreed definition of sustainable HRM is varying interpretations of 'sustainability'. Indeed, Mazur (2014, p. 160) suggests that due to the complexity of the concept, it may not be possible to offer 'one truth or one unified message, but rather various impressions of sustainability'. Exploring various ideas of what sustainability means is an illuminating exercise in developing a deeper understanding of the concept.

The publication of the Brundtland Commission's 'Our Common Future' Report in 1987 brought the concept of sustainability, and sustainable development, to the fore. An outcome of the World Commission on Environment and Development, they state that 'sustainable development is development that meets the needs of the present without compromising the ability of future generations to meet their own needs' (Brundland Commission (Eds.), 1987). The pertinent aspect of this definition is the idea of the replicability of development; that development ought not be undertaken at the expense of the future. Jones (2012, p. 11) suggests this 'is in fact not a definition of sustainability in general, but a definition of a particular kind of economic growth'. The Brundtland Commission's statement on sustainable development has become a common reference in the field, and a starting point for many sustainability discussions. It helped inform Elkington's (1997, 2004) development of the 'Triple Bottom Line' (TBL) concept, whereby sustainability is seen as encompassing three main aspects; economic, social and environmental. This idea of sustainability encompassing these three aspects remains a key feature of the concept of sustainability today, reflected in Kramar's (2014) definition of sustainable HRM cited earlier. The simplicity and universality of the TBL has contributed to its resonance two decades after first being published.

Whilst it can be suggested that the three pillars of sustainability – economic, social and environment – are present in most definitions of sustainability, the emphasis on each or all of these three aspects within sustainable HRM definitions can differ. Milton Friedman (1970, reprinted in 2007) exemplified an economic focus within sustainability when he posited that an organisation operates sustainably when it strives to create long-term success for the organisation's shareholders, which generally translates to generating profit. Those from a corporate social responsibility (CSR) perspective, defined by Carroll (1979) as a business' responsibility to meet the economic, legal, ethical and discretionary expectations of society (the stakeholders and social structures in and outside the organisation), tend to emphasise the social aspect of sustainability (Federica, Silvia, & Arnaldo, 2018; Presley, Presley, & Blum, 2018). Ehnert (2009) and Pfeffer (2010) emphasise the human element within the social pillar, with specific focus on the sustainable development of the organisation's workforce. Those focusing on the environmental aspect of sustainability have developed the term Green HRM, a subset of sustainable HRM (Wagner, 2013). Definitions of sustainability and sustainable HRM also differ according to their consideration of the temporal dimension; Presley et al. (2018) suggest that CSR tends to focus more on the present and short-term, whereas the Brundtland Commission and Kramar's sustainable HRM definition draw attention to the long-term and are more future orientated in perspective. Thus the complexities associated with providing a definitive definition of sustainable HRM become clear.

Exploring the definition of 'sustainability' reveals the potential motivations behind adopting sustainable principles and sustainable HRM. How sustainability is defined can illuminate whether an organisation chooses to operate sustainably because "it is the right thing to do", or if the motivation is that operating sustainably can have positive economic effects for the organisation. Often, there is overlap. For example, countries that have banned the use of single-use plastic bags in major retailers may do so because they see it as a positive sustainability step; however, economic gains also ensue for the organisations who no longer supply bags to customers at the organisation's cost.

Understanding the motivation underlying sustainable HRM, which may differ from one organisation to another, and even within an organisation, is important to help us to understand sustainable HRM. This also begins our understanding of what sustainable HRM might look like. Ehnert, Harry, and Zink (2014) explored this when they considered the possible relationships between each of the three pillars of sustainability in practice. They identified three approaches; first, that each of the pillars are given equal weight and credence in the organisation (following Elkington's 1994 win–win–win principle); second, that economic sustainability takes precedence, with social and environmental concerns only given attention if doing so contributes to economic success; and third, that the environmental pillar is 'in fact the limiting pillar, and therefore needs to be imagined as a "circle"' with the societal and economic "circles" seen as being placed within the limiting environmental circle (Ehnert et al., 2014, p. 15).

In attempting to draw out a workable definition from these diverse perspectives, Kramar developed an encompassing definition of sustainable HRM. This definition brings together the more commonly accepted concepts regarding sustainability; the three pillars of sustainability as underpinned by the TBL, and a long-term, future orientation. For these reasons it is the definition of sustainable HRM that forms the basis of this chapter. Sustainable HRM can therefore be holistically defined as:

> ...the patterns of planned or emerging HR strategies and practices intended to enable the achievement of financial, social and ecological goals while simultaneously reproducing the HR base over a long term. (Kramar, 2014, p. 1084)

Giving consideration to the underlying assumptions involved in defining what we mean by sustainable HRM is important in developing a deeper understanding of the competing motivations of the topic, illuminating the complexity of exploring how sustainable

HRM might be operationalised in practice. In identifying a pathway through these inherit difficulties, this allows us to delve deeper into what sustainable HRM means.

From SHRM Towards Sustainable HRM

A deeper understanding of sustainable HRM can be developed by considering how this concept relates to the more established frameworks guiding HRM in advanced market economies. The most influential of these concepts over the last three decades has been SHRM. SHRM can be defined as 'the strategic choices associated with the organisation of work and the use of labour in firms' (Boxall & Purcell, 2011, p. 65). Underpinned by the resource-based view (RBV) of the firm, an organisation's human resources offer an organisation the opportunity for sustained competitive advantage due to their qualities of being valuable, rare, difficult to imitate and not substitutable (Barney, 1991; Barney, Wright, & Ketchen, 2001). Therefore, SHRM can be described as guiding HR practices and activities that enable the organisation to achieve the objectives of its stakeholders –maximising economic performance (Guerci, Decramer, Van Waeyenberg, & Aust, 2018).

There are two main ways in which sustainable HRM differs from SHRM; first, in the main outcomes that are considered to be part of HRM's remit, and second, the timeframe within which HR's actions are guided. In its most basic form, sustainable HRM can be seen as expanding the focus of HRM from being guided mainly by achieving economic objectives, to adding social and environmental objectives to the HRM sphere of influence; essentially adopting a TBL approach to HRM. Sustainable HRM therefore expands the focus of HRM, taking into account not only the organisation's and society's economic goals, but also giving legitimacy and focus to social and environmental goals and outcomes (Ehnert et al., 2014; Kramar, 2014). In doing so, sustainable HRM takes into account the intended and unintended impacts of HRM practices on social, environmental (and some researchers also suggest human) sustainability (Guerci et al., 2018), together with a broader look at the impacts of striving for economic sustainability. An example is Fuji Xerox's Eco Manufacturing Centre in Australia. Adopting a sustainable approach to operations, the Eco Manufacturing Centre re-engineers faulty, worn or damaged parts that were destined for landfill into 'as new' products for reuse or resale (Benn, Dunphy, & Angus-Leppan, 2012). HRM practices support Fuji Xerox's sustainability goals. Jobs are designed to be meaningful, through the encouragement of autonomous teams; employees, and customers, are offered a range of training and development opportunities to support new ideas in re-manufacturing; and an organisational culture has been developed to support the economic, social and environmental goals of the centre (Benn et al., 2012).

The second way in which sustainable HRM differs from SHRM is each approach's consideration of the temporal dimension. SHRM tends to focus on the short and medium term, employing HRM practices to support the achievement of the organisation's economic goals for its current stakeholders. The regeneration of social and environmental inputs into the achievement of these economic goals is not generally given attention in decision-making. Ybema, van Vuuren, and van Dam (2017, p. 2 referring to Docherty, Kira, & Shani, 2009) describe this as 'a one-sided focus on a rather short-termed efficient and effective exploitation of natural, social and human resources in organisations [that is] no longer desirable'.

In contrast, a sustainable HRM approach, following the Brundtland Commission's definition of sustainability, takes into account the impact of HRM decisions on economic, social and environmental outcomes both now and for future generations. As Guerci et al. (2018, p. 3) explain, sustainable HRM aims to 'simultaneously preserve, regenerate, and develop the economic, environmental, social and human practices of an organisation'. An example of an organisation that takes this longer-term, regeneration approach to its operations is Doterra. Doterra produces essential oils with a focus on sustainable production. They do this by only sourcing and producing oils, often from third world countries, that can be reproduced over time, and by supporting and empowering the local communities that grow their product (Doterra, 2018). From a sustainable HRM perspective, this includes extensive education on the sustainability principles of production for sales staff, encouraging philanthropic donations towards producing communities, and enabling staff to participate in aid trips to third world countries as reward for achieving sales targets. Not only is the longer-term regeneration and production of their product a feature of this business' operations, but a range of stakeholders affected by the business is taken into account.

A sustainable HRM approach therefore

> *recognises that no one facet of organisational life, or the human environment that is cultivated within the organisation, can be separated from the whole. Everything is connected to everything else, and the whole is greater than the sum of its parts. (Wells, 2012, p. 48)*

This stakeholder or 'whole-world' view accepts that an organisation has an obligation to acknowledge that its operations impact not only on the economic sphere, but also on the social and environmental spheres in which it operates, and has a responsibility, and a need, to give its attention to the long-term replenishment and regeneration of its operations. For these reasons, sustainable HRM is being identified as the next phase in the evolution of HRM (Freitas, Jabbour, & Santos, 2011).

Sustainable HRM in Reality

Despite the emerging body of work that has developed over the past two decades, a universally accepted theoretical framework or conceptual model that seeks to offer a generalisable and predictive approach to practising sustainable HRM is yet to emerge. Given the diversity of views within notions of sustainability and sustainable HRM (as discussed), this is unsurprising. Research into sustainable HRM tends to come from varied backgrounds, thus bringing a range of perspectives to the topic. Also, research applying those conceptual perspectives that have been developed has tended to focus on one or two dimensions of the sustainability equation, as opposed to exploring all three pillars of sustainability within the same research project (see Paulet & Holland for review of the Green HRM literature, and De Stefano et al. for CSR review). The result is that sustainable HRM as a whole has not been researched as a holistic concept, and the conceptual frameworks and models that have been developed have not been tested to reveal which, in their entirety or aspects of, do and do not hold when applied in an organisational setting. Ehnert and Harry (2012) argue that this diversity of perspectives is not only inevitable, but also desirable, in that applying and critiquing a range of perspectives will allow for a realistic view of sustainable HRM to emerge.

At this point in developing an appreciation of sustainable HRM it is pertinent to ask the question of what sustainable HRM might look like in practice, and how HRM might be actioned with sustainability principles. Ehnert et al. (2014, p. 7) posit that sustainable HRM adopts a dual role, 'first, in the role of developing and implementing sustainable work and HRM systems (sustainable HRM) and second, in the role of supporting the implementation of corporate sustainability strategies'. In this way, sustainable HRM can firstly be seen as contributing towards sustainability within HRM, through implementing and supporting HR practices that contribute towards sustaining each of the three pillars. A range of findings indicate the ways a sustainability perspective can shape the design and application of various HRM activities. For example, Ehnert (2009) and Kramar and Jones (2012) have explored the way recruitment activities can be undertaken to explicitly recruit for capabilities and skills needed in sustainable organisations. Renwick, Redman, and Maguire (2013), Renwick, Jabbour, Muller-Camen, Redman, and Wilkinson (2016), and Jabbour, Santos, and Nagano (2008) provide a comprehensive examination of how sustainability principles can be integrated through a range of HRM activity areas, with a specific focus on the environmental pillar. Secondly, sustainable HRM can also reach across the whole organisation, assisting and supporting organisation wide sustainability initiatives. Examples include developing specific training programmes to support employees to achieve environmental targets, and facilitating employee voice channels to allow employees to contribute and feedback on sustainability initiatives (Paulet & Holland, 2018). A key way sustainable HRM can support sustainability across the organisation is by the development and maintenance of an organisational culture that supports sustainability within all facets of the organisations operation.

The Pros and Cons of Sustainable HRM: Can it be a Reality or is it Just Rhetoric?

Having established the concept of sustainable HRM, it is important to explore the key debates and arguments for and against a sustainable HRM approach. This is done with consideration to the impact of sustainable HRM on three stakeholders: HRM, the workforce and the organisation.

Key Debates for HRM

The main advantage for HRM adopting a sustainable approach is that doing so expands the breadth and depth of HRM's remit. By enlarging the range of inputs and outcomes, HRM is encouraged to practice their profession in a more holistic way, grounded in the internal and external environments in which they operate. Together with expanding the range of outcomes, a sustainable HRM approach expands the range of inputs into HRM that are considered, explicitly taking into account the macro, organisational and individual influences on HRM (Kramar, 2015, p. 64). Concurrently, it has been argued that HRM is well placed to have a productive impact on helping an organisation towards its sustainability objectives through HRM's experience in navigating behaviour change and communicating organisational values (Harris & Tregidga, 2012; Orlitzky & Swanson, 2006). An additional benefit is research finding that practising sustainable HRM was associated with HR practitioners reporting increased levels of job satisfaction and job meaning, and reduced intention to quit, creating positive effects at both the individual and organisational levels (Guerci et al., 2018).

Whilst a sustainable HRM approach may result in these positive outcomes for HRM, the difficulties associated with practising sustainable HRM may counterbalance these processes. The reality of actually implementing and enacting sustainable HRM requires consideration of complex concepts that may be beyond the skill, time or motivation levels of some HRM employees. Harris and Tregidga (2012) found that HR Managers tended not to actively engage as a strategic driver of environmental sustainability initiatives as it was not seen as a core HR issue. Additionally, in organisations following a sustainability approach throughout the entire organisation, the process would likely be fraught with difficulties, such as questions around which aspects of introducing and supporting sustainability actions are the responsibility of the HRM Department, and which aspects are the responsibility of other departments within the organisation? De Stefano et al. (2018) explore some of these difficulties from a CSR perspective. Citing Gond, Igalens, Swaen, and Akremi (2011) they explore the political problems that can arise for HRM in terms of the actual configuration and share of responsibilities for the CSR function; does CSR fall under HRM, is CSR a separate department, or an organisational hybrid? It is can be suggested that similar conflicts would arise in determining HRM's role in sustainability within an organisation.

Key Debates for the Workforce

There are two key arguments for the adoption of sustainable HRM principles when it comes to the workforce. Firstly, a sustainable approach to HRM, by its very nature, incorporates a sustainable approach to the management of the organisation's workforce. Kira and Lifvergren (2014, p. 65) explain that 'the sustainability paradigm means creating working conditions where the thriving of human resources is possible instead of focussing on coming up with remedies for stress and burnout'. Thus, the nurturing of the workforce has the potential to come to the fore under sustainable HRM through adoption of policies and activities in areas such as work life balance, providing a safe and supportive work environment, and developing the workforce to their full potential. A sustainable approach to HRM can therefore create positives for the workforce through actively renewing the workforce's skill set and regenerating the workforce's "sense of vocation" (Kramar & Jones, 2012). Secondly, sustainable HRM can result in positive synergies for the workforce, by allowing and encouraging the workforce to align their personal sustainability philosophy with their employer. Research from CSR and Green HRM studies have found this alliance between the workforces' and the organisations' sustainability principles can have positive impacts on employee job satisfaction and job meaning (Benn, Teo, & Martin, 2015; Federica et al., 2018; Rayner & Morgan, 2018; Wagner, 2011, 2013; Ybema et al., 2017). Given that sustainability is becoming an important consideration to increasing portions of the workforce, this synergy represents another argument towards organisation's embracing sustainable HRM.

However, one of the problems of sustainable HRM for the workforce is that current models, conceptualisations and research in the field give little attention to employee's voice and role in sustainable HRM (Markey, McIvor, & Wright, 2016; Paulet & Holland, 2018). Whilst there is a scope for sustainable HRM to result in positive implications for the workforce, as discussed above, current literature on sustainable HRM suggests that space is not created for the workforce to express and voice their thoughts, opinions and expertise on sustainability. This is despite multiple findings within the

Green HRM literature of the important role employees have in achieving environmental goals (Boiral, 2002; del Brío, Fernández, & Junquera, 2007; Paille, Chen, Boiral, & Jin, 2014; Ruiz-Quintanilla, Bunge, Cohen-Rosenthal, & Freeman-Gallant, 1996; Temminck, Mearns, & Fruhen, 2015). The literature thus far tends to explore how sustainability impacts on employees (top down), rather than how employees can impact on sustainability (bottom up). Paulet and Holland (2018) explored the implications of a lack of employee voice on sustainable HRM in the following case study.

Case Study

When Employee Voice is Lacking in Sustainable HRM

MetroUni espouses a strong emphasis on its forward-thinking approach to sustainable work practices across its various departments and campuses. In terms of its approach to sustainability, employee voice in MetroUni exemplifies downward voice with no employee input; they have a website and newsletter dedicated to sustainability which are the key voice forums, there are no sustainability committees at the employee level, and all initiatives are seen as taken by senior management and imposed on the workforce. The following examples illustrate implications of this lack of employee voice on MetroUni's sustainability initiatives.

MetroUni and the Mini-Bins

As an initiative to reduce the University's landfill waste and contamination of recyclable waste, MetroUni introduced a 'mini-bin' programme. The programme aimed to encourage recycling of waste by providing a significantly small(er) receptacle for landfill waste (the size of a large cup), a larger paper recycling bin, with all other recyclables to be placed by staff in co-mingle recycling receptacles located in communal areas. Staff had no input in the decision or implementation of this initiative. Whilst the University reported the introduction of the mini-bins as a success, in the workforce's eyes one day their bins were removed and replaced by a bin too small to meet its purpose, with no discussion or opportunity to have input into the changes. Because of the inadequate size of the new bins staff tended to just go to the closest big bin to dispose of their rubbish, having an unknown effect on recycling and contamination rates. It could be argued that had employees been given a voice in this sustainability initiative, a more positive and effective outcome could have ensured. Perhaps employees' needs regarding landfill waste and recycling could have been more embedded in the initiative, likely resulting in higher success rates in reducing landfill waste and recycling contamination. Employee voice and ownership of the mini-bin change may have improved the uptake of the initiative. It could be suggested the mini-bin programme has had a detrimental impact on the sustainability footprint of MetroUni, given the financial and environmental cost of producing 18,000 non-recyclable plastic mini-bins that are not being used to their potential.

Energy Use at Metro Uni

Lighting in the University's photocopy rooms is an example of how a lack of employee voice and consultation in sustainability initiatives can impinge on the achievement of energy reduction goals. Often located in rooms with no natural light, photocopy rooms are generally illuminated with fluorescent strip lighting, with staff asked to turn the light off after using the room. It is not unusual for these photocopy room lights to be turned on and off up to 20 times an hour, despite research that with this type of lighting, frequently turning the light on and off uses more energy that leaving it on. Thus extra waste and costs are incurred due to a decrease in the life expectancy of the globe (Department of Energy, 2018). If employee voice were integrated into sustainability, it is possible a more sustainable – both economically and environmentally – option could have been reached. Employees could have had the opportunity to voice other options, such as placing photocopiers in corridors or areas with natural light, the feasibility of installing automatic lighting could have been explored, and research on optimal times to leave fluorescent light on could be disseminated. However, with no employee voice or consultation on sustainability at MetroUni, staff do not know how to communicate such ideas and initiatives.

Paulet and Holland (2018)

Key Debates for the Organisation

As discussed earlier in the chapter, there are two main ways a sustainable HRM approach can manifest in an organisation:

(1) through enacting HRM policies and activities that support sustainability; and
(2) through supporting the organisations wider sustainability objectives (Ehnert et al., 2014).

Looking firstly at HRM policies and activities that support sustainability, the HR activity area of recruitment is an area in which research has shown positive impacts for the organisation. Organisations that communicate their sustainability credentials during recruitment activities improve their employer brand, positioning themselves as an employer of choice (App, Merk, & Büttgen, 2012; Gully, Phillips, Castellano, Han, & Kim, 2013). Thus a sustainable HRM approach can have positive impacts for the organisation through generating a suitable pool of potential employees, which can be particularly important in attracting new staff in tight labour markets and/or the eco-careerist (Inkson & Parker, 2012; Presley et al., 2018).

Sustainable HRM's support of wider organisation sustainability goals also creates additional advantages for the organisation. Research has shown multiple benefits to organisations that adopt sustainability as part of their business practices, above and beyond the positives that arise from operating in a sustainable manner (such as securing the longevity of the organisation and its resources of production). Benefits include internal advantages such as developing capabilities, enhancing employee morale, attraction and retention of human capital, and reduced turnover, which can lead to external benefits in areas such as corporate reputation, and the market rewarding sustainable organisations (Kramar & Jones, 2012; Schnietz & Epstein, 2005; Wahba, 2008). Notably, research has found that organisations that operate sustainably, supported by a sustainable HRM approach, achieve economic gains (Ehnert et al., 2014; Mazur, 2014; Wagner, 2011, 2013; Wolf, 2013). Therefore, a key argument in support of sustainable HRM is that expanding business focus beyond just economic goals does not mean economic goals are forfeited, in fact economic goals can be enhanced by a wider sustainability approach.

Despite these positives that arise from a sustainable HRM approach, examples of organisations taking an opposite approach to their business operations abound. The Volkswagen emission scandal revealed in 2015 exemplifies an organisation's actions that were the antithesis of a sustainable approach, when it was found that software testing diesel emission in some cars had been deliberately falsified to report low results (Hotten, 2015). This raises the question if a sustainable approach, including sustainable HRM, is feasible or realistic in actually being taken up by organisations operating in this climate. In other words, regardless of the drives towards and benefits derived from sustainability, and sustainable HRM in particular, there are stark examples within the business world that short-term economic goals rule.

Can Sustainable HRM Make a Difference?

This chapter has provided a thorough overview of the main issues associated with the rise of sustainable HRM. The complexity and conflict within the field was considered through definitions, and the implications of a sustainable HRM approach was illustrated by exploring how this approach extends beyond SHRM.

Whilst questions remain over the difficulties in steering organisations away from (for many) a traditional focus on economic goals, the importance of organisations adopting more sustainable principles, supported by sustainable HRM, cannot be denied. Evidence of the negative externalities of a non-sustainable approach abound, from noticeable changes in our climate and confronting images of plastic islands in our oceans, to global housing affordability issues (Woetzel, Ram, Mischke, Garemo, & Sankhe, 2014). Ehnert et al (2014, p. 11) expresses the importance of exploring a sustainable approach when they said 'our traditional economic model fosters an organisational behaviour which produces externalities for corporate natural, social and human environments and individuals even at the risk of their destruction'. The tide is turning. It is time for organisations to give more attention to the way they are managing their resources, including their human resources (Ehnert et al., 2014), in order to meet society's expectations for sustainability. Sustainable HRM is one tool to help organisations achieve this aim.

It is interesting to note that an early piece of work exploring the newly developing concept of SHRM noted many similar issues as raised here. Wright and McMahan's (1992) seminal paper on the (at that time) early stages of theoretical development of SHRM discusses a lack of agreeance on defining the concept of SHRM, and a lack of strong theoretical models to explain the variables within the concept of SHRM. Sustainable HRM, at this early stage of development, is also grappling with these issues, as shown in this chapter. Given the robust theoretical and practical application of SHRM today, it can be anticipated that sustainable HRM will follow a similar path and emerge as a new way of thinking about HRM in the twenty-first century.

References

App, S., Merk, J., & Büttgen, M. (2012). Employer Branding: Sustainable HRM as a competitive advantage in the market for high-quality employees. *Management Revue*, *23*(3), 262–278. doi:10.1688/1861-9908mrev201203App

Barney, J. (1991). Firm resources and sustained competitive advantage. *Journal of Management*, *17*(1), 99–120.

Barney, J., Wright, M., & Ketchen, D. J. (2001). The resource-based view of the firm: Ten years after 1991. *Journal of Management*, *27*(6), 625–641. doi:https://doi.org/10.1016/S0149-2063(01)00114-3

Benn, S., Dunphy, D., & Angus-Leppan, T. (2012). Fuji Xerox Australia Eco Manufacturing Centre: A case study in strategic sustainability. In Benn et al. (Ed.), *Sustainability at work: Readings, cases and policy* (pp. 111–126). Prahran, Australia: Tilde University Press.

Benn, S., Teo, S., & Martin, A. (2015). Employee participation and engagement in working for the environment. *Personnel Review*, *44*(4), 492–510. doi:10.1108/PR-10-2013-0179

Boiral, O. (2002). Tacit knowledge and environmental management. *Long Range Planning*, *35*(3), 291–317. doi:https://doi.org/10.1016/S0024-6301(02)00047-X

Boxall, P., & Purcell, J. (2011). *Strategy and human resource management*. New York, NY: Macmillan International Higher Education.

Brundland Commission. (Eds.). (1987). Report of the World Commission on Environment and Development: Our common future. Retrieved from http://www.un-documents.net/our-common-future.pdf

Carroll, A. B. (1979). A three-dimensional conceptual model of corporate performance. *Academy of Management Review*, *4*(4), 497–505.

del Brío, J. Á., Fernández, E., & Junquera, B. (2007). Management and employee involvement in achieving an environmental action-based competitive advantage: An empirical study. *The International Journal of Human Resource Management*, *18*(4), 491–522. doi:10.1080/09585190601178687

Department of Energy. (2018). When to turn off your lights. Retrieved from https://www.energy.gov/energysaver/when-turn-your-lights

De Stefano, F., Bagdadli, S., & Camuffo, A. (2018). The HR role in corporate social responsibility and sustainability: A boundaryshifting literature review. *Human Resource Management*, *57*(2), 549–566.

Docherty, P., Kira, M., & Shani, A. B. (2009). What the world needs now is sustainable work systems. In P. Docherty, M. Kira, and A. B. Shani (Eds), *Creating sustainable work systems: Developing social sustainability* (pp. 1–32). London: Routledge.

Doterra. (2018). Co-impact sourcing. Retrieved from https://www.doterra.com/AU/en_AU/difference-co-impact-sourcing

Ehnert, I. (2009). *Sustainable human resource management: A conceptual and exploratory analysis from a paradox perspective*. Dordrecht, Germany: Physica-Verlag.

Ehnert, I., & Harry, W. (2012). Recent developments and future prospects on sustainable human resource management: Introduction to the special issue. *Management Revue*, *23*(3), 221–238. doi:10.1688/1861-9908.mrev.2012.03.Ehnert

Ehnert, I., Harry, W., & Zink, K. (2014). *Sustainability and human resource management: Developing sustainable business organisations*. Berlin: Springer.

Elkington, J. (1994). Towards the sustainable corporation: Win-win-win business strategies for sustainable development. *California Management Review*, *36*(2), 90–100.

Elkington, J. (1997). *Cannibals with forks: The triple bottom line of 21st century business.* Stony Creek, VA: New Society Publishers.

Elkington, J. (2004). Enter the triple bottom line. In A. Henriques & J. Richardson (Eds.), *The triple bottom line: Does it all add up* (pp. 1–16). London: Routledge.

Federica, D. S., Silvia, B., & Arnaldo, C. (2018). The HR role in corporate social responsibility and sustainability: A boundary-shifting literature review. *Human Resource Management, 57*(2), 549–566. doi:10.1002/hrm.21870

Freitas, W. R. d. S., Jabbour, C. J. C., & Santos, F. C. A. (2011). Continuing the evolution: Towards sustainable HRM and sustainable organizations. *Business Strategy Series, 12*(5), 226–234. doi:10.1108/17515631111166861

Friedman, M. (2007). The social responsibility of business is to increase its profits. In W. C. Zimmerli, M. Holzinger, & K. Richter (Eds.), *Corporate ethics and corporate governance* (pp. 173–178). Berlin: Springer.

Gond, J.-P., Igalens, J., Swaen, V., & El Akremi, A. (2011). The human resources contribution to responsible leadership: An exploration of the CSR–HR interface. In N. M. Pless & T. Maak (Eds.), *Responsible leadership* (pp. 115–132). Dordrecht: Springer.

Guerci, M., Decramer, A., Van Waeyenberg, T., & Aust, I. (2018). Moving beyond the link between HRM and economic performance: A study on the individual reactions of HR managers and professionals to sustainable HRM. *Journal of Business Ethics*, 1–18. Retrieved from https://doi.org/10.1007/s10551-018-3879-1

Gully, S. M., Phillips, J. M., Castellano, W. G., Han, K., & Kim, A. (2013). A mediated moderation model of recruiting socially and environmentally responsible job applicants. *Personnel Psychology, 66*(4), 935–973.

Harris, C., & Tregidga, H. (2012). HR managers and environmental sustainability: Strategic leaders or passive observers? *The International Journal of Human Resource Management, 23*(2), 236–254.

Hotten, R. (2015, December 10). Volkswagen: The scandal explained. Retrieved from https://www.bbc.com/news/business-34324772

Inkson, K., & Parker, P. (2012). Eco careers. In S. Benn et. al. (Eds.), *Sustainability at work: Readings, cases and policy* (pp. 51–65). Prahran, Australia: Tilde Publishing.

Jabbour, C. J. C., Santos, F. C. A., & Nagano, M. S. (2008). Environmental management system and human resource practices: Is there a link between them in four Brazilian companies? *Journal of Cleaner Production, 16*(17), 1922–1925. doi:https://doi.org/10.1016/j.jclepro.2008.02.004

Jones, G. (2012). Current research in sustainability. In S. Benn et. al. (Eds.), *Sustainability at work: Readings, cases and policy.* Prahran, Australia: Tilde Publishing.

Kira, M., & Lifvergren, S. (2014). Sowing seeds for sustainability in work systems. In I. Ehnert, W. Harry, & K. Zink (Eds.), *Sustainability and human resource management* (pp. 57–81). Berlin: Springer.

Kramar, R. (2014). Beyond strategic human resource management: Is sustainable human resource management the next approach? *The International Journal of Human Resource Management, 25*(8), 1069–1089. doi:10.1080/09585192.2013.816863

Kramar, R. (2015). Sustainable HRM: Beyond SHRM. In R. Kramar & P. Holland (Eds.), *Capstone HRM: Dynamics and ambiguity in the workplace* (pp. 62–87). Melbourne, Australia: Tilde University Press.

Kramar, R., & Jones, G. (2012). Sustainability in strategic human resource management. In S. Benn et Al. (Eds.), *Sustainability at work: Readings, cases and policy* (pp. 80–103). Prahran, Australia: Tilde Publishing.

Markey, R., McIvor, J., & Wright, C. F. (2016). Employee participation and carbon emissions reduction in Australian workplaces. *International Journal of Human Resource Management, 27*(2), 173–191. doi:10.1080/09585192.2015.1045009

Mazur, B. (2014). Sustainable human resource management in theory and practice. *Economics and Management, 6*(1), 158–170.

Orlitzky, M., & Swanson, D. (2006). Socially responsible human resource management: Charting new territory. In J. Deckop (Ed.), *Human resource management ethics*. Greenwich, CT: Information Age Publishing.

Paille, P., Chen, C., Boiral, O., & Jin, J. (2014). The impact of human resource management on environmental performance: An employee-level study. *Journal of Business Ethics, 121*(3), 451–466.

Paulet, R., & Holland, P. (2018). *Sustainable HRM - Is it just rhetoric without employee voice?* Paper presented at the the 32nd ANZAM conference, December 4–7, Auckland.

Pfeffer, J. (2010). Building Sustainable Organizations: The human factor. *Academy of Management Perspectives, 24*(1), 34–45. doi:10.5465/AMP.2010.50304415

Presley, A., Presley, T., & Blum, M. (2018). Sustainability and company attractiveness: A study of American college students entering the job market. *Sustainability Accounting, Management and Policy Journal, 9*(4), 470–489. doi:10.1108/SAMPJ-03-2017-0032

Rayner, J., & Morgan, D. (2018). An empirical study of 'green' workplace behaviours: Ability, motivation and opportunity. *Asia Pacific Journal of Human Resources, 56*, 56–78. doi:10.1111/1744-7941.12151

Renwick, D. W. S., Jabbour, C. J. C., Muller-Camen, M., Redman, T., & Wilkinson, A. (2016). Contemporary developments in green (environmental) HRM scholarship. *The International Journal of Human Resource Management, 27*(2), 114–128. doi:10.1080/09585192.2015.1105844

Renwick, D. W. S., Redman, T., & Maguire, S. (2013). Green human resource management: A review and research agenda. *International Journal of Management Reviews, 15*(1), 1–14. doi:10.1111/j.1468-2370.2011.00328.x

Ruiz-Quintanilla, S. A., Bunge, J., Cohen-Rosenthal, E., & Freeman-Gallant, A. (1996). Employee participation in pollution reduction: A socio-technical perspective. *Business Strategy & the Environment, 5*(3), 137–144.

Schnietz, K. E., & Epstein, M. J. (2005). Exploring the financial value of a reputation for corporate social responsibility during a crisis. *Corporate Reputation Review, 7*(4), 327–345.

Temminck, E., Mearns, K., & Fruhen, L. (2015). Motivating employees towards sustainable behaviour. *Business Strategy and the Environment, 24*(6), 402–412. doi:10.1002/bse.1827

Wagner, M. (2011). Environmental management activities and sustainable HRM in German manufacturing firms: Incidence, determinants, and outcomes. *German Journal of Research in Human Resource Management, 25*(2), 157–177.

Wagner, M. (2013). 'Green' human resource benefits: Do they matter as determinants of environmental management system implementation? *Journal of Business Ethics, 114*, 443–456. doi:10.1007/s10551-012-1356-9

Wahba, H. (2008). Does the market value corporate environmental responsibility? An empirical examination. *Corporate Social Responsibility and Environmental Management, 15*(2), 89–99.

Wells, S. (2012). HRM for sustainability: Creating a new paradigm. In S. Benn et al. (Eds.), *Sustainability at work: Readings, cases and policy* (pp. 36–50). Prahran, Australia: Tilde Publishing.

Woetzel, J., Ram, S., Mischke, J., Garemo, N., & Sankhe, S. (2014). A blueprint for addressing the gloabl affordable housing challenge. Retrieved from https://www.mckinsey.com/~/media/McKinsey/Featured%20Insights/Urbanization/Tackling%20the%20worlds%20affordable%20housing%20challenge/MGI_Affordable_housing_Full%20Report_October%202014.ashx

Wolf, J. (2013). Improving the sustainable development of firms: The role of employees. *Business Strategy & the Environment*, *22*(2), 92–108. doi:10.1002/bse.1731

Wright, P. M., & McMahan, G. C. (1992). Theoretical perspectives for strategic human resource management. *Journal of management*, *18*(2), 295–320.

Ybema, J. F., van Vuuren, T., & van Dam, K. (2017). HR practices for enhancing sustainable employability: implementation, use, and outcomes. *The International Journal of Human Resource Management*, 1–22. DOI:10.1080/09585192.2017.1387865

Chapter 12

Work Design in the 21st Century: A Case of Back to the Future or Forward to the Past?

Peter Holland, Kirsteen Grant and Tse Leng Tham

> *Organisations rely on their employees to introduce new products/services, improve business processes, and develop new working methods ... and job design specifically can create a supportive and stimulating work environment that enhances innovative work behaviour.*
>
> *(Hernaus, 2016)*

Introduction

As the quote above notes, with the accelerated changes we have seen in the twenty-first century in many cases driven by technology, the importance of how work is organised in an increasingly dynamic knowledge and service-based globalised economy is central to the development of effective organisations. On the cusp of the fourth industrial revolution, the existing commentary increasingly reflects divergent views of these changes as both a dystopian and utopian view of the future of work and workplaces in the twenty-first century. We explore the key aspect, the design of work, noting that whilst the fourth industrial revolution (following the mechanisation of production, the massing of production and the automation of production) builds on what has gone before, we note that the increasing move into the digital age of artificial intelligence (AI), robots and big data (Cho & Kim, 2018; Friedman, 2016), has the potential to sideline work or job design in this debate. In particular, the lesson we (should) have learned from the socio-technical era, which focussed on the fusion between humans and technology as the bedrock for ensuring the worst excesses of poor work design are not repeated.

How work is being changed by technology in the twenty-first century is far too broad a scope for this discussion but let us consider this chapter you are reading as a microcosm of this change. It is unlikely you have physically gone to a library or a bookshop to acquire this book. The fact that you can download this book as an e-book or chapter to read, save it in the 'cloud' to read later or comment on it via social media to your colleagues or the authors testifies to how much technology has impacted on academic staff and students' work in the twenty-first century. In addition, where and how you are reading this chapter has changed, you may be at home on the computer or commuting, reading it on a smart phone or tablet. If you are commuting, look up for a second and see how many people around you are reading a newspaper or their smart-phones? The key driver in all this is technology. Technology has fundamentally reshaped the nature of how we work, where we work, when we work and how work is managed. This chapter takes the opportunity to reflect on lessons learnt in the twentieth century to enable our understanding of the relationship between work and technology as the workplace of the twenty-first century becomes increasingly underpinned by technology and again is fundamentally changing the work relationships. We will start with a brief reflection on modern work design, exploring the links to technology to see if we have learnt the lessons of the past as a map to the future of work and work design.

A Brief (but Interesting) History of Work Design

As we move through the various industrial revolutions, we can identify fundamental changes that have been wrought on how we work, where we work and indeed, why we work. The pre-industrial revolution system was dominated by the 'putting out' system which was underpinned by the craft-based skills and cottage-based mode of production. The key to this system was that the craftsmen effectively controlled the pace of production to their own ends. The demands for increased production that emerged with the first industrial revolution saw these traditional patterns of work organisation unable to cope (Berg, 1985; Thompson & McHugh, 1995). Adam Smith (1776), identified that the restructuring of work patterns (job design) would be a central factor in increasing organisational efficiency of production, through the narrowing of the range of tasks and the application of simple machinery (technology) (Smith, 1979). This deskilling of the work set in train the opportunity to firstly, shift the focus of the economics of production away from the craftsmen to the demands of the market and discipline workers to this new demand cycle run through factories (Nichols, 1980; Pollard, 1965; Thompson & McHugh, 1995). Secondly, it facilitated the continued deconstructing of work processes with the development of simple machinery (Berg, 1985; Grint, 1991; Hobsbawn, 1968; Mathias, 1969; Thompson, 1968).

The growth in industrial production and national and international markets towards the end of the eighteenth century coincided with the scientific-technical revolution, which provided advances in many industries (Freidman, 1977; Hobsbawn, 1968). This contributed to increased complexity of organisations and the production process. A key inhibitor at the time was seen to be the organisation of work which was still based upon arbitrary decision-making (Drury, 1922; Merkle, 1980). From this period (and perspective) emerged F.W. Taylor and his concept of Scientific Management (Taylor, 1911). The techniques of scientific management focussed on the elimination of 'rule of thumb' approaches to work organisation and increasing productivity and efficiency underpinned by so-called scientific methodology through what came to be known as time and motion studies (Rose, 1988). Jobs were analysed and reconstructed (eliminating all superfluous actions), 'scientifically – in the one best way' (Friedman, 1961;

Nyland, 1987; Thompson & McHugh, 1995). Despite criticism and resistance (Drury, 1922; Hoxie, 1918; Rose, 1988), scientific management permeated a wide variety of industries in the first two decades of the twentieth century (Chandler, 1977) to become the dominant paradigm in the organisation of work. The overall effect of scientific management on work organisation was the separation of conception and execution and the reduction of jobs into narrowly defined, repetitive tasks (deskilling) under strict conditions of decision-making by management and time (Rose, 1988: Thompson, 1983). Think today how you will check the time when you are going to work, whilst working or when the work day starts or ends – you can thank Taylor for this.

The combination of mass-production and scientific management realised the true potential of combining these work patterns and processes of standardisation, continuity and simplification of the production process and by implication, work patterns and practices (Littler & Salaman, 1982). The success of this mode of production and associated patterns of work (through the reduction of labour and production costs), gave competitors the option of adopting these patterns of work, or surrendering market share, thus allowing Fordism (as it became known) to emerge as the dominant mode of production and work organisation in the twentieth century through eliminating alternative patterns of work (Lipietz, 1987; Thompson, 1983).

In the context of work organisation, the key feature of Fordism was management control (pace and intensity) of production of work and how it was designed around the machines and taken out of the hands of the worker. In other words, technology was the driver of work design rather than the 'scientific manager' effectively reversing the dominant relationship of labour over technology (Edwards, 1979; Gorz, 1976; Kelly, 1982). The foundations of modern job and work design can be traced through the economic expansion associated with the Industrial Revolution described above. However, the deconstructing of work processes was rarely if ever considered in terms of the human and social impact of these changes, despite criticism and resistance (Rose, 1988).

Work Design and the Socio-technical Era

Today, the brutal unfettered concepts of scientific management and Fordism may seem hard to comprehend in terms of what we want from work. When seen in the context of the underlying philosophy of human motivation, the logic becomes clearer. The foundation of traditional work design was the concept of rational-economic man (Schein, 1965). This concept is based upon a belief that a person will take the work that offers the maximum self-reward (Birchall, 1975). The assumption is extrinsic reward (money) is the key driver or motivator. Therefore, in a work context, issues such as working conditions, the environment and relationships are subsidiary to the economic rewards.

However, starting with a series of strikes during the World War I at key factories involved in the war effort in the UK, a series of studies on the issues of monotony and work in the 1920s were undertaken by the UK Government. The research identified a link between social conditions and workers' mental health, productivity and autonomy (Buchanan & Huczynski, 1985; Rose, 1988). Further research identified the importance of working conditions and relationships, and social relationships between group dynamics and monotony above pay (Brown, 1986). These studies provided the first connection between the human aspects of work, technology and productivity, creating foundations for the next generation of researchers.

The Hawthorne Studies

The Hawthorne studies are often cited as the breakthrough in the impact of the social aspects of work on its design and organisation, arguably because they provided a link to productivity (and profits). In addition, these studies were seen as the foundations of what became known as the *human relations school* of research on work and work organisation which was to follow (Thompson & McHugh, 1995). The Hawthorne studies took place between 1924 and 1932 at the Hawthorne plant of the Western Electric Company in Chicago. The Company was seen as an enlightened employer paying high wages and providing welfare facilities for its workers. However, it is often lost in translation that the Hawthorne studies were initiated in a period when scientific management was the central focus of work organisation and industrial efficiency, and the studies were undertaken through this frame of reference in terms of working conditions and performance (Pratt & Bennett, 1985). What this research began to uncover was the relationship between social aspect of work, employee satisfaction and increased productivity (Cole, 1988).

Without getting into various critiques of the research, it is generally accepted that these studies, were the building blocks of contemporary work design (Thompson & McHugh, 1995). The critical point being that the studies recognised the relationship between the social and technical aspects of work organisation, and provided the first evidence that employee engagement, satisfaction and productivity were related to social relations at work. The Hawthorne studies were also the first serious counter critique of scientific management and economic man and in particular, their neglect of human factors in the workplace (Rose, 1988; Thompson & McHugh, 1995). In addition, they introduced the concept of social man into the mainstream context of the work relationship, highlighting the power that these relationships had over workers through the development of informal groups establishing their own values and norms outside the formal organisation. In addition, they could also demonstrate the positive impact of these relations on productivity.

Contemporary Theory of Job and Work Design: The Human Relations School

The human relations school emerged out of the Tavistock Institute of Human Relations in London and ascribes a period of research in work design from around the 1940s to the 1980s (Parker & Wall, 1998). The focus of the work built upon the research undertaken during World War II (Rose, 1988), and was also influenced by the Hawthorne studies and the development of the socio-technical systems approach. The socio-technical approach viewed organisations as a combination of interactions between social and technical networks (Warr, 1987). From this perspective, the socio-technical system approach explored the most favourable relationship(s) that enhance the employment experience for both the employee and the organisation. This approach drew the focus away from simply adding humans to the 'production' (or technological) process as with scientific management and then Fordism, requiring both systems to be designed in unison (Parker & Wall, 1998; Watson, 1995). The importance of this approach lies therefore in the need for a comprehensive understanding of the impact of each system on the other and how this could be managed effectively (Warr, 1987).

In taking a more comprehensive approach, the socio-technical perspective allowed for a wide range of factors to be taken into account. This approach therefore provided a framework of values to understand the organisational systems, rather than a prescriptive map of how to uniformly build systems – as per scientific management (Buchanan & Huczynski, 1985; Warr, 1987). One of the most significant aspects of the socio-technical school was the understanding of the impact of technology at work and effective teamwork in the organisation of work design (Parker & Wall, 1998). The studies by Trist and Bamforth on long-wall and short-wall mining in the UK and Rice's work on the Calico knitting mills of Ahmedabad in northern India identified both the positive social and economic aspects of work relationships and work design. The development of work organisation around autonomous and semi-autonomous work units allowed these groups to decide their own methods of work and handle as many of the operational issues encountered as possible (Parker & Wall, 1998; Passmore, 1998). The success of these work patterns and practices further undermined the logic of scientific management as 'the one best way' (Trist, 1973).

What the human relations school identified was the importance of the relationship between the social, psychological and technological aspects of work and its organisation. In particular, the symbiotic relationships within the organisation of these key elements. The acceptance of these relationships provided a significant understanding in how work design should be understood from both the individual and the group levels to enhance the personal experience and productivity (Pratt & Bennett, 1985; Watson, 1995).

As noted, this chapter is not meant to be a chronology of work and job design but an opportunity to reflect on lessons learnt (or unlearnt) in the midst of fundamental changes to work, underpinned by significant technological change and globalisation at the cusp of the fourth industrial revolution. We acknowledge that much research has built upon the foundation of the socio-technical era. The fundamentals of the building blocks of this approach reflect to us similar overtones to today's challenges between social system and technology. Indeed, many argue that the generation entering the workforce today has been fundamentally rewired by technology in terms of how they think and learn. In this context, we explore a high-skilled work environment that epitomises the advances in work through technology. The aviation sector, which has moved from the domain of the niche professional business person to the mass markets with the advent of economy airlines and deregulation. The following sections explore how technology and the individual have been fused in the context of what we know about work design, but more importantly have we learnt the lesson of the past as we hasten in the fourth industrial revolution?

Case Study: The Shifting Terrain of Commercial Aviation

The global commercial airline industry is undergoing rapid change. Already operating within very small profit margins, the industry is facing intense and growing competition from the large number of new, low-cost carriers (Fraher, 2014; Sarker, Hossan, & Saman, 2012) entering the global market. These changes in the strategic operating environment have resulted in a corresponding impact on airlines' human resource management (HRM) strategy and practices (Bamber, Hoffer Gittell, Kochan, & von Nordenflycht, 2015; Oxenbridge, Wallace, White, Tiernan, & Lansbury, 2010). The management of pilots within many airlines increasingly centres on harder, financially driven models of HRM, as opposed to a focus on developing more people-centric and high-commitment based approaches to HRM. The corollary is that contemporary HRM in this industry is often characterised by precarious forms of employment (Maxwell & Grant, 2018) with minimalistic and low-cost work practices that are likely to result in increased pressure and job demands being placed on pilots (Harvey & Turnbull, 2010). Indeed, such industry changes led Bennett (2006, p. 93) to conclude that airline pilots today face 'a poorly rewarded and risky battle with fatigue, stress and exploitative terms and conditions'.

Commercial airlines exemplify 'high reliability organizations' (Roberts, 1990, p. 160) or 'ultra-safe macro-technical systems' (Amalberti, 2001, p. 110). Yet, the shift towards low-cost and precarious work practices raises important safety concerns, particularly in relation to pilots' readiness and ability to deal with unpredictability and critical incidents (Fraher, 2014). Of particular interest within the contemporary airline industry is the impact of human factors and technology on airline safety. The study of human factors concerns the interactions between human and machine (Gordon, 1998) or the scientific study of the relationship between people and their working environment (Murrell, 1965). As noted above, human factors theory recognises that people work with and within dynamic and complex socio-technical systems (Robertson, Black, Grand-Clement, & Hall, 2016) and is based on the premise that three broad and interrelated components lead to human error: *overload*, *inappropriate response* and *inappropriate activities* (e.g. Friend & Kohn, 2014). Overload concerns capacity and capability, and is influenced by environmental (workplace), internal (physical and psychological) and situational (e.g. risk) factors. Inappropriate response is concerned with how a person responds to a particular condition or situation, and inappropriate activities refer, for example, to undertaking a task without having received adequate training, or perhaps misjudging the level of risk associated with the task.

Importantly, whilst the rapidly increasing sophistication of technology has led to significant improvements in aviation safety, human error has not decreased at a corresponding rate (Liou, Yen, & Tzeng, 2008), accounting for up to 80% of accidents and incidents (Li, Baker, Grabowski, & Rebok, 2001). Indeed, modern technology has also been identified as having the potential to impact negatively on pilots' state of situational awareness (Taylor & Cotter, 2016), for instance, through boredom experienced whilst monitoring systems rather than manually flying the plane. Technology is thus a key factor within high reliability organisations, and 'fly-by-wire' (Oliver, Calvard, & Potocnik, 2017, p. 732) technologies in the case of the aviation industry, is at the forefront of aviation advancement and effectively replaces the conventional manual controls of the aircraft with technology. However, this raises important implications for pilots' cognition, both in terms of their engagement with modern technology and their ability to take in, assimilate and retain information without experiencing overload. Consider, for example, an airline pilot in the flight deck who may be experiencing high levels of fatigue or poor mental health, and is faced with an emergency situation or critical incident. The situation is dynamic and fast moving, requiring the pilot to quickly assimilate and interpret both verbal and computerised information in order to make timely and risk critical decisions.

A recent study comprising in-depth interviews with 28 UK-based commercial airline pilots (Grant & Maxwell, 2018) exemplifies the potential impact of new technology. The study unveiled concern among experienced pilots about a potential imbalance between the technological and manual flying skills of newly qualified pilots. It was suggested that 'Soon pilots will have an electronic flight bag where you have a laptop basically, and everything that's on the flight deck now will be on the laptop or tablet'. Pilots' concerns, however, arise from the resultant competence of newly qualified pilots to deal with technological failure or unpredictable situations. According to one pilot, 'It's about knowing how to use it [technology], understanding how it works and also the limitations that come with it'. For example, pilots highlighted the need to disengage the autopilot and revert to manual flying when a problem arises; which, in their view, are skills which are potentially lacking in newer, less experienced pilots. It was suggested that

> The new pilots have an Xbox, Nintendo mentality, they don't know how to fly and on an Airbus it's all computerised, so they are up close with automation, not real flying. It's a slippery slope – and the irony of all ironies: pilots can't manually fly.

This point was echoed during many interviews, with another pilot explaining that, 'The combination of new pilots not being sure what the aircraft is doing and not being able to fly manually is possibly leading to dangerous situations'.

Therefore, the changing nature of the contemporary airline industry alongside changes to the technological environment raises a number of important implications for HRM. The HRM model and concomitant work practices are central to safety in what is an increasingly deregulated and competitive industry. Considering the paramount importance of safety, it is unlikely that the optimum and sustainable HRM model is the low-cost, 'hard' HR model which appears to be growing in prominence across the global industry. Arguably, a pressing need exists for commercial airline organisations to reconsider and reframe their current approach to the management of their pilots in order to prevent and deal with critical incidents as efficaciously as possible. Demonstrably, it is the pilots who are pivotal and central to a safe and sustainable industry. According to Hobbs (2004, p. 335), pilots may indeed be the 'last frontier of aviation safety'.

This case study also reflects the increasing disjuncture between the human and technological aspects of work and its organisation, so critically identified by the human relations school. As noted in the case, the focus on technology leading the relationship, rather than working in harmony with the human side of flying is leading to some major concerns from those within the sector. Such concern highlights that job design in the twenty-first century might be more of a case of back to the future, or forward to the past.

References

Amalberti, R. (2001). The paradoxes of almost totally safe transportation systems. *Safety Science, 37*(2–3), 109–126.

Argyle, M. (1989). *The social psychology of work* (2nd ed). London: Penguin.

Bamber, G. J., Hoffer Gittell, J., Kochan T. A., & von Nordenflycht, A. (2015). Contrasting management and employment-relations strategies in European airlines. *Journal of Industrial Relations, 51*(5), 635–652.

Bennett, S. A. (2006). A longitudinal ethnographic study of aircrews' lived experience of flying operations at a low-cost airline. *Risk Management, 8*, 92–117.

Berg, M. (1985). *The age of manufactures 1700–1820*. London: Fontana.

Birchall, D. (1975). *Job design*. Essex: Gower Press.

Brown, J. A. C. (1986). *The social psychology of industry*. London: Penguin.

Buchanan, D. A., & Huczynski, A. A. (1985). *Organizational behaviour*. Upper Saddle River, NJ: Prentice Hall.

Chandler, A. (1977). *The visible hand*. Cambridge, MA: Harvard University Press.

Cho, J., & Kim, J. (2018). Identifying factors reinforcing robotization: Interactive forces of employment, working hour and wage. *Sustainability*, *10*(2), 490.

Drury, H. B. (1922). *Scientific Management: A History and Criticism*, (3rd ed). New York, NY: Longmans, Green & Co.

Cole, G. A. (1988). *Personnel management: Theory and practice*. London: DP Publications.

Edwards, P. K. (1979). *Contested terrain*. London: Heinemann.

Fraher, A. L. (2014). *The next crash: How short-term profit seeking trumps airline safety*. London: Cornell University Press.

Friedmann, G. (1961). *The Anatomy of Work*. London: Macmillian.

Friedmann, G. (1977). *Industry and Labour, Class Struggle at Work and Monopoly Capitalism*. London: Macmillian.

Friedman, T. (2016). *Thank you for being late: An optimist's guide to thriving in the age of accelerations*. New York, NY: Allen & Unwin.

Friend, M. A., & Kohn, J. P. (2014). *Fundamentals of occupational safety and health* (6th ed.). Lanham, MD: Bernan Press.

Gordon, R. (1998). The contribution of human factors to accidents in the offshore oil industry. *Reliability Engineering and System Safety*, *61*(1–2), 95–108.

Gorz, A. (Ed.). (1976). *The division of labour: The labour process and class-struggle in modern capitalism*. Brighton: Harvester Press.

Grant, K., & Maxwell, G. A. (2018). Risky business: Pilots' accounts of critical incidents in commercial aviation. Paper presented at 15th International human resource management conference, June 13–15, Madrid.

Grint, K. (1991). *The sociology of work*. Cambridge: Polity Press.

Hakim, C. (1987). Trends in the flexible workforce. *Employment Gazette*, *95*, 549–560.

Hakim, C. (1990). *Core and periphery in employers' workforce strategies*: Evidence from the 1987 E.L.U.S. Survey. *Work, Employment and Society*, *4*(2), 157–188.

Harvey, G., & Turnbull, P. (2010). On the go: Walking the high road at a low cost airline. *The International Journal of Human Resource Management*, *21*(2), 230–241.

Hernuas, T. (2016). Job design at the crossroads: From 'creative' jobs to innovative jobs. In M. Skerlavaj, M. Cerne, A Dysvik, & A. Carlson (Eds.), *Capitalizing on creativity at work: Fostering the implementation of creative ideas in organizations.* (pp. 17–28). Cheltenham: Edward Elgar.

Hobbs, A. (2004). Human factors: The last frontier of aviation safety? *The International Journal of Aviation Psychology*, *14*(4), 335–341.

Hobsbawm, E. J. (1968). *Industry and Empire*. Harmondsworth: Pelican.

Hoxie, R. F. (1918). *Scientific Management and Labor*. New York, NY: Longmans, Green & Co.

Kelly, P. (1982). *Scientific management, job redesign and work performance*. London: Academic Press.

Li, G., Baker, S. P., Grabowski, J. G., & Rebok, G. W. (2001). Factors associated with pilot error in aviation crashes. *Aviation, Space and Environmental Medicine*, *72*(1), 52–58.

Liou, J. J. H., Yen, L., & Tzeng, G. (2008). Building an effective safety management system for airlines. *Journal of Air Transport Management*, *14*, 20–26.

Lipietz, A. (1987). *Mirages and miracles: The crises of Global Fordism*. London: Verso.

Littler, C. R., & Salaman, G. (1982). Bravermania and beyond: Recent theories of the labour process. *Sociology*, *16*(2), 251–269.

Mathias, P. (1969). *The first industrial nation: An economic history of Britain 1700–1914*. London: Methuen.

Maxwell, G. A., & Grant, K. (2018). Commercial airline pilots' declining professional standing and increasingly precarious employment. *The International Journal of Human Resource Management.* DOI: 10.1080/09585192.2018.1528473.

Merkle, J. (1980). *Management and ideology. The legacy of the international scientific management movement.* Los Angeles, CA: University of California Press.

Murrell, K. F. H. (1965). *Human performance in industry.* New York, NY: Reinhold Publishing.

Nichols, T. (1980). *Capital and Labour: Studies in the Capitalist Labour Process.* London: Athlone Press.

Nyland, C. (1987). Scientific planning and management. *Capital and Class, 33,* 55–83.

Oliver, N., Calvard, T., & Potocnik, C. (2017). Cognition, technology, and organizational limits: Lessons from the Air France 447 disaster. *Organization Science, 28*(4), 729–743.

Oxenbridge, S., Wallace, J., White, L., Tiernan, S., & Lansbury, R. (2010). A comparative analysis of restructuring employment relationships in Qantas and Aer Lingus: Different routes, similar destinations. *The International Journal of Human Resource Management, 21*(2), 180–196.

Parker, S., & Wall, T. (1998). *Job and work design: Organizing work to promote well-being and effectiveness.* Thousand Oaks, CA: Sage.

Passmore, W. A. (1998). *Designing effective organisations: The sociotechnical systems perspective.* New York, NY: Wiley.

Pollard, S. (1965). *The Genesis of Modern Management.* London: Edward Arnold.

Pratt, K. J., & Bennett, S. G. (1985) *Elements of personnel management* (2nd ed.). London: Van Nostrand Reinhold.

Roberts, K. H. (1990). Some characteristics of one type of high reliability organization. *Oganization Science, 1*(2), 160–176.

Robertson, K., Black, J. Grand-Clement, S., & Hall, A. (2016). *Human and organisational factors in major accident prevention. A snapshot of the academic landscape.* Cambridge: RAND.

Rose, M. (1988). *Industrial behaviour* (2nd ed.). London: Penguin.

Sarker, M. A. R., Hossan, C. G., & Saman, L. (2012). Sustainability and growth of low cost airlines: An industry analysis in global perspective. *American Journal of Business and Management, 1*(3), 162–171.

Schein, E. H. (1965). *Organisational psychology.* Upper Saddle River, NJ: Prentice Hall.

Smith, A. (1979). *The wealth of nations.* New York, NY: Penguin Books. (First published 1776.)

Taylor, A. K., & Cotter, T. S. (2016). Human opinion counts: Making decisions in critical situations when working with highly automated systems. *Proceedings of the American society for engineering management 2016 annual conference,* October 26–29, Charlotte, NC.

Taylor, F. (1911). *The principles of scientific management.* New York, NY: Harper.

Thompson, E. P. (1968). *The Making of the English Working Class.* Harmondsworth: Pelican.

Thompson, H. (1988). Australia Reconstructed: Australia Deconstructed. *Journal of Australian Political Economy, 23,* 87–96.

Thompson, P. (1983). *The nature of work.* London: Macmillian Business.

Thompson, P., & McHugh, D. (1995). *Work organisation: A critical introduction* (3rd ed.). London: Macmillan Business.

Trist, E. (1973). A socio-technical critique of scientific management. In M. Lockett & R. Spear (Eds.), *Organisations as systems* (pp. 58–65). Milton Keynes: Open University Press.

Warr, P. (1987). *Psychology at work* (3rd ed.). London: Penguin.

Watson, T. J. (1995). *Sociology, work and industry* (3rd ed.). London: Routledge Press.

Chapter 13

Codes of Conduct: Are They Worth the Paper They Are Written On?

Xiaoyan (Christiana) Liang and Peter Holland

Introduction

The concept of an organisational code of conduct is often seen as part of the passive policies that organisations generate, the effectiveness of which in guiding ethical decision-making inside the organisation has been questioned (e.g. Adams, Tashchian, & Shore, 2001; Farrell, Cobbin, & Farrell, 2002). However, as high profile cases explored in this chapter identify, the value placed on code of conduct in terms of its content development and implementation can send a clear message about the culture, governance and ethical values to stakeholders both inside and outside the organisation. It also illustrates in this era of prevalent social media use and 24/7 news, the important role codes of conduct play in helping organisations navigate through high-impact issues and incidents in the public domain. In particular, codes of conduct provide a frame of reference to manage the issues in a way that is perceived to be fair and equitable to all stakeholders. It can also illustrate in 'moments of truth' whether they are merely human resources (HR) rhetoric, which is conveniently ignored or a key anchor around which to make decisions in turbulent times. Through a series of case studies, we analyse the effectiveness of codes of conduct in three different organisations in what could be described as the good, the bad and the ugly of decision-making by management in terms of their code content and management decisions' adherence to their codes.

So What are Codes of Conduct?

A code of conduct is defined as a formal normative written document stating the principles and rules of conduct which help guide intraorganisational and interorganisational relations and behaviours (e.g. Stevens, 1994; Stohl, Stohl, & Popova, 2009). In its simplest form, these policies provide a frame of reference for acceptable standards of behaviour for member of the workforce representing the organisation. This is an important distinction to note, as the focus of interpreting the issues by senior management in formulating a decision on an incident or incidents, needs to be considered in the context of fair and reasonable workplace behaviour. This more than implies a central role for human resources. A second reason why human resources should be central to these issues is that the perceived breach can happen at the level of senior management or senior management do not have the skill to investigate the incident(s) associated with a perceived breach of the code of conduct, nor the objectivity, as this chapter highlights. As such human resources are central to developing and managing these policies and to provide clarity in what Carlzon (1987) described as a *moment of truth* in exposing the true culture of the organisation.

Effectiveness of the Codes of Conduct

Codes of conduct have the potential to create and shape an ethical and effective organisational culture. In many studies, effectiveness of the codes of conduct is assumed to mean generally 'influencing behaviour' (e.g. Adams et al., 2001; Ford & Richardson, 1994). For the purpose of this chapter, we define code effectiveness in organisations as meeting three criteria: (1) evidence of codes with content that explicitly state legal and ethical guidelines governing the behaviours of corporate agents (e.g. employees, managers and senior executives; (2) at times of code violation, transgressions are reported, acknowledged, and promised to be addressed by the organisation to prevent its repetition; and (3) the final decision and outcomes are consistent with the general ethical values and specific ethical guidelines outlined in the codes.

Introducing a code of conduct is just one factor in shaping corporate ethical behaviour (Nijhof, Cludts, Fisscher, & Laan, 2003). The mere existence of a code of conduct alone in an organisation does not guarantee ethical behaviour. Schwartz (2004) interviewed different stakeholders within four organisations (employees, managers, ethics officers) and found that the effectiveness of codes of conduct is influenced by a series of factors that roughly fall into two categories – content and implementation.

Content of the Code

In terms of code content, what is written in the code and how it reads matters. Schwartz (2004) reported that the content, readability, tone, relevance, 'realism' and provision of examples in the code of conduct are factors that determine code effectiveness. Echoing earlier studies (Laczniak & Inderrieden, 1987; Pitt & Groskaufmanis, 1990), Schwartz (2004) suggested that the code content needs to have enough detail to properly guide organisational and individual behavioural. Code of conduct ought to include both general value statements and specific guidelines for behaviour (Hoffman & Driscoll, 2001). This specificity might result in a lengthy code document, thus potentially negatively affecting its readability and effectiveness (Trevino & Nelson, 1995). However, Schwartz (2004) found that code readers use the document as a point of reference, as such, it should be expected to be somewhat lengthy. Contrary to critics (e.g. Harris, 1978; Raiborn & Payne, 1990) who deem the negative tone of the codes as top down, commanding, and controlling doctrines that fall short in employee inspiration, Schwartz (2004) reported that negative tones (e.g. do not do x) are more effective in outlining expected behaviours and are preferred by employees than positive tones (e.g. 'try or strive to do x'), which leaves leeway for inappropriate behaviours or their justifications.

Relevance and realism as criteria of codes content are straightforward. If the activities addressed in the codes are not relevant to the employees in question, the code would lose its purpose, and be deemed ineffective (Brandl & Maguire, 2002; Pitt & Groskaufmanis, 1990). Similarly, if the codes outline behaviours which are unrealistic and difficult to attain, employees will dismiss its legitimacy (Harris, 1978; Murphy, 1988). Provision of examples in the codes or during training programmes is reported to be an important factor in code effectiveness, understandably so as examples effectively increase employees' interpretation of the provisions in the codes (Gibbs, 2003; Murphy, 1995).

This brief overview of the literature reveals that in terms of code content, effective codes are (1) well-balanced in general values and specific guidelines; (2) appropriate in length, and negative (in addition to positive) in tone; (3) relevant and realistic to corporate agents; and (4) strengthened by provision of examples. For the purpose of this chapter, we examine the code content of the case companies using these four criteria.

Implementation Process

How the code is implemented in the organisation has been reported to influence code effectiveness. Code ought to be distributed prior to the commencement of the employment (Schwartz, 2004). Senior management ought to be perceived as supporting the code through speeches and actions (Brandl & Maguire, 2002; Montoya & Richard, 1994). Employees ought to go through a sign-off procedure (Gibbs, 2003; Pitt & Groskaufmanis, 1990). Training ought to be conducted on codes to ensure understanding and influencing behaviour (Benson, 1989; Gellerman, 1989; Messmer, 2003; Pitt & Groskaufmanis, 1990). Reinforcement in the form of regular reminders (e.g. emails, newsletters, speeches) (Trevino & Nelson, 2016) and last, a testing on the content of the code for employees. It is worth noting that some of these suggestions are controversial. For example, the employee sign-off provision has been criticised for its perceived 'pushiness', 'lack of trust' and 'excessive paternalism' (Schwartz, 2004, p. 332) and the testing for its unpleasant nature (Schwartz, 2004). This series of suggestions essentially boils down to the key attitudes and decisions by the senior management within the organisations with respect to the code administration. For the purpose of this chapter, we summarise the key decisions as whether (a) codes are in place prior to violation; (b) there is honest reporting, acknowledgement and communication of transgressions of codes and commitment to address the transgressions; and (c) final decision and outcomes are consistent with the general ethical values and specific ethical guidelines outlined in the codes.

It is worth pointing out that there are also studies which associate code effectiveness with its creation process. Treviño, Weaver, Gibson, and Toffler (1999) propose that employees' perception of the raison d'être of the ethics programme (code included) is a key factor (e.g. company reputation consideration, legal compliance, etc.). Several studies also suggest that employees' direct involvement in the code creation process contribute to its effectiveness (Messmer, 2003; Montoya & Richard, 1994; Sweeney & Siers, 1990).

The Case Studies

We explore three high profile critical incidents in which organisational employees engaged in misconduct or unethical behaviour in three multinational corporations located in three different countries, that is, BBC from United Kingdom, United Airlines from the United States and Seven West Media from Australia.

The BBC *Top Gear* Case

Background

The BBC is the world's oldest broadcaster and one of the largest public broadcasting organisations in the world. Founded in 1922, it has its headquarters in London. It is arguably the world's leading media broadcaster with an international audience estimated in the billions. It employs 35,000 staff. In recent time, its car review show – *Top Gear* – was its premier show and a major source of revenue.

Top Gear

The contemporary version of the television show *Top Gear* has been running since 2002 and at the time of the incident was the most viewed factual television programme in the world. As such the show and its presenters had a very high global profile. In addition, the show was financially lucrative for the British public broadcaster. Jeremy Clarkson, the lead presenter had been credited as the person behind the success of the show, attracting audiences of 350 million a week in 170 countries, with what can best be described as 'blokey' or 'male' humour.

Incident

Whilst filming on location on March 4, 2015, Clarkson punched the show's producer Oisin Tymon, in the face during a brawl over food, which left Tymon with a split lip, Clarkson also referred derogatively to him as 'Lazy Irish c**t' (Sawer, 2015, March 14). In the wake of the incident, the BBC suspended Clarkson, launched an internal investigation and cancelled up coming episodes of the *Top Gear* show. The following week of the investigation saw the BBC management under intense pressure in the media over the incident and how it should be handled. A petition signed by over one million people urged them not to take dismissal action against Clarkson (Sawer, 2015, March 14).

Final Decision/Outcome

On 25 March 2015, the BBC announced that Clarkson's contract would not be renewed, despite the public pressure to reinstate the presenter. BBC director-general Tony Hall said in a statement that 'For me a line has been crossed. There cannot be one rule for one and one rule for another dictated by either rank, or public relations and commercial considerations' (BBC, 2015, March 25). Clarkson accepted the decision taking full responsibility for his actions.

United Airlines

Background

United Airlines is an American airline headquartered in Chicago, Illinois and employs 82,000 staff. It has a comprehensive route network in the Asia Pacific and is one of the largest aviation carriers in the world, with over 3,000 flights a day.

Incident

On 9 April 2017, United Express flight No. 3411 bound for Louisville (Kentucky) from Chicago's O'Hare International Airport was overbooked by four passengers, because United needed to accommodate four airline crew for subsequent flight operation the next day, originating from Louisville. In order to resolve this situation United offered financial incentives/compensation for passenger to give up their set allocation. United first offered $400 for any volunteering passenger, which later increased to $800 vouchers and a hotel stay. After no one volunteered, United used a computer to randomly select four passengers to leave the flight for the next one. One of these four passengers, a doctor, David Dao, refused on the grounds that he had patients to see the next day in Kentucky. Security was called (state police force), and Dao was passively dragged off the plane. In the process of taking him off the plane he was knocked out, suffered a concussion, a broken nose and lost two teeth (Evans, 2017, April 10). This incident was captured in a series of smart technology videos by other passengers on the plane.

Final Decision/Outcome

As the video of the incident went viral, United Airlines management defended the actions it took and over the following days, what could be described as a smear campaign regarding Dr Dao's work and private life emerged. Whilst it is important to note that United Airlines were never directly found to have been involved in this campaign, it needs to be seen in the context of the actions of chief executive officer Oscar Munoz who initially defended the policy of overbooking and its consequences in a letter to employees, saying he 'emphatically' stood behind his employees. Munoz also called Dr Dao 'disruptive and belligerent', and blamed him for defying orders (Khomami & Lartey, 2017, April). However, as the stock of United Airlines dropped by almost US$1 billion along with high profile negative media attention, Munoz reversed his position and unreservedly apologised for the incident. Legal action on behalf of Dr Dao was being considered and by late April, United announced it has come to a confidential settlement with Dr Dao and had completely revamped its policies and practices regarding its dealing with passengers, including not requiring them to be removed from the plane by law enforcement officers and offering up to US$10,000 to passengers who gave up a seat in similar situations. In addition, and specifically because of his role in the incident, the board of United subsequently reversed its decision to make CEO Oscar Munoz the chairman of United from 2018 (ABC News, 2017).

Seven West Media

Background

Seven West is one of Australia's leading media companies with platforms in television, newspapers and magazines. Based in Perth it is the amalgamation of various media outlets, with its present structure being established in 1992. Seven West employs over 5,000 staff.

Incident

Seven West Media's CEO Tim Worner had an 18-month extramarital affair with Ms Amber Harrison, an executive assistant for Seven's Pacific Magazines. The relationship ended in June, 2014. Ms Harrison went public with her affair with the CEO, Mr Worner in December, 2014, following her difficult severance negotiations with Seven – the latter allegedly had dishonoured a confidential redundancy payment of $350,000 entitled to her due to investigation into misuse of her corporate credit card. Ms Harrison had broadcast on social media the text exchanges and picture evidence of the affair, and made claims against Mr Worner of drug use on company time, inappropriate relationships with four other women in the company and misuse of a corporate credit card (Schipp, 2017). Mr Worner admitted to and apologised for the affair but denied all other allegations. Following an independent report by Allens Linklater Lawyers, Seven West cleared its CEO of any serious misconduct. However, the report commissioner Sheila McGregor resigned prior to the board statement (Battersby, 2017). Ms Harrison called Seven West's review of Worner's action a 'white wash' (Schipp, 2017). She had lodged claims in the Federal Court of Australia against Seven for breaches of the Fair Work Act. Recently, Channel 7 has been ordered by Federal Court judge Bromberg to try to resolve this long-running dispute (Cavanagh, 2017).

Final Decision/Outcome
From an apparent settlement on confidential terms, this case has become a major incident for Seven West and front-page news.

Analysis
Using our three-factor codes effectiveness criteria as the analytical framework, we identify the following with regard to codes of conduct.

Evidence of Codes and Comparison of Their Content Effectiveness
As can be seen from **Table 13.1**, at the times of scandal, the BBC's code of conduct is accessible to the public via its official website. This 28-page document provides guiding principles for all those working with and for BBC. Apart from stating BBC's mission, vision and values, this code of conduct clearly spells out guidelines governing three aspects of workplace: people (respecting people), conduct (doing the right thing) and relationships (working with others).

United Airlines' Code of Conduct was a 66-page document at the time of the incident, accessible via the company's website. Upon careful examination, it had two versions combined. The company corrected the duplication when updating this document in June 2017, which reduced the document to 28 pages. But we will keep using this 66–page document as the basis of analysis given it was the version applicable to the time of the incident. It consists of major categories of principles of integrity, ethical decision-making and protecting company information and assets.

Seven West Media's code of conduct for employees either did not exist or was not accessible to the public at the times of incident. However, a code of conduct for employees appeared on their website following the incident in 2018. The two-page document included the following 12 subheadings: work ethics, safety, confidentiality, personal conduct, fair business, working environment, gifts, conflict of interest and ethical conduct, obligation to disclose relevant information, use of company assets, change, environment, Seven West Media's employee assistance programme.

There are also variations amongst the codes with regard to their content effectiveness. First, the BBC's code of conduct is written in plain and simple language and provides clear structure, containing general principles as well as specific guidelines. Hence, it has good readability.

Table 13.1 Evidence of codes and comparison of code content.

Criteria	BBC	United Airlines	Seven West Media
Evidence of codes at times of scandal	Publically accessible via company website.	Publically accessible via company website.	Missing at times of incident. Post-incident: Code of conduct for employees, two pages in 2018 August version, accessible via company website.
Readability	#28 Pages. #Three sections (people, conduct, and relationships). #General principles with specific guidelines.	#66 Pages (two versions merged together). #Focus on conflict of interests and protection of company. Post-incident: Revised and updated in June 2017, 28 pages.	N/A Post-incident: # Code of conduct for employees, two pages in 2018 August version.
Tone (negative vs. positive)	'Never' four times. 'Won't' (at least 12 times).	'Never' 11 times. 'Not' Many times.	N/A Post-scandal. 'not' twice, 'must not' five times.
Relevance	Activities are relevant to employees in question.	Activities are less relevant.	N/A Post-incident.
Provision of examples	If over 40 times, and 'If you…' appeared 27 times.	The word 'Example' appeared 24 times.	N/A Post-incident: Few examples: Listing once under Environment.
Realism	BBC and Employees #Mutuality: behaviour expectations of BBC juxtaposed with those of employees/partners 'What you can expect from the BBC; What we expect from you'.	#Heavily referencing law and regulation.	#Vague.
Code content effectiveness	***** Good	** Bad	* Ugly

United Airlines' combined code of conduct is a 66-page document, which is heavy with legal jargon. This undercuts its readability. Seven West Media's code of conduct post-incident was a two-page document with minimal information, incapable of effectively guiding employee behaviours.

In terms of tones, all codes of conduct from the three case companies used both positive and negative tones, with BBC being a leading user in negative tones, and Seven West Media, the least. With the criterion of relevance and provision of examples, the BBC once again leads. The activities cited in their codes are highly relevant to employees' workplace. There are ample examples given in the format of 'If you...' followed by specific guides for action. For example,

> *If you're directly involved in buying products or services for the BBC, you'll make sure whoever you're buying from has been assessed to make sure they live up to our standards. (BBC, 2017, p. 5)*

United Airlines' code also contained several examples, but most fall under 'ethical decision-making' section that is mostly concerned about protecting the company by avoiding situations of conflict of interests. For example:

Examples of possible conflict of interest situations:

- *when you have a relationship with a co-worker;*
- *when a customer is a family member, friend or co-worker;*
- *when a supplier is owned by or employs a family member, friend or coworker; and*
- *when you have an investment or financial interest in a competitor, customer or supplier (United Code of Conduct, 2016, p. 6).*

Seven West Media had only one example in the format of a list under the section 'Environment', see below:

> *Employees are expected to consider the impact of their actions on the environment and local community, including in relation to the disposal of waste, use and storage of chemicals and use of natural resources. (Seven West Media, 2018, p. 2)*

Finally, along the criterion of 'realism', the BBC's codes present a feature of 'mutuality', each section contains two subheadings named 'What you can expect from the BBC' and 'What we expect from you'. Under these separate subheadings, the behaviour expectations of the BBC are juxtaposed with those of employees/partners, this signals that the expected behaviours are realistic, attainable and mutual. The code has equal binding power regardless of the organisational status of the agents. This arguably enhances the BBC codes' legitimacy and realism. In comparison, United Airlines' codes heavily reference law and regulation centring around situations of conflicts of interests, many of which are not directly relevant to the day-to-day activities of a typical employee. For example,

> *When preparing a government contract or interacting with government per-sonnel, United has an obligation to ensure that the information provided is truthful, current, accurate and complete. Prior to submitting any representa-tion or certification to the government, United employees must carefully review such information to ensure its accuracy. (United Code of Conduct, 2016, p. 13)*

As a consequence, the degree to which its employees perceive the code as relevant is questionable, and its effectiveness potentially diminished. Seven West Media's codes are simplistic, as all 12 subheadings have only one or two sentences outlining the general expectations. For example, under work ethics, 'Employees are expected to perform their duties to the maximum of their ability and deliver acceptable objectives to the company' (Seven West Media, 2018, p. 1). What objectives are acceptable to the company are not specified, which leaves the code ambiguous and interpretation is dependent upon another separate document, for which the information for retrieval is not mentioned.

Based on comparing the code availability at times of the incidents and their content effectiveness along the selected criteria, it is apparent that the BBC's code could be described as 'Good', United Airlines the 'Bad', and Seven West Media the 'Very Poor'.

Attitudes Towards Codes at Times of Transgression
Our second criterion for code effectiveness is during times of violation, whether transgressions are reported, acknowledged and promised to be addressed by the organisation to prevent its repetition. As illustrated in **Table 13.2**:

Table 13.2 Attitudes Towards Codes at Times of Transgression.

Organisation / Criteria	BBC	United Airlines	Seven West
Communication of violations	Suspension of culprit; acknowledge and own the violation; and commitment to address.	Apparent smear campaign towards the victim; blame the victim by the CEO; reverse attitude after share price plummeted by $1 billion.	Deny wrongdoing by CEO; no serious misconduct; chair of investigation resigned prior to official statement supporting above.
On average	***** Good	** Bad	* Ugly

In the wake of the incident, the BBC immediately acknowledged the violations of codes by suspending the culprit, launching an internal investigation, cancelling up coming episodes of *Top Gear* show immediately and making a decision within two weeks of the incident. Hence, we would give this a good score on the second category of code effectiveness. In comparison, United Airlines was slow to own and communicate to the public its misconduct. A smear campaign towards the victim emerged, its CEO 'emphatically' stood behind his employees and called Dr Dao 'disruptive and belligerent', and blamed him for defying orders (Khomami & Lartey, 2017, April). However, he reversed his position in the wake of the company's share price drop by $1 billion following the incident. Therefore, United Airlines scored 'Poorly' in communication of code violations at times of transgression. Seven West Media denied any wrongdoing and launched an internal investigation, which cleared its CEO of any serious misconduct, but the head of the investigation resigned prior to the release of the CEO exoneration. Hence, Seven West Media scored very poorly in communication of codes violations.

The Consistency between Final Decision and Outcome with the Codes
Our third criterion, as **Table 13.3** illustrates, looks at whether the final decision made by the senior management and incident outcomes are consistent with the general ethical values and specific ethical guidelines outlined in the codes.

Table 13.3 Final Management Decision's Consistency with Codes.

Organisation ⟍ Criteria	BBC	United Airlines	Seven West
(c) Consistency between code policy and final decision.	Consistent, final decision and outcome upholds codes.	Partially consistent.	N/A
On average	***** Good	* Bad	* Potentially ugly

On 25 March, 2015, the BBC announced that Clarkson's contract would not be renewed, despite the public pressure to reinstate the presenter. In the BBC's case, the final decision to terminate contract with the codes violator remained consistent with the principles and specific guidelines of their Codes.

Under the section 'People', the BBC's code of conduct clearly states: 'Wherever we are in the world, we respect people and their rights: the people around us, the people we work with and the people we speak for' (BBC, 2017, p. 9). In addition, the need to treat everyone equally is explicitly stated:

> We don't tolerate discrimination of any kind, and we speak up when we see it. We'll take disciplinary action against anyone who crosses the line, including firing them for gross misconduct, if it's serious.

As noted above these principles echoed in the statement made by BBC director-general Tony Hall: 'For me a line has been crossed. There cannot be one rule for one and one rule for another dictated by either rank, or public relations and commercial considerations' (BBC, 2015, March 25). Hence, the BBC upheld its codes principles in its final decision.

In United Airlines' case, under the section of making ethical decision, its Code of Conduct clearly states that 'United supports and respects internationally proclaimed human rights and is not complicit in human rights abuses' and 'United … embraces dignity, respect and diversity in all aspects of its business operations' (United Code of Conduct, 2016, p. 16). However, the brutal treatment Dr Dao received is a gross violation of its codes. The actions taken by United Airlines' CEO in the wake of the incident further depart from its codes principles. Apparently, under external pressure, United Airlines was forced to comply with its codes and completely revamp its policies regarding dealing with passengers. As noted, the board of United also reversed its decision to make CEO Oscar Munoz the chairman of United from 2018 (ABC News, 2017). Hence, it could be said that United Airlines' final decision and outcome upheld its codes, but was forced by external pressure. Seven West Media did not appear to have a code at the times of the incident; hence the question of whether the final decision and outcome is consistent with its code is moot. On the basis of the above analysis, the BBC scores 'Good' in this third criterion of code effectiveness, United Airlines scores 'Poor' and Seven West Media, 'Very Poor'.

Analysis and Conclusion

This chapter explores the role and the effectiveness of a code of conduct in guiding the decision-making of senior management in highly public and controversial situations. It is clear from the analysis of the three cases that in situations which are evolve quickly, a code of conduct can be critical in guiding and justifying a course of action which is perceived to be fair and equitable to all stakeholders.

Echoing Stohs and Brannick (1999), our analysis found that a code of conduct is potentially an important factor influencing the organisational decision-making in ethical incidents. In our analysis of the three companies' codes of conduct, both the BBC and United Airlines were found to explicitly or implicitly establish a code of conduct underpinned by general principles and specific behavioural guidelines. Seven West Media did not have a code of conduct (publically available) at times of the incident, which demonstrates a potential lack of ethical awareness throughout the entire organisation. The introduction of a code of conduct is usually at the heart of the organisation's ethical programmes, supplemented by ethics training and ethics officer who is in charge of ethics-oriented performance appraisal (Ruiz, Martinez, Rodrigo, & Diaz, 2015). It is difficult to understand how Seven West Media could cultivate an ethical culture with the core element of ethics programme missing. Not surprisingly, organisations that do not have a code of conduct at the time of the major incidents can be oblivious to the ethical implications, and potentially turn a deaf-ear to outcries for justice. The Seven West Media's decision not to stand down its CEO amidst the investigation of the incidents could be seen to demonstrate this approach. We are not saying that the adoption of a code of conduct would have prevented the behaviour; the mere lack of it is telling of the apparent insignificance the role of a code of conduct appeared to be for a company the size of Seven West Media.

In addition, the availability of codes is the first step towards making ethical decisions in times of major and often public incidents. However, its mere existence does not guarantee code effectiveness. Our analysis shows that the content of the code (i.e. readability, tones, provision of examples, relevance and realism), communication of codes violation at times of transgression, followed by management decisions and outcomes which uphold the codes are all essential steps that lead to code effectiveness. BBC's code of conduct is a stand out in the way it is written in a manner that demonstrates thoughtfulness, clarity, mutual accountability (both for the BBC as a company and its employees), relevance and practicality. United Airlines' code of conduct is written with apparent reliance on legal doctrines, which affects its readability. Seven West Media presented a simplistic two-page codes several years after the incident, the effectiveness of which in guiding ethical behaviours is questionable. Causal or not, the BBC's communication of codes violation as well as the final management decision both upheld principles in its codes, whereas United Airlines communication of codes violation and management decisions were forced into alignment with its codes by apparent external pressure (negative media attention and share price drop). The Seven West analysis is limited in the accessibility/availability to the code of conduct – which is an issue in itself. However, extrapolating from the code of conduct beyond the incident, it is difficult to establish that they have managed the process in accordance with their codes. It is also interesting in this case to note that the role of the human resource management (HRM) department. Ms Harrison made grievance claims about the misuse of the corporate credit card. Allegations are now surfacing that HR pressured her to drop the action because of the focus on her and her reputation (Wilson, 2017, p. 6). As Peter Wilson the Chairman of the Australian Human Resources Institute stated in reviewing this case: If true, these allegations could be seen as HR offering helpful advice about what Harrison was getting into. Alternately, they could be seen as a more disturbing attempt to move her along (Wilson, 2017, p. 6).

In summing up the relationship between organisational ethical decision-making and the code effectiveness, we would describe the BBC as exhibiting best practice because it had arguable the most to lose from its decision; they followed the code and resolved the issues immediately, in a fair and equitable manner.

What this chapter has attempted to highlight is whether codes of conduct are effective mechanisms to influence behaviour or serve merely as a cosmetic function. The answer is largely dependent on to what extent the organisations put efforts in crafting a codes document which reflects their core principles and which meets essential criteria of content effectiveness and is supported by management. More importantly, to what extent the organisations choose to acknowledge and openly communicate codes violation and to what extent the senior management's final decision complies with the codes in moment of truth/conflict of organisation's economic interest. If ticking all these boxes, it could be argued from the comparative analysis that codes of conduct are definitely worth the paper they are written on.

References

ABC News. (2017). United Airlines reaches settlement with passenger David Dao, who was dragged from overbooked flight. Retrieved from http://www.abc.net.au/news/2017-04-28/united-reaches-settlement-with-passenger-dragged-from-plane/8478816

Adams, J. S., Tashchian, A., & Shore, T. H. (2001). Codes of ethics as signals for ethical behavior. *Journal of Business Ethics, 29*(3), 199–211.

Battersby, L. (2017). Tim Worner thanks Amber Harrison for giving him 'quite a weird feeling'. *The Sydney Morning Herald.* Retrieved from http://www.smh.com.au/business/media-and-marketing/tim-worner-thanks-amber-harrison-for-giving-him-quite-a-weird-feeling-20170207-gu7ba9.html

BBC. (2015, March 25). BBC Director-General's statement regarding Jeremy Clarkson. Retrieved from http://www.bbc.co.uk/mediacentre/statements/jeremy-clarkson-dg-statement

BBC. (2017, March). BBC code of conduct. Retrieved from http://www.bbc.co.uk/aboutthebbc/insidethebbc/howwework/policiesandguidelines/codeofconduct.html

Benson, G. C. (1989). Codes of ethics. *Journal of Business Ethics, 8*(5), 305–319.

Brandl, P., & Maguire, M. (2002). Codes of ethics: A primer on their purpose, development, and use. *The Journal for Quality and Participation, 25*(4), 8.

Carlzon, J. (1987). *Moments of truth.* Cambridge, MA: Ballinger Publishing Co.

Cavanagh, R. (2017). Channel 7 sex scandal: Seven West Media ordered to mediate Amber Harrison case after CEO affair. *Herald Sun.* Retrieved from http://www.heraldsun.com.au/news/law-order/channel-7-sex-scandal-seven-west-media-ordered-to-mediate-amber-harrison-case-after-ceo-affair/news-story/851bed1bd8f231d74b39d21d0998f25f

Evans, P. (2017, April 10). United Airlines forcibly removes passenger from overbooked flight. Retrieved from http://www.cbc.ca/news/business/united-airlines-flight-overbooked-1.4063632

Farrell, B. J., Cobbin, D. M., & Farrell, H. M. (2002). Can codes of ethics really product consistent behaviours? *Journal of Managerial Psychology, 17*(6), 468–490.

Ford, R. C., & Richardson, W. D. (1994). Ethical decision making: A review of the empirical literature. *Journal of Business Ethics, 13*(3), 205–221.

Gellerman, S. W. (1989). Managing ethics from the top down. *MIT Sloan Management Review, 30*(2), 73.

Gibbs, E. (2003). Developing an effective code of conduct. *Financial Executive, 19*(4), 40–41.

Harris, C. E. (1978). Structuring a workable business code of ethics. *University of Florida Law Review, 30*, 310–382.

Hoffman, W. M., & Driscoll, D.-M. (2001). Integrating ethics into organisational cultures. In C. Bonny (Ed.), *Business ethics: Facing up to the issues* (pp. 38–54). London: The Economist Books.

Khomami, N., & Lartey, J. (2017, April). United Airlines CEO calls dragged passenger 'disruptive and belligerent'. *The Guardian*. Retrieved from https://www.theguardian.com/world/2017/apr/11/united-airlines-boss-oliver-munoz-says-passenger-belligerent

Laczniak, G. R., & Inderrieden, E. J. (1987). The influence of stated organizational concern upon ethical decision making. *Journal of Business Ethics, 6*(4), 297–307.

Messmer, M. (2003). Does your company have a code of ethics? *Strategic Finance, 84*(10), 13.

Montoya, I. D., & Richard, A. J. (1994). A comparative study of codes of ethics in health care facilities and energy companies. *Journal of Business Ethics, 13*(9), 713–717.

Murphy, P. E. (1988). Implementing business ethics. *Journal of Business Ethics, 7*(12), 907–915.

Murphy, P. E. (1995). Corporate ethics statements: Current status and future prospects. *Journal of Business Ethics, 14*(9), 727–740.

Nijhof, A., Cludts, S., Fisscher, O., & Laan, A. (2003). Measuring the implementation of codes of conduct. An assessment method based on a process approach of the responsible organisation. *Journal of Business Ethics, 45*(1–2), 65–78.

Pitt, H. L., & Groskaufmanis, K. A. (1990). Minimizing corporate civil and criminal liability: A second look at corporate codes of conduct. *The Georgetown Law Journal, 78*, 1559–1664.

Raiborn, C. A., & Payne, D. (1990). Corporate codes of conduct: A collective conscience and continuum. *Journal of Business Ethics, 9*(11), 879–889.

Ruiz, P., Martinez, R., Rodrigo, J., & Diaz, C. (2015). Level of coherence among ethics program components and its impact on ethical intent. *Journal of Business Ethics, 128*(4), 725–742.

Sawer, P. (2015, March 14). Jeremy Clarkson 'punched producer and called him lazy Irish'. *The Telegraph*. Retrieved from http://www.telegraph.co.uk/motoring/top-gear/11472112/Jeremy-Clarkson-punched-producer-and-called-him-lazy-Irish.html

Schipp, D. (2017). 'Whitewash': Seven CEO's former mistress slams review clearing Worner. Retrieved from http://www.news.com.au/finance/work/leaders/seven-review-clears-ceo-tim-worner-of-misconduct-after-affair/news-story/7d489921f90dd5e08a1e44354fbab38a

Schwartz, M. S. (2004). Effective corporate codes of ethics: Perceptions of code users. *Journal of Business Ethics, 55*(4), 321–341.

Seven West Media. (2018). Code of conduct for employees. Retrieved from http://www.sevenwestmedia.com.au/assets/pdfs/Code-of-Conduct-for-Employees-20-August-2018-website.pdf

Stevens, B. (1994). An analysis of corporate ethical code studies: "Where do we go from here?". *Journal of Business Ethics, 13*(1), 63–69.

Stohl, C., Stohl, M., & Popova, L. (2009). A new generation of corporate codes of ethics. *Journal of Business Ethics, 90*(4), 607. doi:10.1007/s10551-009-0064-6

Stohs, J. H., & Brannick, T. (1999). Code and conduct: Predictors of Irishih managers' ethical reasoning. *Journal of Business Ethics, 22*(4), 311–326.

Sweeney, R. B., & Siers, H. L. (1990). Survey: Ethics in corporate America. *Strategic Finance, 71*(12), 34.

Trevino, L., & Nelson, K. A. (1995). *Managing business ethics*. New York, NY: Wiley.

Trevino, L. K., & Nelson, K. A. (2016). *Managing business ethics: Straight talk about how to do it right*. Hoboken, NJ: John Wiley & Sons.

Treviño, L. K., Weaver, G. R., Gibson, D. G., & Toffler, B. L. (1999). Managing ethics and legal compliance: What works and what hurts. *California Management Review*, *41*(2), 131–151.

United Airlines. (2016). Code of ethics and business conduct. Retrieved in Dec. 2018 from http://ir.united.com/corporate-governance/governance-documents

Wilson, P. (2017). Whose side are we on? *HRMonthly*, March, p. 6.

Index